Understanding Catholic Christianity

saint mary's press

Nihil Obstat: Rev. Peter Cho, STL, PhD
                Censor Librorum
                August 8, 2022

Imprimatur: Cardinal Joseph W. Tobin, CSsR
                Archbishop of Newark
                August 9, 2022

The nihil obstat and imprimatur are official declarations that a book or pamphlet is free of doctrinal or moral error. No implication is contained therein that those who have granted the nihil obstat or imprimatur agree with the contents, opinions, or statements expressed, nor do they assume any legal responsibility associated with publication.

Contributing Authors:

Barbara Allaire
Steven Ellair
Brian Singer-Towns
Thomas Zanzig

This course was developed and designed by the expert teams at Saint Mary's Press.

Cover image: © agsandrew / Shutterstock.com

Printed in the United States of America

1171 (PO6872)

ISBN 978-1-64121-180-2

Contents

1   **Being Human: Hungering for Meaning, Goodness, and Connection** **5**

Spiritual Hungers 6

A Time of Unique Growth 16

The Shared Wisdom of the World's Religions 28

2   **Revelation and Faith: Knowing and Responding to God** **36**

Revelation: How We Come to Know God 37

The Nature of God 44

The Human Response to God: Faith 50

An Overview of the Worldview, Beliefs,
    and Practices of Catholics 58

3   **Judaism: Christianity's Religious Roots** **64**

The Jewish Connection 65

The Beginnings of a People 70

From Slavery to Freedom 74

Living in the Promised Land 81

Crushing Defeat and Painful Exile 86

After the Exile 90

4   **Jesus: Son of the Living God** **97**

Who *Is* This Man? 98

Jesus' Life and Mission Begin 107

The Public Ministry of Jesus 114

5   **Jesus' Death and Resurrection: Experiencing New Life** **127**

The Last Supper: Jesus' Extraordinary Meal 128

Accepting Death on a Cross 134

The Resurrection of Jesus 140

What Does the Resurrection Mean? 149

6   **The Church: Gathering in the Spirit of Jesus** **156**

The Spirit Is Poured Out 157

What Is the Church? 165

The Spirit in the Church through History 173

7   **The Scriptures: Hearing the Inspired Word of God** **185**

The Power of God's Word 186

What Is in the Scriptures? 191

Understanding God's Truth in the Scriptures 205

8   **Tradition: Handing on Living Faith** **215**

Unity in Diversity 216

Tradition: The One Faith Handed on as a Living Reality 220

What All Christians Believe 229

Special Gifts of the Catholic Tradition 235

9   **The Sacraments: Celebrating the Grace of God** **243**

A Sacramental Faith 244

The Sacraments: Celebrations of the Paschal Mystery 249

The Sacraments of Christian Initiation 251

The Sacraments of Healing 261

The Sacraments of Service 267

The Liturgical Year 273

10   **Spirituality and Prayer: Growing in Life with God** **280**

Spirituality: Toward a Full Life with God 281

Prayer: Nourishing a Relationship with God 291

Prayer and Community 306

11   **Christian Morality: Living in the Spirit of Jesus** **311**

A Life of Love: The *Why* of Christian Morality 312

The Law of Love: The *What* of Christian Morality 318

Freedom and Grace: The *How* of Christian Morality 328

Virtue and Character: The *Who* of Christian Morality 335

Our Final Destiny 339

Glossary **345**

Index **353**

Acknowledgments **366**

chapter **1**

Being Human: Hungering for Meaning, Goodness and Connection

IN THIS CHAPTER

Spiritual Hungers   6

A Time of Unique Growth   16

The Shared Wisdom   28
of the World's Religions

Spiritual Hungers

Imagine participating in a study about **religion**. After you have answered all the questions about your values and practices, you are asked to identify your religious affiliation using a checklist something like this:

- ☐ agnostic (I don't know whether there is a god.)
- ☐ atheist (I do not believe a god or any gods exist.)
- ☐ Buddhist
- ☐ Christian (Catholic)
- ☐ Christian (Orthodox)
- ☐ Christian (Protestant)
- ☐ Hindu
- ☐ Jewish
- ☐ Muslim
- ☐ Native or Indigenous religion
- ☐ nothing in particular
- ☐ other

Which box would you check? Would you answer quickly, or would you have to think about it? Would your answer be the same or different from others in your family? A recent study by Springtide Research Institute® shows that 61 percent of young people (ages 13 to 25) in the United

States identify with a religion, leaving 39 percent who indicate they do not belong to a particular religion. This same study shows that almost 75 percent of young people say they are religious, suggesting that many who do not identify with a particular religion still find something valuable about religion.

Regardless of which religious affiliation box you would select on a checklist, this course is for you. It has been designed with awareness of, and respect for, young people regardless of religious tradition. It is not the intent of this course to convince students who are not Catholic to become Catholic; rather, the course provides an opportunity to learn about the faith of your school and also your own faith if you are Catholic. But no matter what your current beliefs are, learning more about the Catholic approach to faith and life can be a rich experience.

Before considering the specific beliefs and practices of the Catholic faith, also called **Catholicism**, this

religion An organized system of beliefs, rituals, and ways of living that gives expression to a particular people's faith in a god or gods.

Catholicism The beliefs, rituals, and practices as lived out by those who identify with the Catholic religion.

course explores religion more broadly. It considers common hungers that people experience and explores this question: What does religion provide that makes it valuable in people's lives? This sets the context for the course's exploration of Catholic Christianity.

People belong to a religion generally because it feeds the hungers of the human heart and mind. Just as we have physical hungers that require nurturing our body, we have hungers related to the parts of ourselves that aren't material or physical. We refer to those as **spiritual** hungers. We'll turn now to exploring three of those hungers: the hunger for meaning, the hunger for goodness, and the hunger for connection.

What does it mean to say that some- one is religious or belongs to a particular religion?

spiritual Relating to the nonphysical, or nonmaterial, aspects of human life and experience.

Hunger for Meaning

Davin met his friends Monica and Charlie for lunch at the neighborhood deli. Halfway through their sandwiches, Charlie asked: "So how is everyone doing? Like how are you really doing?"

Davin took a deep breath before replying. "Well, if I'm really honest, I've been feeling down lately.

Helen Keller on the Best Things in Life

Helen Keller, who lost her eyesight and hearing in early childhood, shares a powerful reflection on spiritual experience in her autobiography, *The Story of My Life:*

I used to wish that I could see pictures with my hands as I do statues, but now I do not voften think about it because my dear (heavenly) Father has filled my mind with beautiful pictures, even of things I cannot see. . . . How happy your little Helen was when her teacher explained to her that the best and most beautiful things in the world cannot be seen nor even touched, but just felt in the heart. Every day I find out something which makes me glad.

One could imagine that Helen could easily have become angry, isolated, or cynical. Instead, her spiritual hungers were nurtured by people who loved her, and Helen's resulting love, joy, and gratitude inspired everyone around her.

It feels like all I've been getting is bad news. First, I bombed the math test a couple of weeks ago. Then we got the news that my uncle Desmond has cancer. Then there was that school shooting down south and the terrible floods up north. It's sometimes hard for me to even want to get out of bed these days."

"Oh no, Davin!" Monica exclaimed. "Will your uncle be okay? Isn't he the uncle you always go hunting with?"

"Yes, that's him," Davin responded. "I don't know yet how bad it is. They're not saying much. He's going in for more tests, and there's probably going to be chemo or radiation. I didn't really want to talk about all this negative stuff, but I needed to tell someone. Since you are my two best friends, I hope it's okay that I shared it with you."

"Of course, it is," Charlie said. "And you're not the only one feeling down. Life can seem overwhelming sometimes, but I have faith that God is there to help us through things like this. Just let us know how we can help you."

"I don't know about God," Monica chimed in. "I can't see why a loving God would let all this bad stuff happen. But I believe the universe wants the best for us, whether there is a God or not. Don't lose hope!"

Davin smiled at his friends. "Thanks, guys. It's really hard to be positive right now. I'm not sure what I believe in, but your support means a lot. Thank you."

We all want our lives to make sense, to have meaning. This is one of the deepest desires of the human heart. Most people find this meaning by believing in something bigger than themselves. Monica and Charlie both believe in something that helps them see the meaning in their lives and the lives of others. Charlie expresses his faith in God, a supreme being that he believes loves and cares for every person. Monica has faith in the goodness of the universe, believing that if we work on being our best selves, good things will result. Davin is still figuring out what he believes in, but he hungers for something that will give him strength and hope in dealing with the challenges of life.

Hungering for life to have meaning is a common human experience. When we feel that our life doesn't have meaning, we can easily despair or feel sad. We all want to know that what we do matters. We also want to know that the things we experience—both good and bad—have a purpose. Even if that purpose isn't clear, it is possible to have faith that it will become clear over time.

Meaning Leads to Faith

The hunger for meaning leads to the idea of faith. Faith means putting your trust in something or someone. Having confidence in this thing or person gives meaning and purpose to a person's life. Understood like this, faith doesn't even require belief in a supreme being. It can mean believing in nature, the human race, your country, or even yourself. The point is that our hunger for meaning points to the belief in something bigger than ourselves.

Do you believe in something bigger than yourself? If so, what role does this belief play in your life? Does it give meaning to your life?

Hunger for Goodness

A few weeks later, Davin, Monica, and Charlie were working on a history assignment together. They had just read *The Hiding Place,* by Corrie ten Boom. This book tells the story of the ten Boom family hiding Jews from the Nazis during World War II (1939–1945) and the consequences of this. Although the book is filled with horrors and injustices, it is also hopeful in showing the depth of human courage and determination.

"This book seems almost unreal," said Monica. "I think most people would just give up when faced with those situations."

"Except they had their faith in God," replied Charlie. "It gave them hope that goodness and love are greater than evil and hate. That's the point of faith. It gives us hope that good will win out, if not in this life then in the next."

"But you don't have to be a Christian to believe in the importance of goodness," said Monica. "I've seen people from many different religions and even people with no religion making sacrifices to bring goodness into the world."

"And does believing that goodness will win out mean having to believe in an afterlife? Can't we believe goodness will triumph over hatred and evil in the here and now?" asked Davin.

"I mean the ten Boom sisters saw moments of kindness and goodness even in the concentration camp. I've been trying to look for the moments of kindness and goodness around me every day. It's like if I look for them, I see them; if I don't look for them, I don't see them."

"That's interesting," Monica replied. "It's almost like you're saying that experiencing the goodness in the world requires a certain way of seeing the world. It's something that's there, but you don't experience it if you aren't looking for it."

A home in the Netherlands showing a place where Jews were hidden during World War II.

We have reasons to wonder whether goodness is really triumphing over evil. Just consider the ongoing news about violence, economic hardships, and injustices. Then there are the racial injustices, marked especially by the hate crimes committed because of race. Concern for global climate change continues to rise as the country experiences more and more weather-related disasters. We've lived through a pandemic during which schools were shut down and many people lost their lives. To make things worse, people in the United States and other parts of the world are sharply split on many of these issues, dividing families and communities.

Any one of these negative experiences can affect someone's life. This is true because human beings have a deep desire for goodness, an expectation that the world is good, and a general belief that people will treat one another with kindness. When something happens that challenges these understandings, it can cause people to feel a sense of hopelessness for the future. Recent years have seen rises in depression, especially among young people, because of struggles with feelings of sadness and hopelessness. A world filled with hate and injustice goes against the desire for goodness that seems built into us.

The hunger for goodness often leads to one of two responses when people face challenging and hurtful experiences. Some people fall into hopelessness and despair. They mainly see pain and grief without much hope that things will get better. Other people face the same situation and say to themselves: "We can get through this. Things can and will get better with time and effort." These people see beyond their current painful situation with the hope that goodness will overcome their pain.

Goodness Is Connected to Hope

Hopelessness and despair are both valid responses to negative, painful experiences. Both come from

Draw a vertical line down the center of a sheet of paper to create two columns. In the left column, write signs of goodness you see in the world. In the right column, write signs of evil you see in the world. Which column is longer, and why?

the same place: the spiritual hunger for goodness. If we didn't have this hunger, experiencing something bad or hurtful wouldn't really bother us (outside of any physical pain). But because it does bother us, we can say that the hunger for goodness points to a reality that is spiritual because it goes beyond the physical or material world.

The hunger for goodness is connected to hope. Hope is the expectation and desire that things can and will be better than they are now. A hopeful person who has failed at something that really matters keeps trying with the belief that they can do better. A hopeful person who is struggling with money believes that their financial situation will improve in the future. A hopeful person seeing the injustice of racism believes that people's hearts can change and that respect for people's dignity will improve. This isn't just wishful thinking.

Hunger for Connection

Davin, Monica, and Charlie were talking after binge-watching their favorite show at Davin's house during their semester break.

"That is so corny," Charlie proclaimed. "As if those two characters could become friends after all the abuse they dumped on each other."

"I think it's great," replied Monica. "A lot of people who start out on the wrong foot end up liking each

Hope and Your Health

Research shows that people with hope are healthier, physically and emotionally. A *Psychology Today* article states: "Many studies have shown a wide range of physical health benefits of increased hope, including a higher-functioning immune system, better prognosis in chronic illness, and decreased sensations of pain." Not surprisingly, researchers have also shown that people with higher levels of hope have lower levels of anxiety and depression. Researchers have also identified practices that help people cultivate hope, including these:

- spending less time consuming news, which tends to focus on and repeat negative stories
- spending less time on social media, especially if your feed is filled with gossip and negative perspectives
- before going to bed, recalling one positive experience that shows the presence of goodness in the world

other. Remember the characters Clare and Chad and how they disliked each other when they first met? Turns out, they were guilty of the very things they didn't like in each other at first. Once they recognized that, they ended up becoming best friends."

"I once heard that the opposite of love isn't hate," said Davin. "The opposite of love is apathy, just not caring about the other person at all. I think our natural desire is to want connection with other people. But sometimes we avoid connecting with other people because we've been hurt in some way and don't want to be vulnerable again."

"I don't know about all that," replied Charlie. "All I know is that I love the two of you."

"We love you too!" said Monica and Davin as they all laughed together.

Every human person hungers for connection. Consider how people thrive and are happy when they are part of a caring and accepting community. Or how people suffer physically and emotionally when surrounded by mean and uncaring people. Or worse, how awful it is to feel alone and completely unconnected to other people. Many studies support the critical importance of being connected to loving and caring people. For example, one study found that being alone too much—often called social isolation—increases the risk of premature death regardless of the cause.

The hunger for connection is not limited to relationships with other people. Think of the role that pets play for many people. Have you ever heard someone with a cat or dog say, "I don't know how I would get along without them"? Human beings also hunger for a connection with nature. During the COVID-19 pandemic, people flocked to outdoor activities in record numbers. When their connection with friends and family was limited, people realized how healing and nurturing it is to be connected to nature.

Many people experience another kind of hunger for connection. It is the connection to a power greater than themselves. Throughout human existence, people have recognized that their connection to a higher power is what gives life meaning and hope. Some even go so far as to say that without this connection, their spiritual hungers are never truly satisfied.

Connection and Love Go Hand in Hand

The hunger for connection is related to love. Loving and being loved are the ways we express our connection with others. Being able to share love with others is an essential part of being human. Think about times you have felt really loved by a family member or friend. Would it be accurate to say that these were times when you also felt the closest to them, the most connected to them? Love and connection go hand in hand.

<D>raw three interlocking circles. Label one "Meaning," one "Goodness," and one "Connection." In the "Meaning" circle, write down things that give meaning to your life. In the "Goodness" circle, write down good things you experience and hope for. In the "Connection" circle, write down things and people you feel connected to. Is there something that all three circles have in common?

spirituality Ways of tending to the part of the self that is not physical. It is expressed through actions, beliefs, values, and attitudes that characterize a person's life.

Thriving, Not Just Surviving

Let's conduct a thought experiment. Assume that the spiritual hungers for meaning, goodness, and connection are part of every person's experience. What do these hungers point to? People will have different answers to this question. Some will say that these hungers are the result of biological evolution—that these hungers are hardwired into our brain for our survival. This answer has some truth to it. The hunger for meaning motivates us to grow and invent, the hunger for goodness motivates us to help one another, and the hunger for connection motivates us to form supportive groups and communities.

Another perspective builds on this survival answer. This perspective says that our ways of satisfying our spiritual hungers do more than help us survive. They help us thrive and grow into our full potential as human beings. People who embrace this perspective believe that human beings exist for more than just survival. We have been created to imagine new and better futures, to create beautiful works of art, to explore and understand the world, to celebrate life with dance and song, to be sources of love and goodness to friends and strangers alike. The hungers for meaning, goodness, and connection call us to use our imagination, intelligence, and creativity in ways that lead to a truly happy and fulfilled life.

The ways we feed our spiritual hungers are part of our **spirituality**. Every person has a spirituality, whether they call it that or not. This is because everyone experiences hungers that go beyond physical needs. A person's spirituality is expressed through actions, beliefs, values, and attitudes that characterize their life.

Responding to our spiritual hungers involves choices. On the one hand, we can choose to nurture our spiritual hungers in healthy ways. A person might do this through connecting with other people, praying, serving others, or intentionally being open to new experiences. This leads to a life that is joyful and thriving. On the other hand, we can starve our spiritual hungers, or worse, feed them in unhealthy ways. This could happen if a person withdraws from others, is resentful and unforgiving, or does not take time to reflect and center themselves. This leads to a life that is joyless, selfish, and often self-destructive. Young adulthood is a time of life when people face these spiritual choices in a more conscious way.

As you read this book, try to see in it an invitation to reflect on any hungers you experience related to the spiritual, or nonphysical, aspects of yourself and to consider the role religion can or might play in helping you satisfy those hungers. The world's religions have long provided wisdom and support for feeding spiritual hungers. First, they provide practices intended to help people grow in their spiritual lives and to become their best selves. They also provide a community of people that support one another.

Second, the world's religions are a source of knowledge and experience about spiritual truths. Over many centuries, religious people have reflected on their spiritual experience. Gifted people within these traditions—they might be called buddhas, prophets, saints, rabbis, and so on—have special

insights. These teachers pass on their wisdom to new generations through writings and oral traditions so that we might benefit from them.

You do not have to belong to a religion to live a spiritual life. Many people throughout human history and from around the world, however, have found that a religion's beliefs, practices, and community have helped them develop fulfilling spiritual lives.

Let's consider the changes that are occurring in the lives of teens and the spiritual opportunities that these changes bring as we continue to think about what religion provides that makes it valuable in people's lives.

For Review

1. Why is the hunger for meaning important in the lives of human beings?
2. Describe two possible responses to challenging and hurtful experiences.
3. Describe three different kinds of connection that most people find important in their lives.
4. Define *spirituality*.

A Time of Unique Growth

Most people don't spend a lot of time thinking about where they are in their life's journey. This is just as true of teens as it is of adults. The demands of school, family life, and extracurricular activities can keep high school students busy. If you are the typical student using this book, you are in the period of adolescence. These are crucial years of human development when a person moves from being a child to being an adult. It is a period of rapid change and physical, mental, and emotional growth. Let's look at some of the growth that occurs during adolescence and how it impacts a person's capabilities and decisions, especially regarding their spirituality.

Growing Body, Mind, and Heart

During adolescence, human beings undergo amazing growth in their physical, mental, and emotional capabilities. The growth in young people's bodies, minds, and emotions is more rapid and extensive during adolescence than at any other time of life, except perhaps during infancy. All this growth leads to new capabilities, new possibilities, and new decisions. You are probably familiar with these changes, but let's review some highlights.

Changing Body

Adolescence is marked by the start of puberty, which typically occurs between the ages of eight and fourteen. These are some of the physical changes that occur during puberty:

- The body grows faster than at any other time of life except between birth and age two. During puberty, young people will grow on average about two inches taller each year over several years.

- The body grows more muscle, becoming stronger, and develops greater physical stamina. Physical reaction times also improve. These changes lead to greater athletic ability, for example.

- The body becomes capable of starting new life.

   Keep in mind that the timing and amount of these changes varies widely between individuals. Growth spurts will also be uneven, sometimes happening quickly and other times more slowly. There is no "normal" except what is normal for each person.

Changing Mind

Although the human brain reaches 90 percent of its adult size during childhood, it continues to go through dramatic changes, sometimes called brain remodeling, during adolescence. These changes in the brain lead to changes in the way you and your peers may think and make decisions. Here are some of the mental changes that occur during adolescence:

- Unused connections in the brain are discarded, while other connections grow. The part of the brain where more connections are pruned away are in the back of the brain, the part that is more primitive and reactionary. Until this pruning process is complete, adolescents tend to be more impulsive, sometimes acting without thinking through the consequences.

What changes in your body, mind, and emotions have you experienced over the last two years?

Consider the view that social media can be harmful to young people's self-esteem. Experts note that when teens compare themselves to the influencers they follow on social media, they often feel inadequate or even deprived. On a scale of one (no influence) to five (high influence), rate the impact you think social media has on your feelings of self-worth.

Think about a big decision you recently had to make. Were you tempted to rush to a decision, or was it easy to take your time thinking about all the possible outcomes?

- The part of the brain that is growing more connections is the front of the brain. This is the decision-making part of the brain, which is responsible for impulse control, problem-solving, and long-term planning. This process takes time and happens later in adolescence. As it continues, adolescents may think through consequences more thoroughly and spend more time thinking about and planning their future.

- The brain's chemistry is changing as new hormones and chemicals are produced, flooding the brain with new sensations. Higher levels of the neurotransmitter dopamine bring new feelings of physical pleasure and satisfaction. Higher levels of the neurotransmitter serotonin help regulate and smooth out moods and behaviors. The experience of alternating quickly between emotional highs and lows is a sign that these hormonal levels have not yet balanced out.

Changing Heart

The rapid physical and mental changes that occur in your body and brain during the teen years are the foundation for changes in emotions, or the life of the heart. This is unavoidable, so you, your family, and your friends should accept these changes as natural and normal. These are some of the common emotional changes you may experience:

- Due to changing brain chemistry, feelings intensify. You might find that things that previously made you a little sad or a little happy can make you very sad or very happy. This can be confusing or even frightening.

- The same changing brain chemistry can lead to big and sometimes sudden mood swings. You might start out the day feeling positive and happy, and by lunchtime be feeling angry, sad, or hopeless—maybe all three!

- Biological changes can lead to sexual attraction, which can lead to dating and close friendships. The attraction can be to someone of the opposite sex or of the same sex, which does not necessarily have any bearing on eventual sexual identity.

- Because of biological changes, you may compare yourself to others. If this happens, it could affect your self-esteem.

- As the front part of the brain continues to develop, you may find yourself thinking more and more about the future. This might lead to feelings of excitement and adventure in anticipation of new experiences. Or it could lead to feelings of frustration, anxiety, or sadness if you do not see a path to a future you want to experience.

If you or your peers are not ready for these emotional changes or do not have caring people to help you through them, there can be negative impacts. For example, changing hormones might make you raise your voice over something that isn't that bad. Or you might have tears in your eyes when hearing something a little sad. These things could cause people to be upset with you or maybe make fun of you, even though your reactions are perfectly normal given the physical and emotional changes you are experiencing.

We could add many more changes to these lists, but these points can help you appreciate the significance and the far-reaching consequences of the changes you and your peers are going through. Of particular concern in this course is the significance these changes have for your ability to think and act spiritually.

Growing Spiritually

Davin, Monica, and Charlie were sitting together in the school lounge during their free period. "How are you guys doing on your religion essay?" Monica asked. "You know, the one where you have to describe your personal spirituality. I don't even know where to start. I mean, I don't pray, and I don't go to church, so what is there to write about?"

"I'm almost done," Charlie responded.

"Yeah, teacher's pet!" Monica laughed. "I mean, your family goes to church and probably prays together and all that stuff. Easy for you to write about."

"Yeah, that's true," Charlie said. "But the essay is supposed to be about my personal spirituality, not just what my family does. It's got me thinking about what God means to me and how I relate to God."

"It really helped me when Mrs. Rhodes said that spirituality is about all of our life," Davin chimed in. "So, I've been writing about my decision to join the football team even when my dad had doubts about it. And about what music means to me—how it calms me and helps me relax. I'm even writing about the time I went to see a counselor about my sadness last year."

"Hmm . . ." mused Monica. "Maybe I'm making this harder than it has to be."

Divide a sheet of paper into three columns. Label the first "Beliefs," the second "Values," and the third "Actions." In the appropriate columns, write down the beliefs, values, and actions that best describe your personal spirituality.

Every person has a spirituality, that is, a way of tending to the part of the self beyond the physical—the part of the self that hungers for meaning, goodness, and connection. As a young person's body, mind, and heart grow during adolescence, their awareness of their spiritual hungers also grows. As teens are more aware of these hungers, the possibilities for their spiritual life also grow.

Children normally mimic what they see, and they often trust the adults in their lives. So as a child, a person's spirituality may be determined primarily by their family and their religious community (if they belong to one). It is common during adolescence to begin to explore spiritual questions more deeply, as Charlie, Monica, and Davin are starting to do. And teens who identify with a particular religion may find themselves wanting to explore for themselves beliefs they have grown up with.

Even if a person doesn't actively participate in a religion, it doesn't mean they don't have a spiritual life. In the conversation between the three friends, Monica initially seems to be assuming that because she isn't religious, she doesn't have a spiritual life. This isn't true. A person does not have to belong to a religion to grow spiritually.

To better understand how young people's spiritual lives grow, consider each of the following five scenarios, keeping these questions in mind as you read through each one:

- Can you see how a change in body, mind, or heart led to the new situation?

- Can you identify the spiritual hungers connected to the situation?

Questions about Religion

As our spirituality develops, we might find ourselves having a lot of questions. Some of those questions will revolve around religion. It is natural to have such questions, especially as a young person. Discussions about religious questions are a good way to understand and grow your spiritual life. But sometimes authority figures discourage religious questions. From the Springtide Research Institute study mentioned earlier, here is one young adult's experience:

> I questioned my religion when I was pretty young, but a lot of my questions were kind of shut down by family members too. So, I couldn't really ask them. But as an adult, probably a few years ago, I started asking questions again.

If you have religious questions, seek out a trusted, caring adult to discuss them with!

A Driving Dilemma

Delores's situation. Delores is old enough to begin taking driver's education classes. Her father is pressuring her to sign up, but she isn't sure she wants to right now. For one thing, it would cut into her time volunteering at the animal shelter. But more importantly, she believes that to battle climate change, people need to drive less, not more. She's checked out the city's bus routes and bike paths, and she's made a plan for using the bus and her bike to get wherever she needs to go. But she hasn't told her father yet because she knows he will not be happy with this decision.

Reflection on Delores's experience. Delores's growing body and mind have made her ready to drive a car responsibly. And her spiritual hunger for goodness causes her to want to make this decision in a way that makes the world a better place. Her spiritual hunger for connection makes her want to please her father, but it also pushes her to do what's best for the whole planet, which is now causing a conflict.

To Play or Not to Play?

Hakeem's situation. Hakeem has really grown in the past year. He's 6 inches taller! He has started questioning if he should join the basketball team this year. On the one hand, it could be a lot of fun and his height could give him a real advantage. But he was on the team two years ago and hated it. He felt awkward and clumsy and sat on the bench most of the time. What if the same thing happens this year?

Reflection on Hakeem's experience. Hakeem's dramatic physical growth has led to this situation. And it is a spiritual issue because his spiritual hungers have been engaged. His hungers for meaning and connection could be satisfied if he tries out and becomes a successful player. But what

© olaser / iStockphoto.com

if Hakeem doesn't do well? Then those hungers could be frustrated. Hakeem is facing one of the great truths of the spiritual life—that growing spiritually often requires taking a risk.

Torn between Two Parents

Ayesha's situation. It's been over three years since Ayesha's parents divorced. She mostly lives with her mom and spends an occasional weekend with her dad. At first, it was great living with her mom, but lately they've gotten into more and more arguments. Her mom is very traditional in her faith and makes Ayesha wear conservative clothing whenever she goes out. Because of this, Ayesha is feeling more and more like an outsider at school and even with her friends. Her father is not as conservative and lets her wear what she wants. He's told her that she can live with

him whenever she is ready. She's wondering if moving in with him might be the best thing for her right now.

Reflection on Ayesha's experience. Ayesha's developing mind and heart are causing her to think about her life in new ways. She's realizing she could have a choice in how she dresses. The increased hormones in her brain are causing her to feel stronger emotions, leading to conflict with her mother. Her hunger for connection is strong right now, and it seems like some of her mother's religious beliefs are keeping her from making new friends.

Friends or *Friends?*

Bruce's situation. Bruce has a problem. He and Cara have been neighbors and friends since grade school. They eat over at each other's houses, they do homework together,

they are in a band together, and they spend time playing games and watching movies together. Lately, Cara's been spending time with Sanjay, and Bruce is feeling some things he's never felt before. Is it jealousy? He's never thought of Cara that way before. But last night when they were watching a movie, she fell asleep with her head on his shoulder. And that felt confusing to him.

Reflection on Bruce's experience. Bruce's growing body and heart might be causing his love for Cara to move from just friendship to romantic love. The spiritual hunger for connection really kicks into overdrive when sexual attraction is added to the mix. Bruce's hunger for meaning and goodness makes him want to respond to this attraction in the best possible way.

Switching Churches

Angel's situation. Angel has been a Pentecostal Christian all her life. She believes in God and considers Jesus her friend. Her church is small, and everyone knows one another, but they have very few youth activities. One of Angel's Catholic friends invited her to a youth activity at the local Catholic parish, and Angel had a great time. She's gone to several other Catholic events with her friend, including a national conference. Everything is so different, and Angel finds that she really likes the Catholic rituals and Eucharistic adoration times. She's thinking about joining the Catholic Church but is afraid people at her church will react negatively.

Reflection on Angel's experience. Angel's growing mind and heart have expanded her understanding and appreciation of different religious traditions. Her hungers for meaning and connection are causing her to explore the possibilities for spiritual growth that a different religion might bring into her life. Her hunger for goodness, though, makes her unwilling to cause pain to the people in the church she grew up in. This is a challenging spiritual situation.

Have you faced an experience like any of these five examples? What new choices have your growing body, mind, and heart brought into your life?

These scenarios may help you appreciate the time of life you are in right now. Your growing body, mind, and heart are making you capable of understanding the role that tending to the spiritual aspects of yourself plays in your life and the lives of others. And because many people find that religious communities—with their organized systems of beliefs and practices—enhance their spirituality, this is the ideal time to study and think more deeply about how religion can be valuable in people's lives.

Being Spiritual and Being Religious

After their teacher handed back their papers about their personal spiritualities, Davin, Monica, and Charlie gathered in the hallway. "What do you think about the question Mrs. Rhodes posed to us?" asked Monica. "Are you spiritual or religious or both?"

"I'm definitely both," responded Charlie. "I believe in God and my church. My church family means a lot to me, and they give me a lot of support. My religion's teachings guide my life."

"I'm still figuring it out," said Davin. "I guess I would call myself religious, but I don't go to services very often, and I have a lot of questions about what my religion teaches. But I can see how important it is to my parents and other people in my family."

"I'm definitely spiritual but not religious," Monica declared. "I think it's important to love others, take care of the earth, and speak for justice. I just don't think I need to be part of a religion to do that."

"I think it's great that even though we have different answers to the question, we can still be friends," said Charlie. "My grandparents told me that when they were growing up, people used to look at people from other religions as enemies. I'm glad it isn't that way anymore."

"Well, hopefully it isn't that way anymore," replied Davin. "Sometimes I'm not so sure."

What are the five most important things in your life right now? How would you have answered this question five years ago?

Think of someone who has different religious beliefs than you. Do their different religious beliefs make them different from you? How?

After reading the explanations of *spiritual* and *religious,* what questions do you have? How would you explain to a friend how being spiritual and being religious are closely connected but not exactly the same?

Charlie, Monica, and Davin's conversation is typical of the way many teens think about spirituality and religion. In this chapter so far, we have been using the words *spiritual* and *religious* almost interchangeably, as if they mean the same thing. And even though these two concepts are closely related in many people's minds, they are not exactly the same. Let's consider how being spiritual and being religious are connected and how they are different.

To be spiritual means that a person recognizes that human life is more than just meeting physical needs, such as the need for food, water, and air. It means recognizing that there are spiritual hungers, such as those discussed in this chapter, and appreciating how experiences such as faith, truth, beauty, justice, and love satisfy these hungers. Being spiritual means recognizing that practices such as prayer, meditation, reflection, and service are also ways to feed those hungers and making these experiences and practices part of one's life. Ultimately, it means sensing that there is something larger than oneself, whether one believes in a supreme being or god.

For most people, to be religious means to identify with an established religion. This means being connected to a community with an organized system of beliefs, rituals, and practices, and a leadership structure that supports these things. A primary characteristic of a religion is the belief that a higher power is at work in the universe. The names for this higher power vary from religion to religion.

Belonging to a religion and following its beliefs and practices are ways many people respond to their spiritual hungers. The world's religions provide opportunities to experience truth, beauty, justice, and love. They provide ways for their members to practice reflection, prayer, meditation, and service. For most people who belong to a particular religion, their spiritual life and their religious life are pretty much the same thing.

As you are on your way to becoming an adult, you have an opportunity to decide which spiritual experiences and practices have value for you, and what role religion will play in your spiritual life. Your developing body, mind, and heart will open you up to a deeper and more fulfilling spiritual life. Along the way, you will probably have more questions about religious beliefs and practices. Your thoughts on what religion provides that makes it valuable in people's lives will grow and change. Before turning to look at the Catholic faith in chapter 2, let's consider the religious truths held in common by most of the world's religions.

Talking about Religion and Spirituality

Conversations about religion and spirituality can help us grow into our best selves if done respectfully. Here are some guidelines for having respectful conversations:

- Honor and respect the other person's religious choices, whether the person belongs to your religion, another religion, or no religion at all. Do not try to convert the person to your beliefs.
- Be genuinely curious about the other person's religious beliefs and practices. Do not attack or belittle their beliefs and practices.
- Be willing to share what you believe and why you believe it, but not in a way that comes across as the only way to believe.
- Be honest about your own religious questions and struggles. Everyone has them!

 ## For Review

1. Give an example of how an adolescent's body is changing.
2. Give an example of how an adolescent's mind is changing.
3. Give an example of how an adolescent's heart or emotions are changing.
4. Give an example of how an adolescent's changing body, mind, and heart can lead to new situations and decisions connected to spiritual hungers.
5. What does it mean to be spiritual?
6. What does it mean to be religious?

The Shared Wisdom of the World's Religions

What are the religious questions young people ask? By *religious questions*, we mean big questions about why we are here, what keeps us alive, and where are we headed. Consider this list of questions.

- How did the universe come to exist?

- Is there a god or supreme power responsible for creation?

- Is the universe basically a machine set in motion by God? Or is it something more?

- Does my life have a purpose?

- Does God care for me?

- When I die, is that the end for me?

How many of these questions have you wondered about? Have you ever talked about them with friends or family members? If you are a member of a religious faith, how does your religion answer these questions?

Since the first humans appeared on our planet, they have thought about questions like these. Over time, different religious traditions developed and provided answers to these questions. The traditions often started out small, associated with a particular tribe or nation. Many died out, but some grew and expanded across the globe. The largest worldwide religions that exist today are Christianity (which includes Catholics, Orthodox Christians, and Protestants), Islam, Hinduism, Buddhism, Taoism, Confucianism, and Judaism. Many other smaller, but still important, religious traditions exist as well. The beliefs and practices of these global religions feed the spiritual hungers of human beings.

People of different religious backgrounds sometimes disagree bitterly, and some of these disagreements have led to violence and war. This may suggest that huge and irreconcilable differences exist among the world's different religions, but this isn't entirely true. When people from different religions talk to one another with open minds and hearts, they find they have as more in common than not. In the last several centuries, religion scholars and religious leaders have recognized that the world's major religions hold many of the same core beliefs. Let's consider some of these core beliefs as one more way to explore what religion provides that makes it valuable in people's lives.

There Is a Divine Creator

Being in nature is a spiritual experience for many people. Walking amid trees, floating on a lake, or looking up at the night sky can bring a profound sense of peace. Even more, it brings a sense of wonder at the beauty, majesty, and diversity of the natural world. And it raises the question, How did all this come to be?

A core belief of the world's religions is that the universe we know came to be as the result of **divine** creation. That is, the universe came into existence through the creative power of a supreme or divine being or beings. The name most used for the supreme being(s) in predominantly Christian countries such as the United States is **God**. Some of the world's religions believe in only one god. This is called **monotheism**. These religions include Judaism, Christianity, Islam, the Bahá'í faith, some forms of Hinduism, and several others. Many religions believe in multiple gods. This is called **polytheism**. These religions include Taoism, some forms of Hinduism, and the ancient Greek and Roman religions. Buddhism does not teach a belief in a divine creator, and for this reason many consider Buddhism a spiritual tradition or philosophy rather than a religion.

This brings us to another point. In addition to believing that the universe was brought into being by God, the world's major religions hold that creation is an expression of divine love, a love that brings all that exists to life. Another way of saying this is that God is in some way part of everything that exists, connecting all creation in divine love. As part of creation, human beings are also connected to one another, and to all of creation, by divine love.

Pope Francis has said on several occasions, "Faith and violence are incompatible." Many other religious leaders agree with him. If this is true, why are so many acts of violence committed in temples, synagogues, and churches or carried out in the name of religion around the world today?

Imagine that someone said to you, "There's absolutely no reason to believe there is a God." How might you respond to this person? Can you give some reasons showing that belief in a divine creator is reasonable?

divine Related to or coming from God.

God A name for the supreme being, creator of all that is.

monotheism The belief that there is only one God.

polytheism The belief that there are many gods.

Can Science Prove That God Exists?

Science cannot prove or disprove the existence of God. The supreme being that created all space and time must exist outside of space and time. So science, the discipline that seeks to understand and measure space and time, cannot measure God. However, this does not prevent human beings from making arguments for the existence of God. It does require using logical arguments, rather than scientific reasoning, when discussing the existence of God.

A person crawling under the edge of the sky represents the human quest to know what exists beyond space and time.

Where and how do you experience love in your life? What are the things that block you from experiencing even greater love? Are these blocks from inside of you or from things outside of you?

Human Beings Are Made for Love

Another belief shared by the world's major religions is that human beings are meant for love. We are created to be in relationship with the divine creator, with God. If you think of God as a power source with outlets to plug into, human beings were created to plug into those outlets. This is a crude image, but you get the idea. And not only do human beings have the ability to "plug into" God, more importantly, God desires to be in relationship with us. Human beings are unique (not more special than the rest of creation, just unique) in that we can freely choose to receive the love of God and share it with the rest of creation.

The world's major religions hold that when we are connected to God, ultimately our lives will be **blessed**; that is, at a deep level we will be happy and be at peace. The flow of divine love will run through us as it is meant to. On the other hand, when our connection with God is blocked, our lives will be unsettled and even unhappy. What blocks this connection? Things like greed, anger, anxiety, injustice, and ignorance can all hamper our ability to be connected to God.

This does not mean that a deep connection with God means never having problems, difficult relationships, grief, or other hardships in life. It can mean just the opposite. It can mean that God knows our pain and the world's pain and does not ignore it. Thus, a person deeply connected to God also experiences pain, grief, and hardship without trying to hide from it. However, having a strong relationship with God can keep a person from falling into complete sadness and despair, knowing that in the end God's love will triumph.

The world's great religions also teach a variety of spiritual practices that are meant to help human beings stay connected to God. Prayer, meditation, religious rituals, forgiveness, serving others, and studying sacred texts, like Islam's Qur'an and Christianity's Bible, are some of the practices shared

Arguments for the Existence of God

Thomas Aquinas (1225–1274), one of the greatest thinkers of the Middle Ages, developed these five well-known logical arguments for the existence of God:

1. Life is in motion. For life to be in motion, there must have been a "first mover" to get everything going. That mover is God.
2. An egg can't just cause itself to be an egg. There must be a cause outside the egg (in other words, a rooster and a hen!) that causes it to be an egg. Likewise, there must be a first cause outside all creation that caused creation to come into existence, and that first cause is God.
3. For the possibility of everything else to exist, there had to be something in existence first. This something is God.
4. There is something we call truest and best against which we measure everything else that is true and good. This something isn't just an abstract concept but is God.
5. The order in nature isn't just a happy accident. An intelligent being exists to direct all things to their natural end, and this being is God.

blessed To receive a favor or gift bestowed by God, bringing happiness.

by many religions. By making these practices part of one's life, people can stay connected with God, the source of love and blessing.

Human Life Has Purpose

Have you ever been asked what you want to be when you grow up or what you want to study in college? You will no doubt be asked these questions more often in your next few years of high school. These questions can feel annoying to young people who are still trying to figure out what they want to do with their lives.

Here's some good news. The world's great religions make a distinction between the work that you *do* and the kind of person you *are*. Your career and the work you do can take many different paths with few wrong choices. You can be a politician, a health care worker, a plumber or an electrician. You might be a minister, an artist, or a sports enthusiast. These are all possible jobs you might do. But they are not who you are. Who you are is more significant than what you do.

It might be better if people would ask what kind of person you want to be. When asked that, most teens give

© FatCamera / iStockphoto.com

Religious Affiliation Worldwide

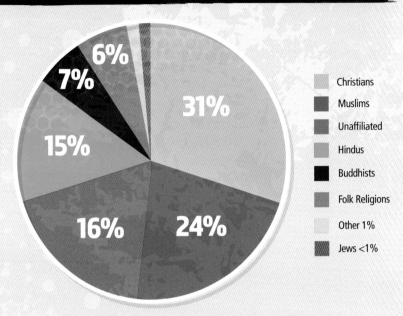

6%

7%

31%

15%

16%   24%

Christians
Muslims
Unaffiliated
Hindus
Buddhists
Folk Religions
Other 1%
Jews <1%

Percentages do not add up to 100 due to rounding. "Christians" includes Catholics. "Folk Religions" includes Indigenous religions. "Other" includes Taoism and Confucianism.

these answers: "I want to be a good friend. I want to help other people. I want to be someone others can count on. I want to be a person who is happy and content." These are all great life goals, and working on them determines the kind of person you will become.

The world's great religions teach that who we are and who we are becoming matters. Human life has a purpose and a goal. Our purpose is to cooperate with God's desire to be a source of beauty, joy, peace, and love. Because God has given human beings free will, we can bring harm to creation—including other humans. But because of our free will, we can also be—we *should* be—sources of healing. We can help creation become what God wishes it to be.

How would you answer the question, What kind of person do you want to be?

Many of the world's great religions believe in some kind of heaven or paradise after death. Some people think of heaven as a reward for doing all the right things, and others think of it as a continuation of a life already lived in union with God's love. What are your thoughts on life after death?

The religions also share a belief that the goal of human life is to be in union with God, to experience the fullness of God's love for us. Some religions teach that we can reach this goal in this life, at least partially. Some religions teach that we reach this goal through reincarnation, living repeated lives in which we keep growing toward spiritual perfection. Some religions believe that we ultimately reach this goal after death, when we see God face-to-face. No matter the specific belief, the world's great religions agree that the goal of human life is to give and receive the love of God, to the greatest degree that we can.

For **Review**

1. What is the difference between monotheism and polytheism?
2. How are creation and divine love connected?
3. Give an example of a logical argument for the existence of God.
4. What happens when human beings are connected to God?
5. According to the world's major religions, what is the purpose and goal of human life?

reflect

Religion, A Love Affair

Suppose someone wants to become a world-class soccer player. Do they only go out on soccer fields by themselves and practice endless hours, teaching themselves how to play? That's not the way the best soccer players achieve their goal. The best soccer players join a good team and find a coach who knows how to bring the best out of them. They study the moves of the world's best players. They value the wisdom and experience of the great soccer players who have gone before them. And they keep practicing, practicing, practicing.

The same is true for our spiritual lives. If we want to become the best version of ourselves, if we want to live lives filled with the most meaning, goodness, and love, it's best not to try to do it all on our own. As you move from childhood to adulthood, you have the opportunity to decide what the best version of yourself will be and how you will become that person. The great religions of the world are filled with wisdom to guide and support you in becoming that person.

The rest of this course takes a deep dive into how one specific faith—the Catholic faith—helps people live lives of meaning, goodness, and connection. The exploration begins in chapter 2, with discussion of the Catholic understanding of how people come to know God.

chapter **2**

Revelation and Faith: Knowing and Responding to God

IN THIS CHAPTER

Revelation: How We Come to Know God 37

The Nature of God 44

The Human Response to God: Faith 50

An Overview of the Worldview, Beliefs, and Practices of Catholics 58

Revelation: How We Come to Know God

An old parable tells a story of six blind men describing an elephant. The first man touched the elephant's ear and said, "This animal seems to be a huge fan." The second blind man touched the elephant's leg. He said, "No, this animal is more like a pillar or a tree trunk." The third man felt the elephant's side and said, "This animal is like a strong textured wall." The fourth, handling the elephant's trunk, exclaimed: "All of you are wrong! This creature is like a large snake." The fifth man touched the tail and said, "I think an elephant is more like a rope." The last man discovered the elephant's tusk and declared: "You are all wrong. This animal is a fierce warrior, shaped like a spear!"

The parable about the elephant has been retold for centuries because it is a clever way to caution people about forming judgments with partial information. Each blind man got stuck at the first part of the elephant he encountered. Sometimes people do that with religion. They encounter one aspect of a religion and base their entire judgment of the religion on that aspect. It's wiser for people to withhold judgment until they've had time to explore many aspects of a religion.

In this chapter, we explore some core Catholic beliefs. The story about the blind men can be read as a cautionary tale of what can be missed if judging things too quickly. No matter what your experience or view of the Catholic faith has been, try to be open to what you might learn and how that could prompt valuable thought and reflection for you. Try to avoid making judgments about the meaning and significance of the Catholic faith until you've explored its many and varied facets.

The spiritual hungers that we experience as human beings point us to the commonly-held belief that all people have a built-in desire for God and a capacity to be in relationship with God. But how do we know what God is like? How do we decide what to believe about God? Where do we get our understandings of God? Let's explore these questions by looking at the Catholic understanding of how we come to know God.

Have you had experiences in which you've learned something about God and God's desires for your life? If so, have you noticed changes in your awareness of God's presence in your life as you have gotten older?

Revelation The communication from God through which human beings come to know who God is.

God Longs for Intimacy with Us

Catholics believe that we can know God because God chooses to be known. Catholics call what God chooses to share **Revelation**. Through Revelation, we can come to know who God is and gain insight about the purpose of creation. This raises the question, Why does God wish to be revealed to human beings? After all, human beings are just created beings. We seem so small and insignificant compared to God.

Just as is true with many other religions, Catholics believe that God created human beings with the ability to have a relationship with God. Our ability to think, imagine, and freely make choices makes it possible for us to be in relationship with our creator. Catholics believe that throughout history God reveals this desire to be in a trusting, loving relationship with us.

Naming the Creator

The world's major religions use a variety of names for the creator. These are some of the most common as written using English-language terms or letters.

Religion	Common Names
Judaism	Yahweh
Christianity	God
Islam	Allah
Hinduism	Brahman (male) or Bhagavati (female)
Bahá'í	Bahá or All-Glorious
Native American	Great Spirit or Creator God

Knowing God through Human Experience and Reason

Catholics believe that God uses many avenues to communicate with us. We'll start our exploration of these avenues with two that are available to us in our day-to-day lives: personal life experiences and logical conclusions we can reach using our own reason.

Experiencing God in the People Who Love Us

One way we come to know God is through personal life experiences. This is particularly true of our experiences with the people who love us. Love relationships can put us in touch with the sense of mystery of God. This is true both when we reach out in love to another person and when we experience another person's love for us. The gift of another's love for us fills us with the sense of the basic goodness of life and with the belief that such goodness can come only from a gracious and loving creator.

Catholics believe that the first way a person experiences divine love is through the love of a parent or caregiver. As infants and children, we learn that the world is good through our family's love for us. This makes believing in a God who loves us more possible. When infants and children do not experience love, they may not trust that the world is good, making belief in a loving God more difficult.

As human beings grow older, their capacity for experiencing love grows deeper. With the changes of adolescence, romantic and sexual love enter the picture. These experiences of love can be intense, overwhelming our thoughts and emotions. They bring the powerful feeling of being loved and accepted for who we are. They also point to a creator who loves us even more deeply. It is for this reason that Catholics have described God's love in passionate, almost romantic, language. A Spanish nun who lived in the sixteenth century, Teresa of Ávila, was

Think of a time when you felt deeply loved. What might that experience and the feelings that went with it tell you about God?

As I Walk

A high school student describes her sense of God's presence in everyday experiences in this poem:

> As I walk into the hallway in school,
> I am kindly greeted by my friends;
> In their acceptance I hear your voice.
>
> At night, during dinner,
> My parents inquire about how
>   my day went;
> In their love and concern I hear
>   your voice.
>
> (Alaine Gherardi,
> in *More Dreams Alive*)

well-known for her holiness and wrote about how she experienced God as the joy of being in a romantic relationship: "The soul is satisfied now with nothing less than God. . . . It is a caressing of love so sweet which now takes place between the soul and God."

Knowing God through Human Reason

Human beings are created with intelligence and the ability to reason. We are able to think about our experiences. We can see ourselves and notice things about the world around us. For many people, this thinking and noticing leads to an awareness of God. Here are a few ways human beings come to understand God through their **reason**.

> **reason** The power of the human mind to think, analyze, and form logical judgments.

From exploring the natural world.
Scientists who study the intricacies of the natural world are increasingly concluding that a world like ours could not exist by chance. The use of their human reason points them to the possibility that creation's wonderful beauty and order point to a divine origin.

We do not have to be a scientist, though, nor an outdoor enthusiast, to be awestruck by the wonders of creation. Most of us can find something to marvel at if we just take the time. If you can, go outside on a clear, peaceful night and stretch out on the grass. Try to find a place away from city lights. Watch the night sky and simply let it speak to you. Avoid trying to analyze anything. Just relax and observe. Or watch ants make anthills in the cracks of a sidewalk, or a spider weaving a web in the corner of a room or window frame. Such moments of contemplating both the immense and the small wonders of creation can expand our heart and mind, opening us to the possibility of God. More than that, we can reasonably assume that creation points to a divine creator who values beauty, diversity, connectedness, order, and love.

Draw a small circle in the center of a piece of paper. Write your name in it. Draw lines connecting three other circles to the center circle. Inside those circles, write: (1) love, (2) nature, (3) the spiritual. In or around those circles, write short descriptions of experiences you've had related to each circle's topic—experiences that could be pointers to God.

From analyzing our spiritual experiences.
Chapter 1 speaks of spiritual hungers common to all human beings. We experience ourselves as more than our physical body. We are conscious, we fall in love, we make deep friendships, we debate, we create, we dream, and we plan for the future. We desire truth, moral goodness, and beauty. All these experiences point to a spiritual dimension in us. They tell us something about God, the one who created us to experience life in this way.

Our experiences and our reason help us understand that belief in God is a reasonable belief. Further, they point to some of the probable characteristics of God. Some people call these experiences the "fingerprints" of God, evidence that God is present and active in the world and in our lives.

Knowing God through Special Avenues

Catholics believe that God chooses to reveal himself in special ways and through specially chosen people. For example, prophets speak about God to others, the Bible's human authors interpret God's work in history, and religious leaders teach about God to their people. Let's explore how we can come to know God through events of history, sacred writings, and official church teachings.

Knowing God through the Events of History

The Revelation of God occurs through the events of history that a community of people experience together. In the Catholic Tradition, this is called **salvation history**. It is the pattern of events in human history in which God's loving presence and actions are revealed. These marvelous events throughout history include the Exodus, when the Israelites were freed from slavery in Egypt, and the death and Resurrection of Jesus. The historical life,

salvation history
The pattern of events in human history in which God's presence and saving actions are revealed.

teachings, and mission of Jesus are understood by Catholics—indeed by all Christians—as the most complete self-revelation of God.

Knowing God through Sacred Writings or Scriptures

Catholics and other Christians believe that the Revelation of God is communicated in a unique and special way through the writings collected in the Bible. They trust that God inspired the human authors and editors of the books of the Bible so that their words would communicate what human beings need to know in order to be their best selves in this life and to spend eternity united with God after death. This is why the Bible is sacred to all Christians. Just how God is revealed in the Bible is a subject of much study and discussion, and we will return to that question in later chapters.

What sacred writings are you familiar with? What do these writings tell you about God and God's relationship with human beings?

Knowing God through Religious Teachings

For Catholics, official teachings and statements of faith have always been a significant means of transmitting God's Revelation. Historical experiences of God happen at particular times with particular groups, and the Scriptures are also written down at a certain point in time. These writings and experiences reveal God to us, but to better understand these "messages" from God, people must reflect on them for a long time and live them out. This is why religious teachings and statements of faith are so important. They take the community's experiences of God's Revelation from the past and try to distill and summarize the community's understanding of these experiences into clearly stated teachings.

Catholics have special teachings called Tradition (with a capital *T*). Tradition contains the teachings that were passed on by Jesus'twelve primary male companions (the Apostles). We look at Tradition in more depth throughout this book, particularly in chapter 8.

For Review

1. According to Catholics, what kind of relationship does God desire with human beings?
2. What is Revelation?
3. What life experiences point us to understanding God and God's love for us?
4. Briefly describe three special avenues through which Catholics come to know the Revelation of God.

The Nature of God

Mr. Farley asked his class, "If you had to describe God in three words, what would they be?"

"*All-powerful, all-knowing,* and *eternal,*" answered Filipe.

"*Loving, forgiving,* and *accepting,*" Cooper responded.

"*Father, Son,* and *Holy Spirit,*" said Beth.

"*Not real, your imagination,* and *wishful thinking,*" said Phoenix.

"Those are all interesting answers," replied Mr. Farley. "Let's explore the Catholic understanding of who God is."

Except for Phoenix's answers, the answers all describe some aspect of God that Catholics believe in. Even Phoenix's answer could be seen as having some truth to it, for on one hand, God is not knowable in the same sense that the moon or a tiger or a person is knowable, because God is not a part of creation in the same way. On the other hand, you could say that God is the most real and knowable thing there is, because nothing would exist without God.

A good piece of wisdom is that human beings must speak of God with a great deal of humility. We need to recognize that no matter who we are or how smart we are, our descriptions of God and how

God relates to us will always fall short. But we can, in our limited human way, come to some understanding of what is revealed to us.

Because God exists outside of time and space, when human beings speak about God, we almost always use a **metaphor**. Metaphors are means of expression that try to describe, by comparison with something else, a trait or characteristic of a person or thing. For instance, a husband might say to his wife, "You are the light in my life." This does not mean that the woman is actually a lamp, of course, but rather that she cheers up her husband and brings him hope and joy, like a lamp in a dark room dispels the darkness and gloom. The metaphor of light tells us something important about the character of this particular woman. Even so, it cannot tell us everything about her. Her husband would be the first to admit that it falls far short of describing her completely!

Catholics use many metaphors to talk about the nature of God. We will look at a few common ones used by Catholics: creator, loving parent, and forgiving judge. These metaphors compare God with human experiences we know and understand. However, it is important to remember that all the images in the world cannot come close to describing the great mystery of God.

God as Creator

The Apostles' Creed is a summary of the core beliefs of Catholicism. A version of it dates back to AD 341. The first line of the **creed** refers to God as creator: "I believe in God, the Father Almighty, creator of heaven and earth" *(Roman Missal).* Most people have the experience of being a creator. Whether it is a drawing, a story, or a song, we have taken an idea and made it exist in the material world. In a similar but infinitely greater way, Catholics believe that God made something that formerly did not exist—the universe!

Which student's answers did you like the most in the exchange with Mr. Farley? What three words would you give in answering Mr. Farley's question?

Think of a metaphor for God that is somewhat original— not one you've typically heard to describe God. What does this metaphor convey about God, and how well do you like it as a descriptor of God?

metaphor A word or phrase for one thing that is used to refer to another thing to show or describe some trait or characteristic of the second thing.

creed A statement that summarizes religious belief.

Chapter 1 discusses how most of the world's religions agree that the universe was created by a supreme being. Many religions have symbolic creation stories that explain how God created the world. In some of these stories, a god or gods created the world out of something that already existed, like a giant turtle or the body of another god. In Hinduism, the god Brahman made the universe out of himself.

The Jewish, Christian, and Muslim religions believe that God (or Allah for Muslims) created the universe out of nothing. Think about this for a minute. Can you imagine creating something from nothing? It sounds like magic, but it isn't magic for God—it is what God does. This is a good example of the mystery of God because it is an aspect of God's nature that human beings cannot wrap their minds around.

Catholics also teach that God created the universe not because God was lonely or wanted some amusement but because creating is what God does. The essence of God is life and love, and life and love must grow, expand, and be shared. We might think of the big bang or however the universe began as the outpouring of God's life and love.

Catholics also believe that besides the material reality that we can experience with our physical senses, there is a spiritual reality that is just as real but that we cannot directly sense. This is what the phrase "heaven and earth" in the Apostles' Creed means. *Heaven* refers to spiritual reality, and *earth* refers to material reality.

Finally, Catholics believe that God did not just create the universe and then sit back and watch it unfold. No, God remains intimately connected to creation. God is somehow part of all that exists. This is not to say that God is a tree or a mountain or a bear; rather, the tree and the mountain and the bear all reflect God's life and love. All creation is a sign of the outpouring of God's life and love into all things, seen and unseen.

Think of something that you created—a story, a song, or a piece of art, for example. What does this creation reveal about you? What part of yourself were you trying to express in your creation? How might a person's experience of creating help them understand belief in God as creator?

God as Loving Parent

Imaging God as a loving parent, Catholics use metaphors of father and mother when talking about God. These metaphors flow from the experience many people have of their parents. Ideally, the experience that most people have of their father and mother includes the following:

- being loved by them just as you are, without having to be someone or something other than who you are

- providing support for you in good times and bad times

- listening to you without judgment; allowing you to vent, try out new ideas, share your mistakes and failures, and share your successes and joys

Human beings realized that these experiences with parents also describe the experiences they have in their relationship with God—even more so with God. When human parents fail to live up to these ideas, however, it is harder for children to understand God as a loving parent.

The metaphor of father is more commonly used than mother by Catholics, because Jesus often called God "father." Jesus called God "Abba," an Aramaic word for father. It was like calling God "Dad" or "Papa," implying an intimate and loving relationship with God. To think about God this way was a challenge for many of the Jews of Jesus' time because they thought about God primarily as a judge or king. Many Christians take for granted the image of God as a loving father, but if it hadn't been for Jesus, we might never have had this understanding.

The Bible also includes images of God as mother. For example, God says through the prophet

Make a list of the qualities you associate with being a mother. Then make a second list of the qualities you associate with being a father. Which of the qualities from either list do you also associate with God?

Isaiah, "As a mother comforts her child, / so I will comfort you," (Isaiah 66:13). Keep in mind that both the Bible and Catholic teaching contain feminine and masculine images of God. This is because God is neither male nor female, so the images of God are not limited to one or the other. Although Catholics honor in a special way the image of God as loving Father, they recognize that any human image we have of God is incomplete. Imaging God as both father and mother can give us a fuller understanding of how Catholics understand God.

God Our Mother

Julian of Norwich (born AD 1342) is a spiritual writer whose work has received renewed attention in our time. In her early thirties, Julian became ill and almost died. During her illness, she had visions of the suffering of Christ and the goodness of God. She wrote a book about her visions, *Revelations of Divine Love*, in which she speaks about God as both mother and father:

> God is our Mother as truly as he is our Father; and he showed this in everything, and especially, in the sweet words where he says, "It is I," that is to say, "It is I: the power and goodness of fatherhood. It is I: the wisdom of motherhood. It is I: the light and grace which is all blessed love. It is I: the unity. I am the sovereign goodness of all manner of things. It is I that make you love. It is I that make you long. It is I: the eternal fulfilment of all true desires."

Julian lived a life of prayer, withdrawn from the world. Some artists' depictions of her reflect the popular belief that she had the company of a cat.

God the Forgiving Judge

Imagine for a moment this scene in a courtroom. A defendant has been found guilty of manslaughter. While driving under the influence, the defendant hit a pedestrian and killed her. Everyone is now back in the courtroom waiting for the judge's sentence. The judge asks the defendant, "Are you truly sorry for your actions?"

"Yes," answers the guilty party. "I truly am. There is no excuse for my actions. I deserve the full punishment for my crimes."

"Then," replies the judge, "I forgive you for your crime. You are free to go." There is a collective gasp in the courtroom as everyone tries to make sense of what just happened!

Catholics believe that there is an order to creation and that order is established by God as the creator. They describe the divine order in the universe through various kinds of laws. Thus, the order in the material reality is described with scientific laws, and the order in the spiritual world is described through spiritual and religious laws.

However, God is not only the lawgiver; God is also the judge of human behavior. The metaphor of judge is often used for God in the Bible. For example, the Book of Isaiah says, "For the LORD is our judge others / the LORD is our lawgiver" (33:22). Jesus emphasizes God's mercy and forgiveness when he talks about the judgment of God, revealing God as a judge who is like the forgiving judge in our scenario. For example, Jesus says, "If you forgive others their transgressions, your heavenly Father will forgive you" (Matthew 6:14). And a letter attributed to the Apostle John says, "If we acknowledge our sins, he is faithful and just and will forgive our sins and cleanse us from every wrongdoing" (1 John 1:9).

Note that the only requirement for receiving God's complete forgiveness is our willingness to forgive others and to admit our wrongdoings (sins).

Think of a time when you did something wrong and were completely forgiven. Was it easy or hard to accept that forgiveness?

Even though one might feel that we deserve punishment, God the forgiving judge only punishes those who will not admit their wrongdoing and who are unwilling to forgive others.

There are other important metaphors for God besides the three discussed here. Some of them are discussed later in the book, particularly the metaphor of God as a Trinity (Community) of divine persons.

For Review

1. Explain why metaphors are often used when Christians speak about God.
2. What are three common metaphors Catholics use to describe the nature of God?
3. What do Catholics believe about how and why God created the universe?
4. Describe two ways Catholics believe God is like the ideal parent.

The Human Response to God: Faith

"Okay, class," Mr. Farley began. "Let's assume that everything we've been discussing about God is true: that God is the creator, the source of all life and love; that God loves us as the most perfect father or mother would love us; that God is the forgiving judge whose law points the way to our best life, but forgives us when we fall short; and that God wishes to be in relationship with every human being. Assuming these things are all true, how should human beings respond to God?"

"We should respond with praise and gratitude," Beth responded.

"I think we should seek out God's plan for us and follow it," said Cooper.

"I think I respond to God every day," Filipe replied. "I mean, when I pray, I put all my concerns in God's hands. I trust that he's helping me get through each day. I look for signs that he's there, working through the people and experiences in my life."

"I just cannot accept that all those things you said are real," Phoenix replied. "I mean, think about the death camps in World War II or the recent earthquakes that killed hundreds of people. How can God be good if he allows all this pain and evil?"

"But God doesn't cause those things to happen," Kayla answered.

"He allows those things to happen because he's given human beings free will, the freedom to make choices. Without this freedom, we'd all be just puppets. If there wasn't the possibility of evil and pain, then there also could be no real goodness and joy. Even though God allows bad things to happen, we can still have faith that he wants the best for us."

"Thank you for your answers," said Mr. Farley. "You are a very thoughtful class, and I appreciate how seriously you are thinking about these questions."

Faith: Trust and Belief

Recognizing the reality of a loving supreme being, or even recognizing the possibility that God may exist, calls for some response. Yes, a person can simply ignore God, but people of many different religions experience a relationship with God as the true answer to the hungers of the human heart, which the first chapter discusses. A relationship with God can bring meaning, goodness, and connection to human life.

Catholicism teaches that God invites all human beings into relationship. All who recognize that invitation have the choice to respond or not. For Catholics, **faith** is responding to God with loving trust and believing what God has revealed. What faith looks like can be different for different people, but it involves both trust and belief, matters of the heart and matters of the head.

It's about Trust

Faith in God, like faith in a human being, is about trust. When we say we have faith in certain friends, relatives, teachers, coaches, pastors, or other important people in our lives, we usually mean that we *trust* them. We all yearn for people who care for us in such authentic ways that we know we can rely on them—friends with whom we can share our deepest feelings and thoughts, and people whose love can give energy and purpose to our lives. When we find a trustworthy friend or older mentor, we realize we have been given a special gift.

In religious faith, a person chooses to trust in God. This process, like trust in human beings, is a matter of the heart—a whole attitude and movement toward God. A person who trusts God is aware of God's love and, in return, loves God, shares their deepest thoughts and feelings with

faith The gift of God by which one accepts the invitation to be in relationship with God. It is a matter of both the heart (trusting in God's love) and the head (believing what God has revealed).

God, depends on God when they are in trouble, and has a sense that God will always be there, even when times are tough or uncertain.

The issue of trust in God is closely related to another question: Is life basically good or not? One answer to this question is yes, life is basically good, and we can approach it with hope. Another is that life is not basically good, and we should live with the attitude that trouble is "just waiting to get me." People who truly place their faith in God believe that God desires the best for them and, because of this, life is basically good. God has created a world where all people, indeed all of creation, should be able to grow and thrive. Human greed, pride, and ignorance can get in the way, causing grief and pain. But having faith in God helps us believe that this is not the last word.

Of the two approaches to describing one's belief about whether life is basically good, which is closer to your own? How does this affect the way you live your life?

It's about Belief

For Catholics, faith in God is not only a matter of the heart, of a trusting attitude toward God; it's also a matter of the mind, of beliefs and convictions about God. Let's return to the answers two students gave to Mr. Farley's question, "How should human beings respond to God?"

Phoenix answered by saying, "How can God be good if he allows all this pain and evil?" Phoenix has a strong belief that if God is truly good, then God should prevent all pain and suffering. Even though Phoenix's heart might like to believe in a God who loves him and wants the best for him, his convictions tell him that a God who does not prevent all pain and suffering is not to be trusted.

Kayla answered by saying, "If there wasn't the possibility of evil and pain, then there could be no real goodness and joy. . . . Even though God allows bad things to happen, we can still have faith that he wants the best for us." Kayla believes that a good God is also a God who gives human beings freedom to follow their own will even if it differs from God's will. God is still good and can still be trusted even if there is pain and suffering in the world.

People with genuine faith in God trust God because of what they *believe*—that God is all-good, that God created them and holds them in love, that God wants their happiness, and in the case of Christians, that God sent Jesus, God's own Son, to save them and the whole world out of love for them. Their trust in God enables them to hold these beliefs with even greater conviction.

A Gift, Not an Achievement

Faith, for Catholics, is trusting in God and holding beliefs or convictions about God. This is the human part of a dynamic relationship with God. But before we go any further, we need to clarify the Catholic understanding of how a person comes to have faith at all.

What personal beliefs or ideas do you have about God?

God Makes the First Move

It would be a mistake to see faith as something a person works at and strives toward, as if it all depends on the person. The Catholic understanding of faith is that human beings are created by God with a built-in desire for God. It is written in their hearts. They may not always recognize it as a desire for God. They may instead experience it as a restlessness or a searching. But Catholics believe it is there, in each and every person.

Having created us with this built-in longing, God does not then abandon us to wander aimlessly on our own. God is constantly trying to reach us, to get through to us, to reveal something of God's own self to us. So God—not us humans—makes the first move. The human yes to God's invitation, the response of faith, is the second move. God longs for a yes response from each of us and pours out the help to enable us to respond.

A Free Gift and a Free Response

It is God's nature to love, to give God's own self freely to us. But it is our nature as human beings to respond to God's love freely. We can choose to put our faith in God—or not. Nothing or no one can *make* us believe—certainly not our parents or teachers or anyone else who seems to be encouraging us to have faith. The response of genuine faith is a free act of giving our trust and belief to God. It cannot be coerced, forced, or bought.

A Lifetime Offer

You may have met people (or perhaps you think this way) who ask if you have been saved, which is a way of asking if you have decided to have faith in Jesus.

Have you ever been approached by someone asking about your religion or religious commitment? If so, how do you feel about that experience?

Would you rather be offered the invitation to faith as a one-shot offer or as a lifetime offer? Explain your answer.

A Question, an Answer

I don't know Who—
or what—
put the question,
I don't know
when it was put.
I don't even
remember answering.
But at some moment
I did answer
Yes to Someone—
or Something—
and from that hour
I was certain
that existence
is meaningful
and that, therefore,
my life,
in self-surrender,
had a goal.

(Dag Hammarskjöld,
    in *Markings*)

"Do you *believe* in Jesus?" is the first question people like this ask, and the next questions are, "*When* were you saved? When did you make your decision for Jesus?" That way of thinking presumes there is one moment in time when we make a definite, once-and-for-all decision to have faith, and after that there is no question about it.

Although that might be the experience of some people, the Catholic understanding of faith is different. It presumes that the response of faith is given through a lifetime of decisions, not just one. Every day, God is offering life, and every day, in many small and large decisions, people can choose to trust in God and try to deepen their beliefs about God. One's faith may vary, being a strong, brilliant torchlight in one season of a person's life and a small, flickering matchlight in another season. At times, the light of faith in a person's life may go out completely. God is, however, always offering the invitation to come back to faith. It is "a lifetime offer" as well as "the offer of a lifetime"!

The invitation to faith from the Catholic perspective, then, is a gift freely offered to every human person by God, and the response of faith must be freely chosen by the person if it is to be faith at all. People of faith do not *achieve* faith. Rather, they choose to *accept* what God is offering them all the time.

The Challenge of Responding

Not all people feel the invitation to respond to God. Some simply do not believe that God exists. Others may not feel certain about God's existence. But many people feel the call to believe and trust in God. We can respond to God's invitation to faith with a yes or a no. One's yes or no may not always be at 100 percent. People are likely to waver and shift as they go through life. And, as was said earlier, a yes or no may be given not all at once but in many opportunities over a lifetime.

For those whose response to God's invitation is yes, questions arise: How do I live out that relationship with God in my life? Each of us must search for the truth with sincerity and open-mindedness. But it is not meant to be a lonely search, undertaken on our own. Perhaps this course in Catholicism will be a significant help in your search. Whether you were raised Catholic or not, this course can offer you insights into the faith heritage that has inspired many of your teachers and those who founded your school, possibly your parents, and millions of great and even heroic people who have gone before you.

What is your opinion on this statement: *No one should be raised to believe in a particular religion; instead, at a certain age, a person should have all religions explained to them and then be allowed to choose which one is most appealing.*

For **Review**

1. How is faith in God about trust?
2. How is faith in God about belief?
3. How do trust and belief influence each other?
4. How does the process of coming to faith get started?
5. Explain why Catholics believe that faith in God is more than a one-time decision.

An **O**verview of the **Worldview, Beliefs,** and **Practices** of **Catholics**

This chapter has introduced three ideas that are important to the Catholic faith: that God chooses to be revealed to human beings, that Catholics use key metaphors to describe God's nature, and that freely chosen faith is the human response to God. These ideas are the roots the Catholic **worldview** grows out of. They are the roots that important Catholic beliefs grow out of. And they are roots for how Catholics live out their faith.

The remaining nine chapters of this book consider the Catholic worldview, Catholic beliefs, and Catholic practices that grow from these root concepts. As in the story of the blind men and the elephant, a person cannot fully appreciate Catholicism without putting together all these pieces. For many who do this, a vibrant, growing, and beautiful religion emerges.

This final section of this chapter invites you to take a brief look at some key aspects of the Catholic worldview and overviews of Catholic beliefs and practices. These things can help give you a sense of the bigger picture before studying the coming chapters, which dive into details.

Catholic Worldview

Just like people from other religions, Catholics have a unique worldview. Many Catholics don't even realize that they have this unique perspective until they spend time with people from other religious or nonreligious backgrounds. These are some of the characteristics of the Catholic worldview:

- Catholics recognize that God is present to, in, and through all creation. Because of this, all creation has the potential to be a source of God's goodness.

- Catholics place their trust in the essential goodness of the human person, who is made in the image of God, even though we are imperfect.

worldview How a person sees and understands the world. A person's worldview is influenced by their experiences and beliefs.

- Catholics appreciate both faith and reason, both religion and science. When we experience conflict between religion and science, Catholics believe it is because we have an inadequate understanding of one or the other.

- Catholics believe that God has revealed all the spiritual truths a person needs to know through the Catholic Church. But Catholics also recognize and affirm the spiritual truths they share with other religions and all people of goodwill.

- Catholics believe in the importance of community in living out their faith. Though Catholics value and nurture their personal relationship with God, they distrust any spirituality that reflects a primary attitude of "it's just God and me—I don't need a church."

- Catholics respect and embrace a wide variety of spiritualities and prayer forms.

Which points from the "Catholic Worldview" list do you find yourself agreeing with? Which points do you need to better understand?

Catholic Beliefs

Catholics have core beliefs that they believe God has revealed and that they accept in faith. These are some of the core beliefs:

- God created human beings to be in perfect loving relationship with one another and with God.

- The sin of the first humans deprived human beings of that perfect loving relationship.

- Throughout human history, God has worked to restore the relationship of love and trust that was lost through sin. God did this by entering into special relationships based on mutual promises, called covenants, with various people throughout history.

- God sent his Son, Jesus Christ, who revealed that God is love. He revealed that God is one being in three persons: Father, Son, and Holy Spirit.

Which beliefs from the "Catholic Beliefs" list do you best understand? Which would you like to better understand?

- Jesus fully restored humanity's relationship with God. He offered himself as the perfect love offering for the forgiveness of sins and the restoration of the relationship of love and trust between God and humankind.

- Following his death, Jesus was brought back to life in the Resurrection. Christ overcame death, and life with God after death became possible for all.

- Jesus Christ established the church with his Apostles as its first leaders.

- The Holy Spirit, always present and active, gives life and holiness to the church.

- All people are destined for life after death. Catholics believe that the baptized as well as others who seek God with a sincere heart can find eternal life with God and complete happiness.

Beliefs of Young Catholics about God

A recent study by Springtide Research Institute asked Catholics ages 13 to 25 what they believe about a higher power, whether it be God, gods, or some other divine source of universal energy. Twenty-eight percent say that they believe a higher power exists and have no doubts about that. Another 22 percent say that they believe in a higher power's existence more than they doubt it. That's 50 percent. The other half say they don't believe, don't know, or doubt a high power's existence more than they believe.

A young Catholic woman the researchers interviewed talked about retreat experiences and shared this reflection on faith and doubt:

> I mostly went to see my friends, but I guess the faith aspect of these retreats was part of it. . . . Like struggling with the idea of even believing in God and knowing what or what not to believe. . . . That's something we talked about in these groups. It actually made me feel a little bit better. It's like, *Oh, like we can have doubts.* We can struggle with these feelings and they're still, we're still, valid, you know? So that was actually kind of refreshing.

The same study found that 87 percent of young Catholics say they are religious, and 85 percent say they are spiritual.

Catholic Practices

Catholic practices are the way Catholics live out their faith in the world. These practices are closely related to Catholic beliefs, and some of these practices could also be listed as a belief as well as a practice:

- Catholics belong to local religious communities called parishes. They gather each week on Sunday (or Saturday evening) with their parish community for worship. Their worship service is called the Mass.

- Catholics celebrate special rituals called the sacraments. The sacraments bestow God's gifts upon those who celebrate them.

- Catholics follow a special calendar with all the seasons and holy days. Some of these seasons and holy days are Advent, Christmas, Ash Wednesday, Lent, Good Friday, and Easter.

- Catholics place a strong emphasis on living morally. Their moral code is based on the Ten Commandments and the Beatitudes of Jesus.

- As part of their moral life, Catholics place a strong emphasis on serving others and advocating for justice. Serving people in need and working to transform society are essential elements of Catholic life.

- Catholics honor the great people of faith who have preceded them, the saints, and in a special way, Mary, the mother of Jesus.

Which of the practices from the "Catholic Practices" list do you witness in the lives of Catholics you know? How does their example inspire you?

For Review

1. What is a worldview?
2. Describe three characteristics of a Catholic worldview.
3. Describe three core beliefs of Catholicism.
4. What are three ways Catholics live out their faith in the world?

reflect

A Testimony of Faith

The Nazi regime under Adolf Hitler, intent on creating a "pure" white race, herded millions of Jews and others they considered undesirable into concentration camps. In the camps, death by execution, disease, or starvation was almost certain. In an attempt to escape such a fate, Anne Frank, a thirteen-year-old Jewish girl, and her family went into hiding in Nazi occupied Holland in 1942. For the next two years, Anne kept a diary. In the following excerpt, Anne writes of maintaining, and even deepening, her faith amid dangerous, life-threatening circumstances:

> We've been strongly reminded of the fact that we're Jews in chains, chained to one spot, without any rights, but with a thousand obligations. We must

put our feelings aside; we must be brave and strong, bear discomfort without complaint, do whatever is in our power and trust in God. One day this terrible war will be over. The time will come when we'll be people again and not just Jews!

Who has inflicted this on us? Who has set us apart from all the rest? Who has put us through such suffering? It's God who has made us the way we are, but it's also God who will lift us up again. In the eyes of the world, we're doomed, but if, after all this suffering, there are still Jews left, the Jewish people will be held up as an example. Who knows, maybe our religion will teach the world and all the people in it about goodness, and that's the reason, the only reason, we have to suffer. . . .

Be brave! Let's remember our duty and perform it without complaint. There will be a way out. God has never deserted our people. Through the ages Jews have had to suffer, but through the ages they've gone on living, and the centuries of suffering have only made them stronger. The weak shall fall and the strong shall survive and not be defeated! (*The Diary of a Young Girl*)

After two years in hiding, Anne and her family were discovered and sent off to concentration camps. Anne died less than a year later, one of six million Jews who died during the Holocaust. Her diary was left behind though, and her father published it after the war. It has inspired tens of millions of readers with its testimony of faith in God and the goodness of humanity. Anne Frank's spirit certainly did survive the Holocaust.

Catholic Christianity is grounded in, and founded on, the history and religious tradition of the Jews. In other words, Christianity was born out of the faith experience and religious expression of the Jewish people. Therefore, if we understand Judaism, we will develop a stronger under-standing of the Catholic heritage. Jesus was born into a devout Jewish family. As a child, he was educated in the Jewish faith, and as an adult he became a Jewish teacher and prophet. He proclaimed his vision of God and the meaning of life to the Jews. The earliest followers of Jesus were Jews, and they were the founding members of the religious community that today we recognize as the church.

So we will turn next to Judaism and the history of God's people in the time before Jesus.

Anne Frank as depicted in a mural in Berlin, Germany.

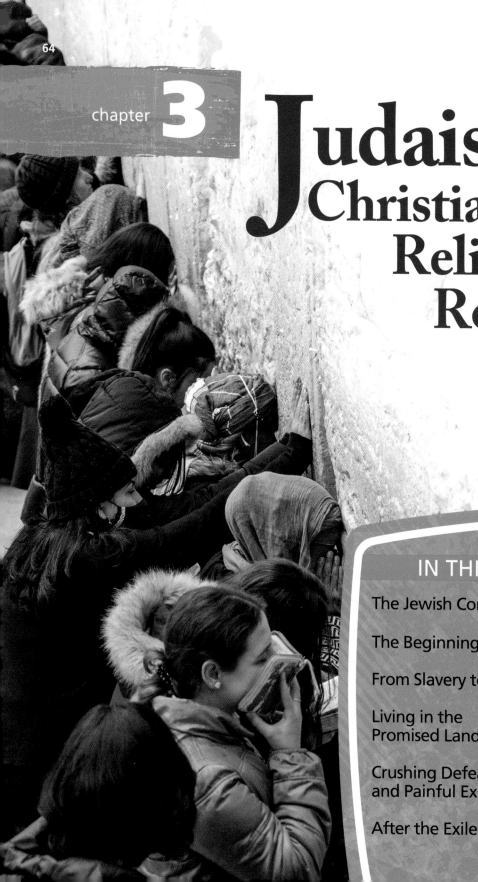

chapter **3**

Judaism:
Christianity's Religious Roots

IN THIS CHAPTER

The Jewish Connection 65

The Beginnings of a People 70

From Slavery to Freedom 74

Living in the Promised Land 81

Crushing Defeat and Painful Exile 86

After the Exile 90

The Jewish Connection

"I've been thinking about the connection between the world's religions," Inesh was telling his friends from religion class. "Did you know that Hinduism and Buddhism started in the same part of northern India? Hinduism began first, almost four thousand years ago. Then along came Siddhartha Gautama, who was a Hindu prince, about five hundred years before Jesus Christ. Siddhartha Gautama founded Buddhism and eventually became known as the Buddha."

"So, are you Hindu or Buddhist?" asked Abby.

"I'm Hindu," replied Inesh. "I believe in the god Brahman as the supreme being. Most Buddhists don't believe in a supreme being, I guess. But Hindus and Buddhists share some of the same religious words, such as *karma* and *dharma,* and even some similar religious practices."

"So, it is the same as the connection between Jews and Christians," said Lily. "I mean Jesus was a Jew, and he became the founder of Christianity. And Christians and Jews use some of the same religious words like *covenant* and *sin.*"

"Well, I don't know if it's exactly the same," said Inesh. "After all, Buddhists do not consider the Buddha to be God. But it does seem similar. I do think that just like you cannot really appreciate Buddhism without knowing something about Hinduism, you cannot really appreciate Christianity without knowing something about Judaism."

"And don't forget about Islam," said Oman. "We believe our religion started with Abraham, just as Jews and Christians believe their religions go back to Abraham."

"Huh," thought Abby. "I wonder what all these connections mean?"

God's Special Bond with a Chosen People

Catholics understand their relationship with God as much more than a matter of "me and God." God reaches out to all creation and desires to enter into a loving relationship with all human beings, not just individually but also as a community. To reach all humanity, thousands of years ago God chose to have a special bond with one group of people *as a people*, acting in their history. Those people were the Jewish race, known also as the Israelites. Through them, God intended that all human beings might eventually come to know and love God.

The solemn promise between God and the **Chosen People**, the Jewish people whom God chose, is called the **covenant**. Like marriage promises (which are even called a marriage covenant), God's covenant with the Jewish people was a pledge of faithfulness forever—a pledge that God would never give up on them and would love them "in good times and in bad." For their part, the people pledged their faithful love too—to love God, one another, and all that God had created. But as we will see, they were not always good at keeping their part of the promise.

Jews and Christians Share a Heritage

Ultimately, God chooses all people and desires union with all of them. But this chapter tells the story of a particular People of God: the Jews, who were chosen by God at a specific time in history, and with whom God continues to have a special relationship. In ancient times, long before Christianity came onto the world scene, the Jews were the ones who carried God's promise of faithful love.

We know that Jesus was a Jew. He felt their hopes and dreams and longings, spoke in their language, thought as they thought, prayed their prayers, remembered their history, celebrated their holy feast

If you want to have a good relationship with someone, why is keeping the commitments you make to that person so important? Who has been really good in keeping their commitments to you?

Chosen People
The Jewish people, with whom God chose to have a special bond.

covenant In general, a solemn agreement between human beings or between God and human beings in which mutual commitments are promised to each other.

days, read their Scriptures, heard and told their wisdom. He was a Jewish man in every respect. The story of the Jews and their relationship with God is also Jesus' story, his "family background." We cannot understand Christianity without understanding the meaning of Jesus' life and message. And we cannot do this without understanding his Jewish roots. Thus, the story of the Jews before Jesus is part of the Christian story as well.

Christianity has emerged out of a history that stretches back nearly four thousand years, to the beginning of what would come to be known as Judaism, the religion of the Jews. We cannot expect to understand Catholicism without a sense of that past. In this chapter, then, we briefly explore the history and heritage of the Jewish people up to the time of Jesus.

Christian and Jewish Relations

Christians' treatment of Jewish people has often been immoral. Some Christians have promoted stereotypes of Jewish people. Some have blamed Jews for killing Jesus, even though only a few religious leaders were responsible. Jews were attacked, killed, and forced from their homes during the Catholic Crusades (religious wars). And most horrible of all, approximately six million Jews were killed by citizens of a predominantly Christian country during World War II.

Things have improved in the last fifty years. The Catholic Church has asked forgiveness for the sins against Jewish people. Catholic and Jewish leaders are working together to build a future that is marked by mutual respect as brothers and sisters worshipping one God.

Located at the Jewish Museum in Berlin, Germany, more than ten thousand faces cut from iron disks memorialize Jews murdered during the Holocaust.

The Bible as Guidebook

The story of the Jews goes beyond history in our usual sense of that term, for we are dealing with more than a series of ordinary historical events. Rather, we are exploring salvation history, the story of God's action among a people throughout their history. That story revolves around the covenant God made with the Jews, the promise to be faithful to them and to bring salvation to the whole world through them as a people.

The story of salvation history is told primarily in the Bible. Here's a quick overview of the Bible as we get started (chapter 7 takes a deeper look at the Bible). The Bible is not just one book but a collection of books, written and collected for over one thousand years. Christians believe that God, through the Holy Spirit, inspired the writers of these books.

The **Old Testament** in Christian Bibles is essentially the same as the Hebrew Scriptures, just organized differently (and with a few more books in Catholic versions). The Old Testament contains many different types of writings: symbolic stories, religious histories, poetry, the words of the prophets, and collections of wise advice, to name a few. Taken together, these books capture the ups and downs of God's relationship with the Chosen People.

The **New Testament** focuses on Jesus Christ. It begins with the four Gospels, which each give an account of the life, death, and Resurrection of Jesus Christ. The rest of the New Testament tells how the first Christians grew in their understanding of the meaning of Christ's life and message, and how they worked to spread this Good News around the known world, fulfilling God's promise to Abraham.

This chapter focuses on the part of the story covered in the Hebrew Scriptures or Old Testament. Some of it may be familiar to you, but some of it may not. It will help you to refer to the time line of events in biblical history on page 71.

Old Testament
The Christian name for the first main section of the Bible, which contains the writings that record God's Revelation to the Chosen People.

New Testament
The name for the second main section of the Bible, which contains the books whose central themes are the life, teachings, Passion, death, Resurrection, and Ascension of Jesus Christ and the beginnings of the church.

Literary Genres in the Bible

Understanding a passage's literary style, also called the literary genre, is a key to grasping what a passage is communicating. Here are some of the genres in the Bible.

Literary Style	What You Can Expect
Symbolic or Figurative Story	A story that teaches religious truth symbolically, as in the accounts of Creation
Law Code	A collection of laws to instruct people on how to live in right relationship with God and one another
Religious History	An interpretation of historical events that focuses on the religious meaning of those events
Prayer	A passage containing emotional and poetic dialogue with God
Proverb	A short, wise saying for living a good and holy life
Parable	A short story used to teach religious truths, based on everyday events and often with surprising endings
Letter	Communication addressed to a person or a community giving encouragement or advice, found mostly in the New Testament

For Review

1. Why did God choose to have a special bond with the Jewish people?
2. Describe the covenant between God and the Jewish people. How is it like a marriage covenant?
3. Why is it necessary to understand Judaism in order to understand Catholic Christianity?

The Beginnings of a People

Abraham, Father of Faith

Abraham lived in a region of the Near East about eighteen hundred years before Jesus. He belonged to a group of tribal people known as the **Hebrews**.

The Covenant Begins

According to the Hebrew Scriptures (known as the Old Testament in Christian Bibles), God called Abraham out of his obscure life as a wandering shepherd, or nomad, told him to go to a new land where God would be with him, and gave him a remarkable promise. God promised that from Abraham and his family would come a great nation, and that all families of the earth would be blessed through him. Abraham's descendants would be more numerous than the countless stars in the heavens. Because Abraham's wife, Sarah, had never had any children and was now old and past her childbearing years, this seemed like a strange promise. But Abraham trusted in God and set off with his family to Canaan, the Promised Land.

Hebrews A tribal people, living in the land of modern-day Israel, who would become the Israelites, and eventually, the Jewish people.

This relationship between God and Abraham was the beginning of the covenant that God would renew again and again with the Jews throughout their long history. As a physical sign of the people's commitment to that covenant, their male children from Abraham's time on were circumcised.

Read Genesis 17:1–10 in the Bible. In this passage, what is God promising to Abraham, and what does God ask Abraham to promise in return?

Time Line of Biblical History

BC

1900 — Abraham's move to Canaan
1800

1700 — Joseph in Egypt
1600
1500
1400
1300 — Moses and the Exodus
1200 — Israelites in Promised Land
1100
1000 — David, King of Israel
— Building of Temple by Solomon
900 — Division into northern and southern kingdoms
800
— Fall of Israel to Assyrians
700
600 — Fall of Judah to Babylonians; beginning of Exile
— Persian defeat of Babylonians; Jews return home
500 — Rebuilding of Jerusalem and Temple
400
— Greek rule of Jews
300
200
— Jewish revolt and independence from Greeks
100 — Roman rule of Jews
— Birth of Jesus
AD —
— Death of Jesus
— Roman destruction
100 of Jewish Temple

King David reigned from c. 1010 to 970 BC.

The One God

The religious world in which Abraham lived was polytheistic. This means that people worshipped many gods. Abraham struggled with the mystery of the many gods. However, once he had been called by the God of the covenant, he began to realize that there was one God above all other gods. He decided to be faithful to that God and no other.

This faith of Abraham developed into monotheism, or the belief that only one God exists. That belief would later become central to the three world religions that today trace their origins back to Abraham: Judaism, Christianity, and Islam. These three religions are connected by their common worship of the One God, the God of Abraham.

Abraham's Descendants, the Israelites

Amazingly, Abraham's wife, Sarah, did give birth to a son, whom she named Isaac. (Another son of Abraham by a different woman was Ishmael, from whom Muslims believe they are descended.) Isaac married, and his wife, Rebekah, had a son, Jacob, to whom God later gave the name Israel, meaning "one who has contended with divine and human beings." (This name came from the story of Jacob's wrestling with a mysterious, angel-like being one night. See Genesis 32:22–31.)

These descendants of Abraham and his son Isaac are known by several names. Originally, Abraham belonged to a tribal people known as the Hebrews. Later they became known as the **Israelites**, called this because of the new name God gave to Abraham's grandson Jacob. Hundreds of years later, they would be known as the Judeans, or Jews, named after the land they lived on (Judea).

Do some research on the religion of Islam. Find out at least one belief or practice that is similar to something in Christianity or Judaism.

Israelites The descendants of Abraham and his son Isaac, who become God's Chosen People.

Patriarchs and Matriarchs

So the origins of Judaism are traced to Abraham, his son Isaac, and his grandson Jacob. These three men are called the **patriarchs** of the Jewish faith, and their wives—Sarah, Rebekah, Rachel, and Leah—are called the **matriarchs**.

Joseph in Egypt

Jacob had twelve sons altogether, with his favorite being his beloved Joseph. Jacob demonstrated this by giving Joseph a special long robe, often referred to as the "coat of many colors." Joseph's favored status caused his brothers to become extremely envious of him. In their hostility, the brothers tried to kill Joseph, but then decided instead to sell him as a slave to some merchants who were on their way to Egypt.

Joseph, however, was so talented that he gained great authority and status in Egypt. Moreover, he was as virtuous as he was talented. Years after he had been sold into slavery, Joseph forgave his brothers for what they had done to him, and he invited them and his father to leave the famine-stricken Canaan and join him to live comfortably in Egypt.

Under a series of kindly Egyptian pharaohs, or kings, the Israelites (Jacob's descendants) continued to live prosperously in Egypt. If the story had ended there, we might be able to say that they lived happily ever after. But the story is only beginning.

Think of a situation in which you, someone you know, or a whole group of people could be as forgiving as Joseph was of his brothers. How difficult would it be for you, the person you know, or the group to forgive those who hurt them? What good might come from that forgiveness?

patriarchs The father or leader of a tribe, clan, or tradition. Abraham, Isaac, and Jacob were the primary patriarchs of the Israelite people.

matriarchs The mother of a tribe, clan, or tradition. Sarah, Rebekah, Rachel, and Leah were the primary matriarchs of the Israelite people.

For **Review**

1. What promise did God give to Abraham?
2. What three monotheistic religions trace their roots back to Abraham?
3. Define *patriarch* and *matriarch*. Name the patriarchs and matriarchs of the Jewish faith.
4. Why were the people who were eventually called Jews known as the Israelites?
5. How did the Israelites end up living in Egypt?

From Slavery to Freedom

The time of peace and prosperity in Egypt under sympathetic rulers ended for the Israelites when they were enslaved by cruel pharaohs who burdened them with the backbreaking jobs of making bricks and constructing public buildings. This oppressive slavery devastated the Israelites, and they yearned for freedom. Hundreds of years later, the answer to their dreams came in the man who is still revered to this day by faithful Jews. That man was Moses.

© Pete Linforth / Pixabay.com

Moses, the People's Greatest Leader

The story of Moses is an epic story of a great hero. Moses was the son of Hebrew slaves, but he was raised in the pharaoh's palace. The baby Moses narrowly escaped death when the ruthless pharaoh ordered the execution of all baby boys under two years of age. His mother put the newborn baby in a basket hidden on a riverbank. There he was found by the pharaoh's daughter, who raised him as her own son.

The Revelation of a God Named Yahweh

When Moses grew up, personal encounters with God led him to realize he had a mission—to save his people. God told Moses to lead the Israelites from slavery to freedom. As God's sign of intimacy with the people, the holy name of God—"I AM WHO I AM," or Yahweh in Hebrew—was revealed to Moses.

The name Yahweh is difficult to translate into English. Some other translations are "I am the One who is present," "I bring into existence all that is," or simply, "I am." The Jews later held the sacred name in such reverence that they refused to pronounce it out loud, even passing over the word *Yahweh* when reading it in their Scripture and substituting for it a Hebrew word meaning "Lord." Out of respect for this practice by Jews, this book will continue by using God in place of Yahweh.

The Exodus: Escape from Slavery

After a mighty moral struggle with the Egyptian pharaoh, Moses eventually led the Israelites out of Egypt. But the pharaoh had second thoughts and sent his soldiers and chariots to catch the Israelites and bring them back. Perhaps you have heard the awesome story of how God saved the Israelites by parting the waters of the sea and leading them across on dry land, then making the waters close back over the Egyptian charioteers when they tried to cross in hot pursuit. The Egyptians drowned in the sea, and the Israelites were free.

This miraculous event of God's freeing the Israelites from slavery, called the **Exodus**, became the central story of God's saving love for Israel. (Historians date the event at about 1250 BC.) Ever after that, the people recalled with joy and gratitude how God had freed them from slavery so they could return to Canaan (modern-day Israel), also called the

Exodus The great event in which God led his Chosen People from slavery in Egypt to freedom in the Promised Land.

Have you ever felt like your freedom to do something was unfairly taken from you? Describe what it was like. If your freedom was restored, tell how it happened and what you experienced.

Promised Land
The land God promised to his Chosen People, which has been known in different times as Canaan, Judea, and Israel.

Passover The feast that celebrates the deliverance of the Chosen People from bondage in Egypt.

Seder The Jewish ceremonial meal, celebrated at home during Passover, in commemoration of the Exodus of the Chosen People from Egypt.

Promised Land. Whenever they doubted God's love for them, the Israelites only had to remember that God had acted directly in their lives and their history. They believed that God's promises to Abraham would be fulfilled—that they would be a great nation someday in their own land, a light to all the other nations. They were a people with a destiny.

The Passover Feast

The Exodus and the events leading up to it are remembered every year in the Jewish Feast of **Passover**. It is called this because the angel of death passed over the Jewish households, sparing their firstborn sons from death. Passover is celebrated with a special memorial meal, the **Seder**. In this meal, Jews recall how the Israelites ate a meal of lamb, sacrificed to God, and unleavened bread before they fled Egypt in great haste, to be freed and saved by their God. Later in this course, the role of this ritual meal in the life of Jesus and in the sacrament that Christians call the Eucharist is explored.

In the Desert

Having escaped from Egypt, the Israelites knew that God was with them. However, once out of Egypt, while they traveled in the desert, they grumbled at Moses about their severe surroundings and lack of food. They even moaned that they would rather be enslaved in Egypt than die in the desert. Despite their doubts, God took care of them by sending them manna (a bread-like substance that they found on the ground) and quail (small birds) to eat.

The Sinai Covenant

After many days, the Israelites encamped in the desert at the base of Mount Sinai, waiting for direction from Moses about where to go and what to do next. In an encounter on the mountaintop

A teenager participates in a Seder.

between Moses and God, which is told with great drama in the Book of Exodus, God sealed the loving relationship with the people that had begun with the promise to Abraham hundreds of years before. This pledge between God and the Israelites became known as the Sinai Covenant.

The scriptural story depicts God calling Moses to the top of the mountain and directing Moses to remind the Israelites how God had brought them safely out of Egypt. Now God wanted to enter into a covenant with them, a covenant that would make the Israelites God's Chosen People. If they kept their covenant with God, they would be God's treasured people, a holy nation.

Moses returned to the people and told them what God had said, and they agreed to do whatever was asked of them. In one of the most powerful

Sinai Covenant
The covenant God made with the Israelites through Moses at Mount Sinai.

scenes in the Bible, God again encountered Moses on the mountaintop and presented Moses with the sacred law. Called the **Mosaic Law**, it described the Israelites' end of the bargain—in other words, their responsibilities in keeping the sacred covenant between God and them. The cornerstone of the Mosaic Law is what we now call the Ten Commandments.

Mosaic Law (or Law of Moses)
The laws given to the Israelites by God as part of the Sinai Covenant. It describes the Israelites' responsibilities in keeping the sacred covenant.

A Law That Frees

With their acceptance of the Law as a code of both individual and communal behavior, the Israelites forever changed and elevated the human understanding of morality, our sense of what is right and wrong. It was a great moral leap forward, a code that truly did make the Jews "a light to the nations" (Isaiah 42:6), that is, a light to all peoples.

© isparklinglife / Shutterstock.com

Mount Sinai, Egypt. This is the place described in the Bible where Moses encountered God and the Sinai Covenant was established.

The Mosaic Law did not carry the restrictive or negative meaning for the Israelites that people today may associate with laws. For example, some people see moral laws as limiting our freedom and locking us in. For the ancient Israelites and for faithful Jews today, the Law promotes freedom because it is an expression of God's loving intention for the people. The Law is all about how to love God and one's neighbor.

Although the Ten Commandments are the most familiar part of the Law for Christians, the Mosaic Law is far more extensive than that, speaking to almost every aspect of the lives of the Jews. In Jesus' time, some Jews were very strict in their understanding of the Law, trying to live exactly by the letter of the Law rather than by its loving spirit. For example, some Jews, citing God's commandment to rest on the Sabbath, were hesitant to do work to help someone in trouble on the Sabbath day.

Divide a sheet of paper into three columns. Label the first column "Rules for Loving God," the second "Rules for Loving Other People," and the third "Rules for Loving Myself." Under each heading, write down the rules you live by for that heading.

The Ten Commandments

This is the account from the Book of Exodus of God giving the Ten Commandments to Moses:

Then God spoke all these words:

. . . You shall not have other gods beside me. . . .

You shall not invoke the name of the LORD, your God, in vain. . . .

Remember the sabbath day—keep it holy. . . .

Honor your father and your mother. . . .

You shall not kill.

You shall not commit adultery.

You shall not steal.

You shall not bear false witness against your neighbor.

You shall not covet your neighbor's house. You shall not covet your neighbor's wife . . . or anything that belongs to your neighbor.

(20:1–17)

Wandering for Forty Years

Once again, it would be wonderful to say, "And they lived happily ever after." But that is not what happened.

The Israelites, who had been chosen and freed by a tender and loving God, soon lost sight of how gracious God had been to them. While Moses spent forty days on the mountaintop receiving the Law from God, the people down below grew impatient. As a diversion, they built an idol of metal—a golden calf made of melted-down jewelry—had a festival to honor it, and offered sacrifices to it. Already they were worshipping a false god.

Although Moses was furious with the people when he found out what they had done, he and God did not abandon them. As punishment, most of them would never see the Promised Land. For forty years, they were lost and wandered in the desert, learning through many mistakes, hardships, and triumphs to trust more deeply in the God who had saved them.

Recall a time when you felt "lost in the desert," wandering around not knowing what to do about some problem, making mistakes and going through hardships. How did you make it through this time?

For **Review**

1. Who was Moses, and what mission did God give him?
2. What was God's name as revealed to Moses?
3. What was the Exodus?
4. How do Jews to this day celebrate and remember the Exodus?
5. What was the Sinai Covenant, and how is the Law given to Moses related to that covenant?
6. What is the cornerstone of the Mosaic Law?

Living in the Promised Land

Moses himself never reached the Promised Land. He died just before his people entered the fertile territory of Canaan, promised to Abraham's descendants by God as a land "'flowing with milk and honey'" (Exodus 3:8). Today, this land is variously identified as Palestine, Israel, or the Holy Land.

Taking over the Land

Joshua, Moses' assistant, led the Israelites into Canaan. But it was not a peaceful entry. The people who already lived there were not happy to see the Israelites laying claim to the land. The period that followed was filled with warfare between the Israelites and other tribes, as well as between the Israelites and the city dwellers of the region. Under Joshua's leadership, the Israelites laid claim to the Promised Land, taking it over from the people who lived there. Joshua divided the land among the Twelve Tribes of Israel, and each tribe settled on their portion (except for the priestly tribe, who was scattered among the other tribes). Each tribe governed itself with only God as their king.

Just as they had in the desert, the Israelites at times abandoned God, choosing to worship false gods instead. It was in those times of infidelity to God that foreign peoples invaded the Promised Land. When the Israelites relied on their own power instead of God's, they met with disaster and were defeated by these enemies.

Realizing their sin, the Israelites would eventually remember their covenant and call upon God to rescue them. In response, God called charismatic people to lead the people back to freedom. These eleven men and one woman were called **judges**, but Israel's judges were not the same as modern-day judges. A judge was more of a ruler or a chief. But unlike a kingship, which is passed on from father to son, judges were recognized by the ways they made the spirit of God evident. For example, Samson, perhaps the most familiar of the judges, was capable of superhuman feats because "the spirit of the LORD rushed upon [him]" (Judges 14:6).

judges The eleven men and one woman who served the Israelites as tribal leaders, military commanders, arbiters of disputes, and inspirations of faith.

A portion of one of twelve windows depicting the Twelve Tribes of Israel, by modern Jewish artist Marc Chagall. This window honors the tribe of Asher. The light of the menorah, fueled by olive oil, is a sign of the tribe's fertile land.

A Kingdom for the Israelites

During the time of the judges, the moral life of the Israelites got worse and worse. At the end of the Book of Judges, there is a terrible story of rape and murder, which led to a civil war during which all the men in one tribe were massacred. Faced with this breakdown of their community and the threat of outside invaders, the Israelites began to ask God for a king, with the hopes that things might get better.

The United Kingdom under David

A man named Samuel was the last judge of Israel, and he was against the people's request for a king. For him, God was the only king Israel needed. Despite Samuel's misgivings, God granted the Israelites' request for a king. After the first king failed, God directed Samuel to anoint a shepherd boy, David, as the second king. David turned out to be a brilliant military leader and led the Israelites in military battles, reclaiming the original territory of the Twelve Tribes. David set up the capital of the new nation at Jerusalem, and the era of his royal kingdom became synonymous with the "glory days" of Israel.

David was a human being with many failings; he made some significant mistakes and sometimes violated the trust of his people. But he was completely devoted to God and kept the people faithful to the covenant. The story of David shows us that God can act through people who have great weaknesses and flaws and who sin.

After David's death, his son Solomon became king and built a beautiful Temple in Jerusalem. This became the focus of the people's worship. With such a magnificent Temple for God and a luxurious palace for the king, it seemed that the glory days would continue. But that was not to be the case for Israel.

Why is it important that God can work through imperfect people? What examples can you think of that show how God is working through someone who is less than perfect?

Jerusalem The city that King David established as the capital of the united kingdom of Israel.

Temple The building complex in Jerusalem where the Israelites' religious sacrifices and worship were performed.

© Flik47 / Shutterstock.com

The tomb of Samuel, near Jerusalem.

Things Break Down

Solomon was rich, powerful, and famous for his wisdom, but he was far from a model king. He ruled the people oppressively and began to fall away from true worship of God. The unity of Israel under David and its faithfulness to the covenant broke down. After Solomon's death, the kingdom split into two—the northern kingdom, called Israel, and the southern kingdom, called Judah—with constant rivalry between them. Judah retained the capital city of Jerusalem with its great Temple.

A succession of kings of both kingdoms followed, many of them corrupt and idolatrous. Injustice to poor people and worship of false gods were the sinful practices of many kings and their wealthy courts, which broke the Israelites' covenant with God. The people were not well served by these kings; they were a disgrace to the memory of King David, who, though a flawed person, had loved God with all his heart.

Prophets: Calling the People Back to God

In response to these corrupt kings, God called individuals to speak his Word to the Israelites and their rulers. These people were called **prophets**,

and in both Israel and Judah great prophets questioned the injustices of the wicked kings and tried to call the people back to their covenant with God.

Contrary to the image we may have of prophets, their role was not simply to predict the future; rather, they were critics of their society and of the injustices that were a sign of the people's failure to be faithful to the covenant. They told what could happen if the people did not turn back to God. Some prophets were fiery critics of empty religious practices—empty because they were not accompanied by justice for the poor.

The prophet Isaiah told of God's distress at how the people had turned their backs on God and the covenant:

Hear, O heavens, and listen, O earth;
for the LORD speaks:
Sons have I raised and reared,
but they have rebelled against me! . . .

Ah! Sinful nation, people laden with wickedness,
evil offspring, corrupt children!
(Isaiah 1:2–4)

prophet A person God chooses to speak his message. In the Bible, primarily a person who called the Chosen People to change their lives, not necessarily a person who predicted the future.

Sometimes the prophets succeeded in bringing the nation to its senses. All too often, however, they were rejected, ridiculed, and scorned. But the goal of the prophets was not to be popular; it was to interpret events from God's point of view, no matter how angry it made the king or the people with power. You may be familiar with the names of some of the prophets besides Amos and Isaiah—for instance, Elijah, Hosea, Micah, Jeremiah, and Ezekiel. These prophets, some of the greatest figures in Jewish history, were outsiders and loners, speaking the truth and suffering the consequences.

Who are some modern-day prophets, people who are speaking a truthful message to society or the world that others may not want to hear? Describe one such prophet and their message.

Jeremiah, the Young Prophet

Jeremiah, one of the major Jewish prophets, was called to be a prophet at a young age. Because of his prophecy, Jeremiah was whipped, accused of treason, imprisoned, and even thrown into a muddy cistern, or pit, and left to die of starvation in the mud.

Through it all, Jeremiah remained faithful to what God had requested of him. He delivered a message that was at once pessimistic because of Israel's failure to keep the covenant, and optimistic because he believed in a God of hope and promise, whose love was unending.

In the opening passage of his book, Jeremiah recounts God's call to him and his own reluctance to answer:

The word of the LORD came to me:
Before I formed you in the womb I knew you,
 before you were born I dedicated you,
 a prophet to the nations I appointed you.
"Ah, Lord God!" I said,
 "I do not know how to speak. I am too young!"
But the LORD answered me,
Do not say, "I am too young."
 To whomever I send you, you shall go;
 whatever I command you, you shall speak.
Do not be afraid of them,
 for I am with you to deliver you—oracle of the Lord.
(1:4–8)

For Review

1. What was the role of the judges in the Promised Land?
2. Who was David, and why was he so important?
3. After the Israelites' kingdom split in two, what were the names of the two kingdoms?
4. How did the Israelites' faithfulness to the covenant break down, and how did the prophets try to intervene?

Crushing Defeat and Painful Exile

Although a few kings attempted to reform the nation, the Israelites and their kings by and large did not heed the warnings of the prophets. The prophets said that the people were paving the way for their own destruction by turning away from the covenant, and they were right. Eventually, the greater powers of the region crushed both kingdoms.

The northern kingdom of Israel with its capital, Samaria, fell to the huge empire of the Assyrians, in about 722 BC. The Israelite citizens of the north were dispersed and never returned again to their land. This was the beginning of what would become known as the **Jewish Diaspora**, the settling of the Jews outside the Promised Land.

The Babylonian Exile

Later, in 587 BC, Jerusalem, the capital of the southern kingdom of Judah, fell under the enormous might of the Babylonian Empire. Many of the survivors were forced to march about 600 miles to their place of exile in Babylon. Babylon was a sophisticated city

Jewish Diaspora The settling of Jews outside the Promised Land, usually during times of war and foreign invasions.

devoted to the accumulation of wealth and power. The Israelites were strangers in a strange land, having apparently lost everything.

The experience of the **Babylonian Exile** was about as crushing a blow as the Israelites could imagine. Their beloved city of Jerusalem and their magnificent Temple were destroyed. Everything familiar to them was gone, with little hope of its return. And the haunting questions kept coming before them: Where was God in all this? Had God abandoned them? Maybe God was not so powerful after all. Maybe the Babylonians had a mightier god.

Read Psalm 137 in the Old Testament. How do the verses in this psalm express the pain and sorrow of living in exile?

Babylonian Exile
The period in Israelite history during which the Israelites of the ancient kingdom of Judah were held in captivity in Babylon.

A Poem of Pain

The destruction of Jerusalem is the most devastating time in the history of the ancient Israelites. One can only imagine what it would be like to see half the people you know killed, and the other half led off in chains to live in a foreign land. One short book in the Old Testament, called Lamentations, has five poems describing the Israelites' sorrow and pain. Here are a few verses from that book:

> As children and infants collapse
> in the streets of the town.
> They cry out to their mothers,
> "Where is bread and wine?"
> As they faint away like the wounded
> in the streets of the city,
> As their life is poured out
> in their mothers' arms.
> (2:11–12)

Sabbath A sacred day of rest and worship, kept by Jews from Friday evening to Saturday evening, and by most Christians on Sunday.

Renewal in the Midst of Exile

This devastating experience for the Israelites in exile, however, did not ultimately defeat their spirit. True, some lost their faith during this period and tried to blend into their pagan surroundings. But for many others, the Exile led to serious reflection on the meaning of the prophets' words. They began to see that God had not abandoned them in Jerusalem; rather, they had abandoned God, and that was why they were in exile. This led them to repent and recommit to their covenant with God.

Instead of losing heart because they had no glorious temple to offer sacrifices in, the Israelites began to worship more informally. They held simple services in which they prayed and retold the ancient stories of how God had saved them so many times in so many ways. They prayed intently, singing psalms from the heart about how they longed for Jerusalem (or Zion, as they also called their beloved city). They poured out their souls honestly to God. They praised God even in their sorrow.

The Israelites were purified by the experience of the Exile. They grew closer to God, not through a powerful kingdom or a magnificent temple, but through the communal process of turning around their hearts. They began to realize that God was making a *new* covenant with them: "I will place my law within them, and I will write it upon their hearts; I will be their God, and they shall be my people" (Jeremiah 31:33). Now God would work in each person's heart, as well as in the people as a whole. This was a marvelous gift of the Exile.

A Sabbath for the Jews

The practice of the **Sabbath**, the sacred day of rest and worship, became extremely significant to the Israelites during the Exile. It marked them as different from the Babylonians, who carried on their business every day. It also reminded the Israelites that although business and work were important, ultimately they were a people chosen by God, given a promise by God, and never abandoned by God. This relationship with God was honored by setting apart a special, sacred time away from all the earthly concerns that dominate day-to-day life. The Sabbath was an important practice at the time of Jesus, and it continues to be central to Jewish life and worship today.

How do you take time to rest and renew yourself? How might you do this better?

People of the Book

Another development during the Exile was the collection of the people's ancient stories into what became the Hebrew Scriptures (later known as the Old Testament among Christians).

Prior to the Exile, some of the Israelites' religious stories were told by word of mouth. Other stories, rules, prayers, royal records, and songs had been written down, but they were not pieced together and edited into a whole. During the Exile, Jewish leaders called **scribes** began the process of creating written books from these oral stories and writings. This was one of the most significant outcomes of the Exile, because without it we would not have the Bible as we know it.

scribes People who were able to read and write in the Hebrew language. They were teachers of the Jewish Law and Scripture.

For **Review**

1. What was the Babylonian Exile?
2. What was the new covenant proclaimed by the prophet Jeremiah?
3. Why did the Sabbath become so important to the Israelites during the Exile?
4. What significant development during the Exile made it possible for the Jews to bring their faith and worship along with them wherever they went?

After the Exile

Approximately fifty years into the Exile in Babylon, the Persian Empire conquered the Babylonian Empire. The Persian king set the Israelites free and allowed them to return home to Jerusalem. The Israelites who had remained faithful, called the Remnant, returned joyfully to their homeland of Judah. The terms *Judaism* and *Jew* are derived from the word *Judah.* Those terms began to be used after the Exile to describe the religion and people of ancient Israel.

The Faithful Practice of Judaism

The returning Jews rebuilt the city of Jerusalem and built a new Temple, although they never regained the political power that the Israelites had known in the days of David. However, the events of the Exile and the return to Jerusalem led to a deep religious conversion of the Jewish people. God's Law, as the prophet Jeremiah had said, had been written on their

hearts. The people no longer engaged in the kind of idolatry and extreme oppression of poor people that had brought them into ruin and exile. Jewish leaders were conscientious about maintaining a strict and pure form of their faith.

A Series of Oppressors

After rebuilding Jerusalem and the Temple, the Jewish people were mostly under foreign rule. At first, they were ruled by the Persians, the people who had let them return to their homeland. But this did not last for long.

The Greeks

Persia was defeated by Greece under the empire builder Alexander the Great, so the Greeks became the Jews' overlords for nearly three hundred years. Some of the Greek kings tried to enforce the Greek religion on the Jews. Some of the most powerful stories of the Jews' courage emerged from this period, as they faced their Greek dictators and tried to fight them off, meeting with some success. Eventually, they gained their independence and kept it for seventy years.

One Jewish holiday, **Hanukkah**, or the Festival of Lights, comes from the remembrance of how the Jews rededicated the Temple after the Greeks had defiled it.

The Romans

Just sixty-three years before the time of Jesus, Palestine (the name given by the Greeks to the Promised Land) came under the rule of the Romans. By then, many Jews were scattered all over the Roman Empire, and Jerusalem had become the religious capital for all these far-flung, dispersed Jews.

Ask Jewish friends or acquaintances or search for and read about the story behind the Feast of Hanukkah.

Hanukkah The Jewish festival remembering the rededication of the Temple after the Jewish victory over Greek occupation.

The Hanukkah menorah is a key religious symbol during this eight-day holiday.

© ungvar / Shutterstock.com

It is estimated that 10 percent of the population of the Roman Empire was Jewish. The Romans were generally tolerant of other religions, but they were intolerant of any criticism of or attempts to overthrow Roman rule. But despite their religious tolerance, Rome's identity as an oppressive dictatorship was never in doubt.

The Longing for a Messiah

During this time, many Jews longed to be free of foreign rule and domination. They had hope that God would send them a new king, a savior descended from King David, who would lead them to freedom. Some of the prophets' writings in the Jewish people's Scriptures, especially Isaiah's, pointed to the coming of someone sent by God to bring lasting joy and peace to the people. The Jews thought that perhaps now was the time.

They called this hoped-for savior the Messiah. *Messiah* meant "anointed one," and the word was used for kings and prophets of old who were often anointed with oil when taking their positions. The people saw the coming of this new Messiah as the fulfillment of the covenant; this Messiah would fulfill God's promises of a prosperous and peaceful homeland. Yes, the Jews were under Roman rule, and yes, times were bad, and yes, many were poor and oppressed. But God would not abandon them in their need.

Groups among the Jews

These are some of the groups active in Jewish society at the time Jesus was born.

Group	Description
Chief Priests	Led religious services and conducted animal sacrifices at the Temple in Jerusalem
Pharisees	Known for strictly adhering to all the laws in the Scriptures and for believing in the resurrection of the dead
Sadducees	Known as a largely elite, wealthy class of Jews, many of whom were also chief priests. They did not believe in the Resurrection of the dead.
Zealots	Believed that God wanted Israel to be an independent nation again, free from foreign rule. Zealots preached a violent overthrow of the Roman occupiers.

What Happened Just after Jesus?

Into this situation of division among the Jews and oppression by their Roman overlords, Jesus was born. The next chapter focuses on his life and mission.

Judaism certainly continued after the death and Resurrection of Jesus, although not with its center at the Temple in Jerusalem. The Temple was destroyed by the Romans in AD 70 as a response to a Zealot revolt. It was never again rebuilt. But the Jews had been well prepared by the Exile for carrying on their faith without the Temple. They knew they did not have to offer sacrifices in the Temple to please God, that they could worship through devotion to God's Word, their Scriptures. The Pharisees further developed the tradition of **synagogue** worship, centered on the Hebrew Scriptures (later referred to as the

synagogue A Jewish center for worship and community life.

People gather at the Western Wall, which is located in close proximity to the destroyed Temple in Jerusalem. The site is sacred for Jews, and many go there to pray.

Look up the story of the destruction of the Temple by the Romans in AD 70, and the valiant but losing defense of the fortress, Masada, where the Jews held out against the Romans. Share with someone what you learn about those events.

Old Testament by Christians), as the basis of Jewish religious life. Because the Scriptures could be taken anywhere, Judaism spread all the more throughout the known world.

Jesus: Fulfillment of the Longing for a Messiah

The story of the Jews is essential to understanding the Christian faith because it marks the beginning of the Christian story. Christians recognize Jesus as the Messiah longed for by the Jews. Jesus brings people to spiritual freedom and helps them understand and live God's Law, just as Moses did. Jesus speaks God's Word of truth, calling people to a holy way of life, just as the Hebrew prophets did. And he offered himself as a sacrifice to unite the people with God, just as the Jewish priests offered their sacrifices.

The next chapter takes up the story and message of Jesus, whose life and mission Christians see as God's fulfillment of the covenant made so long ago with Abraham.

For Review

1. After the Exile, how did the Jews who returned to Jerusalem practice their faith?
2. Which empires oppressed the Jews after the Exile and up through the time of Jesus?
3. During the time of their oppression by foreign powers, what did many Jews hope for to end their suffering?
4. What happened to Judaism soon after Jesus' death?
5. Who is recognized by Christians as the Messiah longed for by the Jews?

The Gifts of Judaism

Judaism did not develop like any other religion the world has ever seen. God's grace, along with an incredible degree of faithful persistence and steadfastness, combined to make Judaism truly a light to the nations.

In ancient times, whenever a tribe of people turned from a nomadic life of wandering to an agricultural way of life as the Hebrews did, their god became just one more god among many worshipped by the people in that locale. But this did not happen to the Jews and their God. Through great determination and by overcoming what seemed unbeatable odds, they remained true to God.

Again, after the Jews were scattered first by exile and then by the final destruction of their Temple,

Arrange with a rabbi to visit a synagogue in your community or in a city nearby to learn about the contemporary life and concerns of the Jewish congregation there.

a historian might predict that their religion would come to an end. But instead, the Jews discovered a renewed sense of their faith.

Based on what has usually happened throughout history to small nations with no military power, the Jews should never have survived. In the twentieth century, the Holocaust destroyed six million Jews—fully one-third of their entire population. Still, this remarkable people and their religion continue to survive.

Its extraordinary history alone makes Judaism a religion worthy of admiration. Christians are sure that God is with the Jews today, keeping the covenant with them and rejoicing in their great gifts of faith in the One God and their keen sense of morality. These are gifts that Judaism continues to give to the world.

chapter **4**

Jesus: Son of the Living God

IN THIS CHAPTER

Who *Is* This Man?   98

Jesus' Life and Mission Begin 107

The Public Ministry of Jesus   114

Who *Is* This Man?

When Jesus stood up to read from the scrolls in the synagogue in Nazareth, as described at the end of chapter 3, he was known to people there as a local boy, now a grown man. Jesus had been raised in Nazareth in the home of Joseph, a carpenter, and Joseph's wife, Mary. At some point in his life, Jesus learned Hebrew and became devoted to the Law and God's covenant with the Chosen People. In the **Gospels**, Jesus followed the Jewish practices like the Sabbath rest and the dietary customs. He participated in the Jewish festivals and went on pilgrimage to the Temple in Jerusalem. He was familiar with the Hebrew Scriptures and could quote them from memory. Jesus was thoroughly Jewish in mind and heart. He identified with his people's longing that God's promise to them would be fulfilled—that they would be a great and free people, living in peace and justice with one another and being the source of light and hope to all other peoples.

© Bakusova / Shutterstock.com

> **Gospels** The four books of the New Testament—Matthew, Mark, Luke, and John—which tell about the life, death, and Resurrection of Jesus.

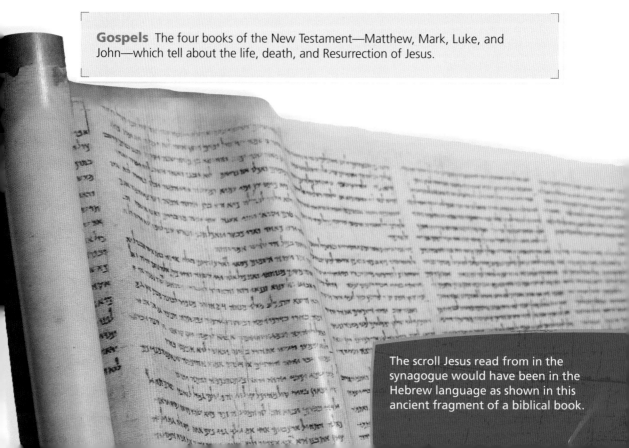

The scroll Jesus read from in the synagogue would have been in the Hebrew language as shown in this ancient fragment of a biblical book.

So picture the scene, as the Gospel of Luke recounts, when Jesus stood up that day in the synagogue and read from the prophet Isaiah: "The Spirit of the Lord is upon me, / because he has anointed me / to bring glad tidings to the poor" (4:18). Then he finished the passage, sat down, and said, "Today this scripture passage is fulfilled in your hearing" (4:21). Jesus' fellow Nazarenes must have been startled. They probably wondered: Who does Jesus think he is? Does he think *he* is the fulfillment of God's promise to Israel? Isn't he just one of us, a hometown boy? Or is he more than that?

Preacher? Prophet? Or More?

Many of Jesus' followers, admirers, and even detractors in his day wondered about this same question: Who *is* this man? At the time Jesus began his ministry, it was not uncommon for wandering preachers to gain a following, often with a message that God was about to make everything different for the Jews. Was Jesus another preacher or rabbi, great and gifted but nothing more than that? Or was he a prophet like Jeremiah and Isaiah, chosen by God to speak to the Hebrew people? Or was he something else?

Matthew's Gospel tells us that toward the end of Jesus' life and ministry, when he asked his disciples, "'Who do you say that I am?' Simon Peter said in reply, 'You are the **Messiah**, the Son of the living God'" (16:15–16).

I magine yourself at age thirty announcing to people who knew you in your childhood that you have an important mission—to bring peace and justice to others. How do you think they might react?

Messiah Title based on a Hebrew word meaning "anointed one" given to the saving leader hoped for by the Jews. The equivalent Greek term is *christos*. Christians apply the title Christ to Jesus.

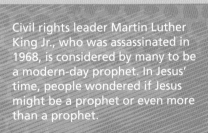

Civil rights leader Martin Luther King Jr., who was assassinated in 1968, is considered by many to be a modern-day prophet. In Jesus' time, people wondered if Jesus might be a prophet or even more than a prophet.

Truly God, Truly Human

The answer Peter (also referred to as Simon or Simon Peter) gave is the one that Christians have echoed for nearly two thousand years. Christians believe that this man from Nazareth, Jesus, is also the hoped-for Messiah and the Son of God. Within a few centuries of Christianity's beginning, the understanding that Jesus Christ is both fully God and fully human was expressed as the doctrine of the Incarnation.

What does the word *incarnation* mean? At its root, it means "made in flesh." In Christian belief, Jesus is God's own Son made present in human flesh—truly God and truly a human being. Jesus has both a divine nature and a human nature.

Why would God become a human being? That is a great mystery of love. Perhaps a parable—a story about ordinary, everyday reality that points to a greater truth—will help us understand why. Read this story about a little boy, his mother, and a fish.

A Boy and His Fish

Jack was a boy about six years old who lived in public housing in New York City. He often went out into the alley behind his apartment building with some older neighbors to bounce a ball off the walls or to pick through the garbage to find something to play with.

One day while scavenging, Jack found a glass bowl covered with grime. Because he had so few things, Jack saw a beauty in that bowl that many others would miss. He took his discovery gently in his hands and climbed the steps up to his apartment. Then he carried the bowl to the kitchen and began to clean it. When he was finished, Jack was delighted because he discovered that his bowl was perfect. Jack gingerly carried the bowl to the kitchen table, sat down, and admired the bowl. He was happy.

After a short time, however, the thrill of discovery began to wear off, and Jack started to get bored. Then he had an idea. He would decorate his bowl. So he went down to the street and picked up a handful of shiny pebbles and pieces of wire and sticks. Back at his apartment, Jack placed the pebbles on the bottom of the bowl and pretended they formed a roadway. Next he placed the wire and sticks among the pebbles and pretended they were bushes and trees. Then Jack had another idea. He got an old tin can, cut it in half lengthwise, placed it over the roadway, and pretended

Incarnation The mystery of Jesus being both God and human. It literally means "in flesh." The term refers to the belief that God took on flesh in Jesus in order to become united with people.

it was a tunnel. When Jack was finished, he looked upon his bowl with great pride. It was beautiful! He was happy again.

Once more, however, the wonder of the bowl began to fade for Jack, and he realized what he was missing. He had no one with whom to share his bowl, no one to enjoy what he had created. So Jack went to his mother. "Mama," he said, "can I buy a goldfish to put in my bowl?" Jack's mother thought for a long time, knowing they had little money. When she looked into Jack's eyes, however, she did what mothers tend to do. She said, "All right, Jack." She found a couple of dollars and placed them in his hand.

Jack's feet seemed to fly above the sidewalk as he ran to the store on the corner. He bought a beautiful goldfish, ran back to his apartment, filled his new bowl with water, and gently dropped the fish into it. Then Jack began to talk to his fish: "Swim along the roadway, fish. That's why I put it there—to make you happy." The fish merely swam around and around in the bowl, unaware of Jack's handiwork. "Hey, why don't you swim among the trees I made for you? That's why I put them there—to make you happy." The fish just kept swimming in circles, ignorant of Jack's pleas.

Jack ran to his mother in tears. "Mama, why doesn't my fish listen to me? I keep telling him what's going to make him happy, but he won't do what I say. Why?"

Jack's mother had been watching what was going on. Gently, she took Jack on her lap and said: "Jack, the trouble is that you and the fish speak different languages. He doesn't understand what you're trying to tell him. The only way he could understand would be if you could become a fish, jump into the bowl, and swim along the roadway, among the trees, and through the tunnel. Then maybe the fish would watch you, see how you live in the bowl, and follow you."

Consider what the story about Jack might mean, based on what you know about Christianity. What might Jack symbolize? The fishbowl? The fish? Jack's desire to become a fish? The wisdom of Jack's mother?

God's Longing to Reach Us

From a Christian perspective, the world we live in can be likened to the fishbowl. God created the world and filled it with beauty. God, like Jack, wanted to share this creation, this goodness. Out of that great longing to share, God created people—you and me. God's wish was that we would live together with God, sharing the wonders of creation in harmony and love. With this gift, God was sharing not just the world, but God's own self. Christians call this great gift **grace**—God's life and love poured out as a gift to all people.

But the Old Testament tells us that even though God reached out to share life and love with human beings, humans did not always accept that love. They sinned. **Sin** means ignoring God and turning away from God; it means insisting on having things one's own way. Sinful human beings can seem remarkably dense—unable or unwilling to understand the love that God tries to offer them.

The Old Testament also tells us that God tried to get through to the people by acting in wondrous ways in their history, freeing them from slavery in Egypt through the Exodus. And when the people sinned, God sent great prophets—people who remind us of Jack getting frustrated as he tries to get the fish to follow his commands. Like the fish in the story, the people could not or would not understand what God was trying to say. So they kept wandering around, ignoring the great life that God was holding out to them.

Jack, through his mother's wise words, developed a great dream—the dream of becoming a fish so he could show his little fish how to enjoy the wonders of his bowl. Jack could only dream his dream. But Christians believe that God did become one of us to show us the way to fullness of life, for God became human in Jesus.

Think about what it means to say that God sent Jesus to save human beings. What bad things do human beings need to be saved from? What good things are human beings saved for?

grace The gift of God's unconditional and undeserved love, present in every person's life.

sin A deliberate thought, word, or action that ignores God's will or turns a person away from God.

God took on human nature in Jesus in order to travel along the roadways, among the trees, and through the tunnels of life just as we do, so that we might look at Jesus, see how he lived, and then follow his living model of life in God. One of the writings in the New Testament explains that the awesome reality of the Incarnation gives human beings the opportunity "to share in the divine nature" (2 Peter 1:4). By becoming human for us in Jesus, God offered us a share in divinity.

Really God?

Some people might say: "I really can't believe that Jesus is God. I can buy his being a good man, even a great prophet, and maybe the greatest human being that ever lived. But this God stuff—that's going too far!"

Ultimately, accepting that Jesus is fully God as well as fully human is a matter of faith, but that does not make it unreasonable. Here is one way to think of it.

Recall your own experience of friendships. When we really like someone, we want to be with that person. We try to communicate with them in as many ways as possible. When we are separated, we feel lonely and think about getting together again. This drive for togetherness is true of all love relationships.

© fizkes / Shutterstock.com

The joy people feel when reuniting with loved ones provides a glimpse into how Christians understand God's desire to be with us.

Mahatma Gandhi on Jesus

A person does not have to believe in the divinity of Christ to respect his life and teachings. The great Hindu social reformer, Mahatma Gandhi (1869–1948), had a great respect for Jesus and his teachings, even though he felt that most Christians failed to live up to Christ's teachings. Gandhi once said: "What, then, does Jesus mean to me? To me, he was one of the greatest teachers humanity has ever had." Another time, Gandhi described Jesus this way: "A man who was completely innocent offered himself as a sacrifice for the good of others, including his enemies. . . . It was a perfect act" ("My Life Is a Message").

Now consider this scenario: God loves us, and that love is total, infinite, and unconditional because God *is* infinite love. Wouldn't God then want to be with us, to communicate with us, just as we do with our friends? There would be no better way for God to *be with us* than for God to *become one of us*.

One of the Gospels expresses this mystery as Jesus' own words: "For God so loved the world that he gave his only Son, so that everyone who believes in him might not perish but might have eternal life" (John 3:16).

Really Human?

Although some people have difficulty accepting that Jesus is truly divine, others have an equally hard time accepting that Jesus is truly human. They want to push him off into the heavens or make him God in a human disguise. This is somewhat the way the thinking goes:

> Jesus was human, maybe, but certainly not like me. Surely he didn't feel down in the dumps as I do so often, or get as frustrated and angry as I do. He was always nice and kind and understanding. He wasn't even tempted to be anything but good. Certainly he never suffered the loneliness or the gnawing questions that I do. I mean, he was God, right? So how could he be like me?

Accepting Jesus as fully human is as important as accepting him as fully divine. If someone does not accept Jesus as one who experienced life as we do—with all its limits, frustrations, loneliness, and fears—they will not be able to identify with him and try to live as he did.

Saint Paul, the great Apostle who spread the Gospel message on several missionary journeys and through letters to young Christian communities, emphasized that Jesus became one with us in all things except sin. In other words, besides the joys of human life, Jesus experienced the same pain we do in being human—the stress, loneliness, anger, and longing for acceptance. But he chose never to respond sinfully to these human experiences. Given the choice between popularity and telling people hard truths, he chose the path that ultimately turned others against him. Faced with a violent death, he did not command his disciples to kill in his name. He responded with humility—a total openness to the call of God that is the exact opposite of sinful self-centeredness. In a letter to Christians living in Philippi, Greece, written about three decades after Jesus' death, Saint Paul urged them to have the same humble attitude as Christ Jesus:

> Who, though he was in the form of God,
>> did not regard equality with God
>> as something to be grasped,
> Rather, he emptied himself,
>> taking the form of a slave, . . .
>>> becoming obedient to death
>>> even death on a cross.
>>>> (Philippians 2:6–8)

Remember the question Jesus put to Peter: "Who do you say that I am?" (Matthew 16:15). It was not obvious to Peter the first time he met Jesus

Reflect on which part of the mystery of the Incarnation is harder for you to understand: (1) Jesus is God. (2) Jesus is human.

that the answer to Jesus' question was "You are the Messiah" (16:16). Peter discovered that over time. Peter got to know Jesus as a man, discovering him as a remarkable teacher, a loving guide, a generous friend, a gifted healer, and a courageous prophet. Peter also witnessed Jesus' acts of wisdom and power: healing the sick, casting out demons, quieting storms, having amazing insights into human behavior, and being incredibly brave in confronting political and religious injustice. Gradually, Peter began to understand that Jesus was a man, yes. But more than that, he was "the Messiah, the Son of the living God" (16:16). Christians have been embracing Peter's proclamation since the earliest days of the church.

The Great Councils on Jesus

Early church leaders gathered in ecumenical (meaning "worldwide") councils to clarify the truth that Jesus is fully God and fully human and to counter mistaken ideas, or heresies. Out of the councils of Nicaea in 325 and Constantinople in 381 came the Nicene Creed, which Catholics and many other Christians hold today as a basic statement of their beliefs. This is the creed recited at Mass by Catholics.

The Council of Ephesus in 431 gave Mary, the mother of Jesus, the title Mother of God. This affirmed Jesus' humanity (because he was born of a human mother) and his divinity (because Mary was Mother of God).

Then, in 451, the Council of Chalcedon responded to a heresy claiming that Jesus was divine but not human, that he only acted human while on earth. Once again, the church leaders affirmed the Christian belief in the Incarnation: Jesus is truly God and truly human.

Image in public domain

For Review

1. How did Peter answer Jesus' question, "Who do you say that I am?"
2. What Christian belief is expressed in the doctrine of the Incarnation?
3. Using the images from the parable of Jack, explain why God became human in Jesus.
4. What did Saint Paul emphasize about the humanity of Jesus?

Jesus' Life and Mission Begin

We have made several references to Jesus' life and message without giving much detail. Let's take a closer look at how the four Gospels describe his life and mission, starting from the beginning.

Jesus' Origin

The Gospels make it clear from the start that Jesus is worthy of special attention. His conception itself was miraculous. According to the accounts written by Matthew and Luke, Jesus was not conceived in the usual way, but by the power of the Holy Spirit.

Jesus Is Conceived

Here, in summary, is how the Gospel of Luke describes the event known as the **Annunciation** (so called because of the angel's "announcement"):

A young Jewish girl, Mary, engaged to Joseph, a carpenter, was surprised one day by the appearance of an angel in her hometown of Nazareth in Galilee. The angel, Gabriel,

---

Annunciation The angel Gabriel's announcement to Mary that she would be the mother of a son named Jesus.

announced to her that God had chosen her to bear a son who would be named Jesus and known as the Son of God. (The name Jesus means "Yahweh saves.") When Mary asked the angel, "How can this be, since I have no relations with a man?" (1:34), the angel told her that this child would be conceived in her womb not by a man but by the power of the Holy Spirit. Though perplexed, Mary gave her willing response: "I am the handmaid of the Lord. May it be done to me according to your word" (1:38). Thus God became human through the power of God's Spirit and the consent of a young, unmarried Jewish girl who was open to surprises—especially to God's surprises.

As a pregnant, unmarried young woman, Mary could easily have been publicly disgraced. But her fiancé, Joseph, kept faith in her and in God's plan.

Read the account in Matthew 1:18–25 of Joseph's dilemma over Mary's pregnancy. Imagine an inner monologue, or conversation with himself, that Joseph might have had in wrestling with what to do.

Mother of Jesus, Mother of God

Catholics believe that God prepared Mary for the birth of Jesus by uniting her closely with God from the first moment of her existence. Unlike all human beings besides Jesus, Mary was born free of the condition known as Original Sin, the alienation of the whole human race from God (see chapter 11 for more on Original Sin). She was "full of grace" from the moment she was conceived in her mother's womb. This special favor given to Mary is known as her **Immaculate Conception**.

Mary is honored by both Muslims and Christians for her holiness and obedience to God. Catholics go further by honoring Mary with a special title: Mother of God. This is because Jesus was the divine Son of God and Mary was his human mother. This title does not mean that Catholics believe Mary is divine; rather, it means that they believe she is closer to God than any human being who ever lived, except Jesus.

Although hesitant at first, Joseph stood by Mary and married her even though Jewish Law would have justified his breaking off the engagement. Joseph was of the house (or lineage) of David, out of whose descendants the Messiah, you may recall, was expected to come. Joseph had to try to understand the blessing that was happening in Mary, which must have been very difficult for him. But his faith in God was stronger than his questioning.

Jesus Is Born

Stories of Jesus' birth, known as the Nativity, are given in two of the Gospels: Luke and Matthew. Jesus was born in the City of David, Bethlehem, during a census that was being taken at the order of the Roman emperor. Luke's account tells of poor shepherds

> **Immaculate Conception** The Catholic teaching that the Blessed Virgin Mary was free from sin from the first moment of her conception.

coming to the stable to worship the newborn baby. Matthew's account has Wise Men, or Magi (foreigners from the East), traveling long miles, led by a brilliant star, to see and offer homage to the child.

Nativity scenes that you might see at Christmastime sometimes merge elements from the two accounts. Luke's account lets us know that Jesus came as a source of hope for poor people and those on the fringes of society. Matthew's story adds the insight that Jesus came as a light to the nations—that is, to the Gentiles, or non-Jews, as well as to the Jews.

The stories of Jesus' origin are wondrous accounts. They indicate what an amazing thing had come about for humankind through the birth of this child.

Symbolic Meaning in the Birth Stories

Only two of the Gospels, Matthew and Luke, have narratives about the birth of Jesus. The basic elements in these two accounts are the same—Mary is the virgin mother, Joseph is the foster father, and Jesus is born under unusual circumstances. But almost all the details—where Mary and Joseph are living, who the angel speaks to, who visits the infant Jesus, and what happens after the birth—are different.

These differences are important because they give us clues about the human authors' focus. One difference is what happens after the birth in the Gospel of Matthew. In Matthew, Joseph and Mary flee to Egypt with the infant Jesus, returning to Israel only after King Herod's death. This is meant to recall the Israelites' time in Egypt, and their liberation by God through Moses. With this detail, Matthew is symbolically establishing that Jesus will be a great prophet like Moses, leading all people to spiritual freedom.

Mary is sometimes depicted as a refugee because of the Gospel account of her fleeing to Egypt with Joseph and Jesus.

His Early Years

Luke's Gospel recounts Mary and Joseph having Jesus circumcised at eight days old, according to the custom of their ancestors. Several weeks later, they presented Jesus, as firstborn male, to the Lord in the Temple, fulfilling another requirement of the Law.

Luke summarizes Jesus' years growing up in Nazareth with the words, "The child grew and became strong, filled with wisdom; and the favor of God was upon him" (2:40). We can imagine that Jesus learned the carpentry trade of his father and that they worked together in Joseph's shop. The boy must have been an extraordinary young person, learning great sensitivity and compassion from his parents and becoming a keen student of Hebrew and religion in the synagogue.

The Gospels say little about Jesus' childhood, other than the story of how his parents, on a visit from Nazareth to Jerusalem when he was twelve years old, lost track of him there. The boy Jesus, mature for his age, busied himself by having an intense discussion with the learned teachers of the Temple. During years of growing into manhood, no doubt he was noticed by people in his hometown as being an unusually perceptive, faith-filled, and devout young person. Mostly, however, he led an ordinary life of obedience to his parents.

Baptized in the Jordan River

The next we hear of Jesus in the Gospels, he is about thirty years old, and he is presenting himself to John the Baptist—his cousin and a wandering prophet—to be baptized in the Jordan River. Jesus must have admired John's zeal in preaching a message of repentance. John had an urgent sense that things were about to change drastically, and he wanted people to get ready for what was to come by being baptized (dunked underwater) as a sign of the washing away of their sins.

Imagine you are one of Jesus' friends growing up with him in Nazareth. What do you imagine Jesus may have been like at your age?

When Jesus appeared at the Jordan, John recognized that Jesus was greater than he, but Jesus insisted on being baptized by John. In Matthew's account of the baptism of Jesus, we are told that just as Jesus came up from the water, suddenly the heavens were opened to him and he saw the Spirit of God descending like a dove and alighting on him. And a voice from heaven said, "This is my beloved Son, with whom I am well pleased" (3:17).

Jesus knew that the great mission of his life lay before him, and that it was now beginning. He knew the mission would involve pain and suffering, but he also knew that he would be sustained by his loving relationship with his heavenly Father.

Tempted in the Desert

Before Jesus began his ministry, he was led by the Holy Spirit to go away for an extended time of prayer, fasting, and solitude in the desert wilderness.

By relying totally on God, Jesus prepared for his life's mission.

The Gospels tell us that the forty days in the desert was a time of great trial for Jesus—not unlike the forty years of trial the Israelites experienced wandering in the desert after they escaped from Egypt. In what is known as the Temptations in the Desert, Jesus was tempted by the devil three times to give up his complete dependence on God and to accept the easy and attractive forms of power that the devil offered. Jesus prevailed in the struggle with temptation. Imagine Jesus keeping his focus on the only true source of power that would sustain him during his ministry—his heavenly Father who announced that Jesus was the beloved Son.

After his struggle with temptation, Jesus was filled with the Spirit and an unshakable sense of purpose. He returned to Nazareth, in his home region of Galilee, to preach. It was there that he entered his hometown synagogue, took up the scroll, and proclaimed the powerful words from Isaiah: "The Spirit of the Lord is upon me . . ." (Luke 4:18). Jesus took the prophetic words as his own, and he knew that God was with him completely, filling him with divine power and love. Jesus was now ready for whatever was to come.

For Review

1. According to the account in the Gospel of Luke, how was Jesus conceived?
2. What two different insights about Jesus' mission are given to us in the birth stories in the Gospels of Matthew and Luke?
3. What was the intimate message Jesus received from his heavenly Father at his baptism?
4. What happened to Jesus during his forty days in the desert wilderness? How did this prepare him for his coming ministry?

The **P**ublic Ministry of **Jesus**

A Community of Disciples

One of the first things Jesus did as he began his ministry was to gather a community of disciples around him, people who would learn from him and carry on his mission even after he was gone. The closest of Jesus' male disciples were the Twelve Apostles. You may be familiar with some of their names—like Peter (also called Simon), Andrew, James, John, and Judas Iscariot, the one who eventually betrayed Jesus.

All four Gospels portray Jesus calling some of the Apostles to follow him. A few were common fishermen who seemed to be unlikely candidates to lead a spiritual and religious revolution, but Jesus saw in them something they did not see in themselves. He had a way of drawing people out, recognizing and affirming those who thought they were not particularly talented or gifted. Picture the scene and the magnetism of Jesus as he attracts followers:

> As he passed by the Sea of Galilee, he saw Simon [also called Peter] and his brother Andrew casting their nets into

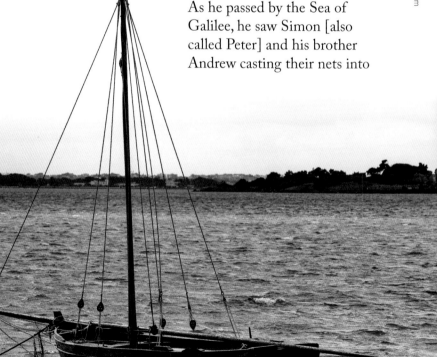

into the sea; they were fishermen. Jesus said to them, "Come after me, and I will make you fishers of men." Then they abandoned their nets and followed him. (Mark 1:16–18)

Jesus apparently had quite an effect on people. Several times, the Gospels report that individuals left everything behind to follow him. And Jesus *needed* to affect them deeply if they were to join him in the work to which he was dedicated.

The Mission: Proclaiming the Kingdom of God

What was the mission given by God that Jesus was so passionately set on? It was to proclaim the Kingdom of God—to preach it as a reality that was coming, but even more than that, to live the Kingdom in the present. Jesus knew that people would never catch on to the goodness and glory of God's Kingdom unless they experienced it for themselves. So Jesus dedicated himself to *living* the Kingdom amid the people, not just talking about it.

What was Jesus trying to get across about the coming Kingdom by his own life and example? Many ideas were circulating at the time of Jesus about how God would restore Israel to its glory. Many people thought God's Reign, or Kingdom, meant that the Jews, led by a military or political messiah, would triumph militarily and reestablish the ancient kingdom of Israel, as in the glorious era of King David.

Jesus had to be certain that people did not expect him to be that kind of messiah. He had no interest in setting up a geographical nation with borders and worldly power. Most important, that was not the kind of kingdom his heavenly Father wanted either. The Kingdom that Jesus proclaimed and lived was entirely different from what so many people expected. It was a Kingdom of love, not of political rule or power.

Think about what someone would need to say or do to get you to follow them. What would it take for you to commit yourself to their cause?

Imagine a high school student today who is pressured to do something or fit someone else's expectations but seeks to follow their own heart. Develop a brief scenario of what a situation like this might look like, and record it in a way that allows you to share the scenario with others.

Kingdom of God
A realm Jesus proclaimed, characterized by love, in which God's will for all creation is brought about and justice reigns.

Change the prayer from "Our Father . . ." to "Our Mother . . ." and then reflect on the meaning of each phrase. What insights, if any, about the Christian understanding of God does this shift in language give you?

Abba A word meaning "my father," which Jesus sometimes used to address God the Father.

Lord's Prayer Another name for the Our Father, the prayer Jesus taught his disciples.

God the Father

How did Jesus know with such confidence what God wanted? Jesus *knew*, according to the Gospels. He knew it with all his being because of his deep relationship with his heavenly Father. He was confident that he knew his Father's will, and he was empowered by his Father's love.

We can imagine that Jesus knew that the God of his ancestors—of Abraham and Sarah, Isaac and Jacob, Moses and David—was also the One who called him beloved and Son at his baptism. At times, Jesus seems to emphasize his intimate, personal relationship by addressing God as **Abba**, a word meaning "my father."

Although Jesus' relationship to his Father was unique, Jesus did not think of it as exclusive. He told the crowds who followed him that God was not only "*my* Father" but "*our* Father." He taught people to pray simply, with trust in God as their Father. When he taught his disciples how to pray, Jesus taught them a simple and profound prayer that had roots in Judaism. This passage from the Gospel of Matthew shows Jesus teaching that prayer, known by Christians as the **Lord's Prayer**:

> Your Father knows what you need before you ask him. . . .
>
> This is how you are to pray:
> Our Father in heaven,
> hallowed be your name,
> your kingdom come,
> your will be done,
> on earth as in heaven.
> Give us today our daily bread;
> and forgive us our debts,
> as we forgive our debtors;
> and do not subject us to the final test,
> but deliver us from the evil one.
> (6:8–13)

God's Love Includes Everyone

The Gospels convey that living in the Kingdom of God means living in the Father's love, surrounded by that love, breathing it, being saturated by it, and letting it guide social and community life. Jesus knew the love of his heavenly Father in the closest way. That experience of love became a fire in him that he longed to share with everyone. He wanted everyone to know God's love for them and to realize not only in their head but in the depths of their being what it meant to be a child of God.

How did Jesus live the reality of God's love for everyone? As God's own Son, Jesus was the embodiment of God's love. He made real God's love. In the Gospel of John, Jesus says, "Whoever sees me sees the one who sent me" (12:45). It was as if Jesus was throwing open his arms to all people to say: "If you need proof of God's love, look to me and my words. God's love is wider and deeper than anything you can imagine. We are all God's children. Come and join us in this great, wide love!"

Think about the nature of fire. What does it do? If the experience of love is likened to fire, what does that say about love?

The Kingdom of God Is among You!

"I'm not sure that I buy into this Kingdom of God idea," said Francisca. "You know, the belief that we can experience heaven on earth in this life. There's just too much pain and suffering in the world to believe that."

"I too am not sure that we can experience heaven on earth," agreed Michael. "Someone would really have to show me what it looks like."

Jesus' Actions: Signs of the Kingdom

The Gospels are full of stories of how Jesus made God's love and God's Kingdom present in this world. Let's look at some of the ways he did this.

Think about wheth-er you have ever seen healing take place in a person—a healing of body or spirit that seemed like a special gift, perhaps even a miracle of grace. If so, what did you see or experience?

Give three examples of kinds of people who tend to be excluded in our society or in your school—that is, people rejected by others as inferior and not deserv-ing of respect. Who has stood up for these people? Describe their actions.

Healing and life-restoring miracles. Jesus cured sick people and relieved suffering of all kinds. Many people in his time were considered unclean and were outcasts because of a disease such as leprosy or a long-term bleeding disorder in a wom-an. Conditions like blindness and epilepsy were believed to be results of sin. But Jesus saw true faith in these suffering people. He embraced them and offered the healing power of God, for their spirit as well as their body, whenever they presented them-selves to him in genuine faith. Three Gospel stories even tell of Jesus bringing people back to life after they had died.

Nature miracles. The Gospels record that on several occasions, Jesus performed miracles in nature. In the miracle of the loaves and fishes, he fed thousands of people by relying on God's providence to provide food when there was not enough for all. Another time, he calmed a fierce storm that terrified the disciples who were with him in a boat at sea.

The Gospel accounts of miracles may challenge our modern way of understanding nature and sci-ence. But most significant is what the miracles reveal about Jesus and his teaching. Jesus was so filled with the love of God that when faced with suffering, he compassionately healed; when faced with chaos, he restored calm. These actions reveal vital characteris-tics of the Kingdom of God that Jesus proclaimed.

Inclusion of outsiders. Jesus welcomed chil-dren when others saw them as a bother or not worthy of his attention. He ate dinner with sinners and those who were considered "lowlife." He treated as his friends those who were rejected or thought inferior in his society: people who were foreigners, female, unclean, insane, poor, sick. He stood up for people who had no power and no esteem from others.

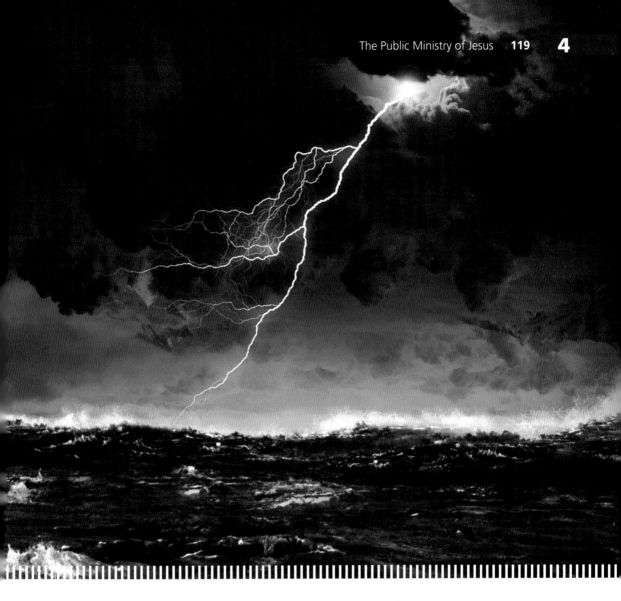

Love of enemies. Jesus taught that people should love not only their friends but their enemies as well:

> But to you who hear I say, love your enemies, do good to those who hate you, bless those who curse you, pray for those who mistreat you. . . . For if you love those who love you, what credit is that to you? Even sinners love those who love them. And if you do good to those who do good to you, what credit is that to you? Even sinners do the same. (Luke 6:28,32–33)

Jesus not only taught love for enemies, he lived it. He forgave those who persecuted him and betrayed him. Even as he hung on the cross dying, he forgave those who put him to death.

I magine Jesus in our society today. What kind of hypocrisy would he confront? What kind of religious legalism might he question? Give two examples of hypocritical attitudes or behaviors that Jesus would criticize.

Confronting hypocrisy and religious legalism. Sometimes when Jesus conveyed the mystery of God's love, the message was harsh. He could not stand hypocrisy and injustice, and he let people know that. In particular, groups of Pharisees and Sadducees debated with him about the fine points of the Jewish Law. In one incident in a synagogue, Pharisees questioned Jesus about healing on the Sabbath, which they understood to be a day of total rest. But Jesus responded by asking the Pharisees: "Which one of you who has a sheep that falls into a pit on the sabbath will not take hold of it and lift it out? How much more valuable a human person is than a sheep. So it is lawful to do good on the sabbath" (Matthew 12:11–12). Then he healed the withered hand of a man in the synagogue. Angered by this, the Pharisees plotted against Jesus.

Jesus loved the Law, but he could not bear to see it interpreted in rigid ways that made people less free or less loving. He demonstrated God's love for all by challenging hypocrisy and showing that religious legalism had no place in God's Kingdom.

Beatitudes: Turning the World's Values Upside Down

In the Sermon on the Mount, Jesus proclaims the Beatitudes, the values and the lifestyle that turn the world's values upside down. Here are two of the eight Beatitudes:

Blessed are the poor in spirit,
for theirs is the kingdom of heaven.
Blessed are they who mourn,
for they will be comforted.
(Matthew 5:3–4)

Can you imagine the crowd thinking, "How could the poor in spirit and those in mourning be blessed? I want to be rich in blessings and happy!" But Jesus has a different way of looking at the world. The poor in spirit are blessed because they recognize their need for God and by seeking God will find the Kingdom of heaven. Those in mourning recognize the pain and injustice in the world, and because they bring their pain to God they will be comforted by God's love. Find the rest of the Beatitudes in the Gospel of Matthew (see 5:3–11) and see what other people Jesus proclaims will be blessed.

The Least Are the Greatest

In the Kingdom of God as Jesus lived it and taught it, the usual values and priorities of the world are turned upside down. Those who have less really have more. The poor are truly rich. Those who want to be in the highest places of prestige are really in the lowest places. People considered unworthy are the most worthy. The most powerful ones are really the weakest, and those who are weakest are really strongest. The foolish are really wise, and those who think themselves wise are foolish. A person who wants to lead must first become a servant. Those who want to gain their life must first lose it.

Jesus lived these values by paying attention to the poor and those on the margins of society, by insisting on serving his disciples rather than lording over them, and, most of all, by giving his life on the cross.

Parables of the Kingdom

Jesus had another way besides the example of his actions to convey what the Kingdom of God is like. He taught truths about God and the

Think of someone who seems lost or alone in life. How could a caring person express God's love to that person so that they would not feel so alone?

parable A short story used to communicate religious messages, based on everyday events and often with surprising endings. Jesus used parables frequently to teach about the Kingdom of God.

Kingdom by using **parables**, intriguing stories and images that piqued people's curiosity and then delivered a point they were not expecting to hear. The images were familiar—a sheep, a coin, a seed—so his audience understood that Jesus knew them and their concerns. Jesus kept his listeners on their toes. With his talent for telling just the right story, Jesus was probably one of the most fascinating teachers of all time.

In the parable of the lost sheep, a shepherd seeks out the one lost sheep in a hundred, leaving the other ninety-nine to take care of themselves. Jesus was trying to give the message: "God is like that. God cares about the people who are lost, the sinners, the ones everyone else has given up on. If you want to be like God, then you too must seek out the lost ones who have gone astray."

The parable of the good Samaritan tells a story of a man who is robbed, beaten, and left for dead on the side of the road. Several prominent and respectable religious men pass by and do not help him. Only a man from Samaria stops to help, a person who, in the eyes of Jesus' Jewish audience, is a despised foreigner. Jesus' message about the Kingdom was something like: "Don't be surprised if people you see as outsiders are the ones who enter the Kingdom before you 'respectable' ones! God's Kingdom is for all who are open to God, regardless of what they own, how much power they have, or how high a position they hold in society."

Jesus' message was of God's love for all, and his whole ministry was about inviting people to share that love with one another. Despite this, he became a controversial figure and the subject of much concern by the ruling authorities.

Think of a children's book that is a type of parable. For example, *The Giving Tree*, by Shel Silverstein, is a parable about sacrificing yourself for the good of others. What is one of your favorite childhood books, and what is its message?

Present-Day Samaritans

Pope Francis referred to those who have peacefully protested the killing of George Floyd in 2020 in Minneapolis as "collective Samaritans." "The protesters" did not pass by on the other side of the road when [seeing] the injury to human dignity caused by an abuse of power," said the pope (in *Black Catholic Messenger*, October 17, 2021). He likened them collectively to the Samaritan in Jesus' parable who did not pass by the injured man on the side of the road. It is important to note, however, that the pope was not affirming the protesters who used violence.

Imagine what kind of responses Jesus would get if he came physically as a human person into our world today. What social media posts might you encounter describing how various groups react to him?

What do you find most interesting or intriguing about Jesus' life and teachings? Why?

The Response to Jesus

When a remarkable and loving figure passes through history—the kind of person who demands a response from those who encounter them—two things can happen.

First, many people take notice of, and cling to, the person. Some people reacted to Jesus this way. He came among a people who at the time were under the thumb of the Romans. The Jews' long and difficult history had led them to a passionate yearning for the one who would relieve them of their suffering—the Messiah.

Jesus was hardly what many Jews expected. They were looking for a take-charge military leader; Jesus told them to turn the other cheek. They wanted to become powerful; Jesus told them to humble themselves and to serve. They wanted wealth; Jesus told them to give everything to the poor.

Despite all this, many Jewish people found Jesus irresistible. They knew he offered them the kind of freedom that could not be gained from wealth and war. Surely, many people listened, found Jesus' message impossible to accept, and walked away. Many others, however, followed and staked their lives on this man and his message. The world is so hungry for love that when a loving person is finally met, many find that person especially attractive. So when Jesus came on the scene in dramatic fashion, people began following him in great numbers.

Second, when this kind of leader emerges in history, often the powers that be—the political, social, and religious leaders of the time—feel threatened by the new leader and new ideas they cannot control. Many Jewish leaders refused to accept Jesus as the Messiah. They were also irate that Jesus dared to criticize them. He criticized the legalists, who taught a spiritless form of the law. He criticized the pompous leaders, who deemed themselves superior to the poor and the powerless. These elites deeply resented Jesus. And even the Romans feared him. He threatened their base of power by stirring up the people's desire for freedom and equality. No doubt about it, this fellow was not just controversial; he was a threat to their power.

Eventually, a plot was arranged to get rid of Jesus by having him executed as a criminal. He was crucified, died, and was laid in a tomb for burial. But that was not the end of the story; it was just beginning. Chapter 5 looks at the events surrounding Jesus' death and the remarkable happening that followed three days after. It also searches out the meaning of those events today.

For **Review**

1. How was Jesus' idea of the Kingdom of God different from what people expected the Kingdom to be?
2. How did Jesus address God? What name for God did Jesus sometimes use that indicated his intimate, personal sense of sonship?
3. What powerful message about God did Jesus preach and live by his example?
4. What are five examples of the upside-down values of the Kingdom of God?
5. Give an example of a parable of Jesus, and describe the point it makes.

reflect

Love One Another

Jesus left his followers with the example of his love for them, a love that went so far as to give up his life for them. John's Gospel recounts that at the meal shared with his disciples the night before he was put to death, Jesus said to them: "This is my commandment: love one another as I love you. No one has greater love than this, to lay down one's life for one's friends. You are my friends if you do what I command you" (15:12–14).

For Jesus, it all comes down to love—love for God, love for others, and love for oneself—a love he not only proclaimed but also lived out in an exceptional way. The events of his last three days on earth showed just how committed Jesus was in his love for his heavenly Father and his love for all people.

Think about a group or community you are a part of, such as your school, neighborhood, or wider community, whether Christian or not. If the members were to take Jesus' message "Love one another as I love you" to heart, how might things be different in that community?

chapter **5**

Jesus' Death
and
Resurrection:
Experiencing New Life

IN THIS CHAPTER

The Last Supper: 128
Jesus' Extraordinary Meal

Accepting Death on a Cross   134

The Resurrection of Jesus   140

What Does   149
the Resurrection Mean?

The Last Supper: Jesus' Extraordinary Meal

"My grandmother told me that her church used to hold a Jewish meal ritual called a Seder shortly before Easter each year," Olivia said. "It was the church community's way of remembering the Passover meal Jesus shared with the disciples the night before his death. But they quit doing it out of respect for people who are Jewish."

"I kind of get why they stopped," Sadie replied thoughtfully. "After all, the Seder is an important Jewish ritual that celebrates God's action to save the Jewish people from slavery in Egypt. Think about how you might feel if the Jewish synagogue started having Easter Mass in honor of Jesus."

"Wouldn't we be honored if they did that?" asked Olivia.

"A lot of Catholics would be offended, I think," Sadie responded. "It can be disrespectful to recreate another religion's core traditions. Remember the mission trip to the Lakota Reservation? How the elder there said that many Indigenous people are offended when people who aren't Indigenous hold sweat lodge ceremonies?"

"I never thought of it that way before," said Olivia. "I'm beginning to see your point."

© kevin laminto / Unsplash.com

Christians throughout the world call the Passover meal, or Seder, that Jesus shared with his friends the night before he died the **Last Supper**. Catholics believe that during that meal Jesus instituted the **Eucharist**, the ritual meal through which Jesus nourishes his followers through the bread and wine that have become his Body and Blood. This occasion is remembered every year on the Thursday before Easter, which Christians call **Holy Thursday**. The circumstances in which that meal took place will help us understand its meaning today.

The Passover Seder

The place was the city of Jerusalem, center of Judaism and home of the revered Temple. The season was the Feast of Passover in the spring, the holy days when faithful Jews remembered how God had freed the Israelites from slavery in Egypt so many centuries before. Every year, they recalled with passionate gratitude how God had not abandoned them to their oppressor, the pharaoh. They told the story of the Exodus again and again, of how God had rescued them by parting the sea and leading them on dry land to freedom on the other side.

Every Passover, the Jews kept that memory alive with a special meal, the Seder, in which they retold the story of the Exodus. This meal also kept alive the hope that God would not abandon them now in the midst of their trials, and that God would one day free the Jewish people from every form of oppression they suffered.

Toward the Final Confrontation

It was this deeply joyful memorial meal that Jesus longed to share with his disciples during the Passover in Jerusalem. But the occasion was not a lighthearted, happy moment for Jesus and his

Imagine sharing a "thankfulness meal" with family and friends to celebrate some significant moment that has made a great difference in your life. Describe the moment you would focus on and what you would do at the meal to express your gratitude.

Last Supper Jesus' final meal with his disciples before his death, in which he instituted the Eucharist.

Eucharist The special meal, also called the Mass, in which Jesus nourishes his followers through the consecrated bread and wine that have become his Body and Blood.

Holy Thursday The Thursday before Easter, on which Christians prayerfully celebrate Jesus' Last Supper.

friends. Something ominous was in the air; they recognized that some of the Jewish authorities were closing in on Jesus, plotting to destroy him.

Jesus had entered Jerusalem with a triumphal welcome the week before the Passover. Jewish crowds who were there for the feast days waved palm branches and cheered his arrival on a humble donkey. Christians now remember this event every year on **Palm Sunday**, also known as **Passion Sunday**.

It was clear to the authorities that Jesus had a tremendous following. Furthermore, he was claiming to be sent from God—that was **blasphemy**! As if that were not enough, this wandering preacher had the nerve to challenge the operations of the Temple itself, claiming that the Temple might even be swept away someday. Jesus' challenge to the authorities reached a highly dramatic point during a visit to the Temple:

> They came to Jerusalem, and on entering the temple area he began to drive out those selling and buying there. He overturned the tables of the money changers and the seats of those who were selling doves. . . . The chief priests and the scribes came to hear of it and were seeking a way to put him to death, yet they feared him because the whole crowd was astonished at his teaching. (Mark 11:15,18)

Jesus was confronting the very guardians of the Law, the **chief priests** of the Temple and the Pharisees. No way could they tolerate such a bold attack on all they stood for. In addition, the Roman rulers were beginning to see that Jesus' presence in Jerusalem at Passover time could stir up trouble, inciting the passion of the crowds and possibly causing a riot against the Romans. He had to be done away with. As Jesus and his disciples gathered for the Passover Seder, Jesus knew that his final confrontation with the authorities was near.

Bread and Wine: "My Body . . . My Blood"

With the awareness that his time of great suffering was close, Jesus led his friends in the celebration of the Passover meal, or Seder. They told the ancient story of the Exodus, poured

---

Palm (Passion) Sunday The Sunday on which Christians remember Jesus' triumphal entrance into Jerusalem and his Passion and death.

blasphemy To claim to be divine or to act in a way that is mocking or being irreverent to God.

chief priests Jewish priests of high rank in the Temple, who had administrative authority and presided over important Temple functions.

out thanks to God, and sang the psalms of liberation. Then it came time to bless and share gratefully the unleavened bread and the cup of wine, as their ancestors had done for centuries. But at that meal, when Jesus blessed the bread and the cup, he did something different than the usual ritual. With tender love, he identified the bread, blessed and broken, with his own body, which was soon to be given up and broken in death for all humankind. And he identified the cup of wine with his own blood, which was about to be poured out in sacrificial love for all.

Here is the way Matthew's Gospel tells it:

> While they were eating, Jesus took bread, said the blessing, broke it, and giving it to his disciples said, "Take and eat; this is my body." Then he took a cup, gave thanks, and gave it to them, saying, "Drink from it, all of you, for this is my blood of the covenant, which will be shed on behalf of many for the forgiveness of sins. I tell you, from now on I shall not drink this fruit of the vine until the day when I drink it with you new in the kingdom of my Father." (26:26–29)

Jesus driving merchants from the Temple.

In John's account of the Last Supper, we get another glimpse of Jesus' great love. During the meal, Jesus got up from the table, took a towel and a basin of water, and washed the feet of his friends, as a servant would do. This was his way of teaching them by his example to serve one another in love.

The Last Supper is the origin of the Eucharist, which is discussed further in chapter 9. When Catholics celebrate the Eucharist, also called the Mass, they break bread as Jesus did at the Last Supper, in memory of him.

They recognize that Jesus himself is present with them in the bread and the wine—that the bread *is* the Body of Jesus broken for them, and the wine *is* the Blood of Jesus poured out for them. In sharing the bread and the wine, they proclaim that Jesus' sacrifice of love is now and forever with them. They believe that in the presence of Jesus they are united in love with God and one another. For Catholics, this is the great meaning of the Eucharist, which literally means "thanksgiving."

© Sipa USA/Newscom

Pope Francis washes the feet of Muslim, Christian, and Hindu refugees on Holy Thursday in remembrance of Jesus' foot washing at the Last Supper.

Breaking the Bread

During a Mass, Pope Francis shared this reflection on the meaning for Catholics of Jesus breaking the bread at the Last Supper:

> In the Eucharist, we contemplate and worship the God of love. The Lord who breaks no one, yet allows himself to be broken. The Lord who does not demand sacrifices, but sacrifices himself. The Lord who asks nothing but gives everything. In celebrating and experiencing the Eucharist, we too are called to share in this love. For we cannot break bread on Sunday if our hearts are closed to our brothers and sisters. We cannot partake of that Bread if we do not give bread to the hungry. We cannot share that Bread unless we share the sufferings of our brothers and sisters in need. ("Homily of His Holiness Pope Francis," June 6, 2021)

For Review

1. What was the purpose of the Passover Seder, at which Jesus celebrated the Last Supper? On what day of the year do Christians now remember the Last Supper?

2. How did Jesus deviate from a typical Seder when he blessed the bread and the wine at the Last Supper?

3. What do Catholics believe about the meaning of the Eucharist?

Accepting Death on a Cross

The Gospel accounts tell us that before the supper ended, Judas Iscariot, one of the Apostles, left the room. Jesus had an idea of what was in Judas's heart—that Judas was about to betray him by handing him over to the authorities. Jesus also realized that most of the other disciples would soon desert him, leaving him to face his persecutors alone. They would be too frightened to stay by his side. Jesus would go to his death abandoned by most everyone around him. The terrible ordeal of suffering that he was about to face is called his **Passion**.

The Agony in the Garden

Before his Passion, Jesus walked with his friends across a valley to the Mount of Olives, where many people

Passion The suffering of Jesus during the final days of his life: his agony in the garden at Gethsemane, his trial, and his Crucifixion.

© Dan Rata / Shutterstock.com

The garden at Gethsemane on the Mount of Olives in Jerusalem.

who came to Jerusalem for the Passover would camp at night. There, in the garden at Gethsemane, among the olive trees, Jesus prayed in dreadful anguish to his Father that he might be spared from "drinking the cup" of suffering and death that awaited him: "Abba, Father, all things are possible to you. Take this cup away from me, but not what I will but what you will" (Mark 14:36).

As Jesus agonized over what was about to happen, he came to accept it because he trusted in his Father's love for him. He was ready for what lay ahead. Meanwhile his disciples slept, unaware of what Jesus was going through.

The Arrest and Trial

Judas arrived in the garden with the chief priests, the elders, and their soldiers. Judas indicated who Jesus was by greeting him with a kiss. The authorities then moved in on Jesus. A disciple, rushing to Jesus' defense, drew his sword and cut off the ear of the high priest's servant. Jesus insisted there would be no such violent resistance: "Put your sword back into its sheath, for all who take the sword will perish by the sword" (Matthew 26:52).

Now deserted by his terrified disciples, Jesus was led off to face his accusers. Before the **high priest** of the Temple, he was accused of blasphemy (claiming a divine status) and of threatening the Temple. Those holding Jesus mocked him, blindfolded him, spat in his face, beat him, and hit him in the face. Then Jesus was handed over to the Roman governor, Pontius Pilate, who had the legal authority to sentence someone to death. After having a conversation with Jesus, and seemingly finding Jesus innocent, Pilate still condemned Jesus to be crucified.

Recall a time when someone let you down. How did that person fail to be there for you when you needed them?

Think about other people in history who have been falsely accused of crimes they didn't commit. Explain why this is such an injustice.

high priest One who led the religious services and conducted animal sacrifices at the Temple in Jerusalem. The high priest was appointed by the Jewish king with the approval of the Roman governor.

The Crucifixion and Death

Death by crucifixion was one of the cruelest, most torturous methods of capital punishment known in the ancient world, a method so horrifying that the Romans would not inflict it on Roman citizens. Crucifixions were not uncommon at that time in Palestine.

The Scourging

Recall an incident from your experience when a person—you or someone else—was being ridiculed or mocked. Reflect on what the person was thinking or might have been thinking during their mockery.

First Jesus was scourged with a whip, probably made of metal- and bone-tipped strips of rawhide; his flesh was literally torn from his body. He was mockingly dressed in a purple robe, the color of royalty, and a crown made from a thorny bush was pounded onto his head. He was then ridiculed by the Roman soldiers as "King of the Jews." In all this suffering, Jesus was alone; his friends and followers were nowhere in sight.

© Daisy Daisy / Shutterstock.com

The Pain of Ridicule

Being humiliated by ridicule can be as painful as a physical blow, or even more so. And people can be cruel, especially when protected by the anonymity of social media. A young woman committed suicide after a former boyfriend posted embarrassing photographs of her online, and a young man jumped to his death after being humiliated because of his sexual orientation. These anecdotes might sound like they come from a television series, but they are real-life stories. Jesus knew the pain of ridicule. He calls his followers to respect and protect every human person—no exceptions.

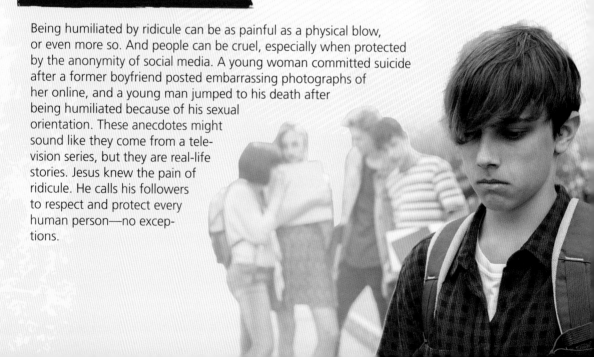

Nailed to the Cross

The Gospels do not say much about the Crucifixion itself. From descriptions of other crucifixions of that era, we have an idea of what happened. It is likely that Jesus, already weak from loss of blood and beatings, was forced to carry a heavy wooden beam on his shoulders for the quarter-mile walk to Golgotha (meaning the "place of the skull," the hill where crucifixions in Jerusalem took place). Some of the Gospel accounts say a man named Simon of Cyrene was pulled from the crowd to help Jesus, to prevent him from dying before he got to the execution site. When he arrived, his garments were stripped off him,

reopening all his wounds, and he was laid with his arms stretched out along the wooden beam. The soldiers pounded spikes through his wrists into the beam. Next, the beam, with Jesus nailed to it, was lifted up and lashed to an upright beam, which Jesus' feet were then nailed to.

Jesus hung in this tortured state for several hours. In a crucifixion, death usually came by suffocation, as the victim struggled to push up their body and gasp for air. As Jesus hung there writhing in pain and gasping for air, he must have felt alone and abandoned by God. At one point, as the Gospel of Mark tells it, he cried out, "My God, my God, why have you

Read the story of Jesus' death on the cross in the Gospel of Luke (see 23:33–49). What things most strike you in this account of Jesus' death? What do these things say about the kind of person Jesus is?

Recall the account of Jesus showing his trust in his heavenly Father, even when faced with death. How do you show your trust in God or in something else greater than yourself?

forsaken me?" (15:34). These are words from one of the Psalms, which would have been familiar to Jesus from his participation in Jewish life and prayer.

As Jesus suffered and died on the cross, the Gospels tell us that some of the women who had followed him watched in shock and grief from a distance. John's Gospel reports that several women, including Jesus' mother and one male disciple ("the disciple there whom [Jesus] loved" [19:26], assumed to be John himself) stood near the cross. The others abandoned Jesus out of fear for their own lives.

Love and Trust from the Cross

Despite his struggle with feeling abandoned, Jesus did not despair. Calling on the great source of his love, his *Abba*, Jesus prayed for those who put him to death: "Father, forgive them, they know not what they do" (Luke 23:34). Finally, with his terrible agony at an end and being at the point of death, Jesus yielded himself over in trust to God with a loud cry, "Father, into your hands I commend my spirit" (23:46). With that, he died.

Freely accepting his death, Jesus remained faithful to his Father to the end. The giving of himself—his Body and Blood—at the Last Supper came to its full meaning in the sacrifice of his life on the cross the next day. Jesus' death was an act of perfect love for all humankind and of total trust in God's love for him. Christians each year commemorate the day Jesus died as **Good Friday**.

Joseph of Arimathea, a wealthy disciple of Jesus, went to Pilate and received permission to take Jesus' body away to be buried. Joseph then wrapped Jesus' body in a linen cloth and laid it in a new tomb, carved out of a rocky hillside. A large stone was rolled in place to cover the entrance. Because it was Friday evening, the beginning of the Sabbath, the women who were to prepare Jesus' body for burial with ointments and spices had to delay their work. Following Jewish Law, they would rest on Saturday and come back to the tomb on Sunday.

Martyrdom, Dying for Faith

People who defend their faith knowing that doing so puts their lives at risk and who die as a result are called **martyrs**. The numbers are difficult to estimate, but it's safe to say that they are in the millions. Here are a few modern Catholic martyrs to be familiar with:

- Maximilian Kolbe, a Catholic priest who was killed when he took another condemned man's place in a German concentration camp in 1941
- Edith Stein, a German Jewish philosopher who became a Catholic nun, killed in a German concentration camp in 1942
- Óscar Romero, a Catholic archbishop who was killed in 1980 by a death squad because he spoke out for justice in El Salvador
- Ita Ford, Dorothy Kazel, Maura Clarke, and Jean Donovan, missionaries in El Salvador, killed by the military because of their work with the poor
- James Miller, a Christian brother who was killed in 1982 by vigilantes, possibly because he spoke out against forcing young men into the military

Edith Stein.

Good Friday The day on which Christians prayerfully remember Jesus' Passion and death on the cross.

martyr Someone who dies with courage for their religious faith.

1. What did Jesus agonize about while praying in the garden at Gethsemane? How did he resolve his struggle?
2. Who was responsible for the death of Jesus?
3. Describe the kind of suffering Jesus probably endured during his Crucifixion.
4. What were Jesus' disciples doing during his Passion and death?
5. What were three of the last things Jesus said, according to the Gospel accounts quoted in this chapter?

The
Resurrection of Jesus

To Jesus' followers, it must have seemed that all was lost after his death. They remembered his passionate preaching that God's Kingdom was right in their midst. His examples of a loving God who cared for poor people and outsiders would never abandon them. They remembered the healings and miracles Jesus had performed, examples of God's power breaking through into their world, making things good and right again. It had seemed that God's ancient promises to the Jewish people were coming together in the Good News of Jesus. But now he was dead. Had all that been just a false hope?

Jesus' followers were a fearful, defeated group at the time of the Crucifixion, their hopes crushed by their leader's execution. Although some faithful followers stayed close to Jesus, viewing the terrible events at a distance, most of the disciples just hid, afraid that Jesus' whole purpose and mission had been destroyed in his death. They thought it was all over and that they would be lucky to escape with their lives. But Jesus' death on the cross was not the end of the story.

"He Has Been Raised!"

Here is one Gospel's account of what happened when the women came back to the tomb on Sunday to prepare Jesus' body for burial:

> After the sabbath, as the first day of the week was dawning, Mary Magdalene and the other Mary came to see the tomb. And behold, there was a great earthquake; for an angel of the Lord descended from heaven, approached, rolled back the stone, and sat upon it. His appearance was like lightning and his clothing was white as snow. The guards were shaken with fear of him and became like dead men. (Matthew 28:1–4)

The angel told the women to not be afraid, for Jesus had risen from the dead. The angel further told them to tell the other disciples this Good News. The women ran to tell the disciples and, on the way, ran into the Risen Christ himself! Filled with amazement, they knelt before him and embraced his feet.

Mary Magdalene depicted fallen to the ground in front of the Risen Jesus.

© Brooklyn Museum of Art / Bridgeman Images

Religious Views on Resurrection

Christianity is not the only religion that believes in the resurrection of the dead or life after death. As mentioned, the Pharisees of Jesus' time believed in the resurrection of the dead, and most Jews today share that belief. Muslims also believe that the dead will be resurrected on judgment day. Hindus believe in a continuous cycle of life, death, and rebirth, some believing that one can break out of the cycle to eternal life.

The reality that Jesus was raised from the dead by God is called the **Resurrection**. It is the core belief of Christianity. Christians celebrate that central mystery of their faith every year on **Easter Sunday**. In fact, every Sunday is "the day of the Lord's Resurrection," a kind of "mini-Easter," a day to recall with joy that Jesus has risen and is with us in glory. For this reason, the Sabbath for Christians is on Sunday.

The Appearances of Jesus

The Gospels tell us that Jesus appeared to various people following the Resurrection. These appearances give us fascinating insights into the Christian understanding of resurrected life, or life after death. The appearances also offer a strong sense of the meaning and power of Jesus' presence to his disciples. They can help believers understand the nature of Jesus' presence in the world today.

No Trumpet Blasts

The Gospels do not record that blazing trumpets, magical signs, or roaring crowds accompanied Jesus' appearances. On the contrary, he appeared simply and without fanfare. In the account in the Gospel of John, Mary Magdalene at first thought Jesus was a gardener. Yet when he called her name, she suddenly recognized him. In another appearance, on the road to Emmaus, Jesus took a long walk with two terrified disciples who felt lost after the Crucifixion. They did not

Resurrection The passage of Jesus from death to life on the third day after his death on the cross; the basis of Christian hope in the resurrection of the dead.

Easter Sunday The day on which Christians celebrate Jesus' Resurrection from the dead; considered the most holy of all days and the high point of the Church's liturgical year.

recognize him until he broke bread with them. Jesus also appeared to some shocked and frightened disciples who at first thought they were seeing a ghost. He told them they had nothing to fear and then asked if they had anything to eat. Jesus also shared a simple breakfast of fish by a lakeshore with Peter and others.

In all these accounts, the people were shattered by what had happened in the Crucifixion. They were unprepared for the Resurrection and amazed by the One who was now present among them. In all cases, Jesus brought overwhelming peace and joy.

Really?

Did the Resurrection and the appearances afterward actually happen? Or was it all a hallucination, a figment of the imagination of the followers of Jesus? Or perhaps it was a hoax, a deception pulled off by a few close friends of Jesus who stole his body and hid it, then claimed he had risen? Could the Christian faith that has spread around the world for almost two thousand years be based on a falsehood? Let's consider this challenge to the Christian faith.

What is your reaction to the statement "God shows up in our lives in unexpected ways and at unexpected times"?

In one of his appearances after the Resurrection, Jesus shared a simple fish breakfast with Peter and others on a lakeshore.

Differing Accounts

The four accounts of the Resurrection in the Gospels of Matthew, Mark, Luke, and John tell a similar story: The women return to the tomb on Sunday to find that Jesus' body is not there. They are afraid, but then they are told by someone that there is nothing to fear, that Jesus has been raised from the dead. They go off to tell the news to others.

Yet inconsistencies exist among the four accounts. For instance, they differ in details such as these:

- who arrived at the tomb first

- which of the Apostles came next to the tomb

- who informed the women that Jesus was raised (An angel? A man? Two men or angels?)

- whether the women saw an angel roll away the stone or whether they discovered it already rolled away

- where the message was given that Jesus was raised (Inside the tomb? Outside the tomb?)

- whether Jesus himself appeared in the garden where the tomb was located

To a reader who is looking for a literal history of events, such inconsistencies can be disturbing. The reader may wonder why the Gospel writers couldn't "get the story straight." Is it because the whole thing was just made up?

It helps if we understand that the Gospels were written down some forty to seventy years after the events they describe. In the decades after

Jesus' death, the stories of his life, death, and Resurrection were passed on by word of mouth among
different communities of Christians. Naturally, some
of the details were lost or changed in the telling
and retelling of the stories before they were written
down. In addition, each Gospel was written within
a particular Christian community of the first century. The people in these communities had different
struggles and challenges, and the Gospel writers
often arranged their accounts of Jesus' life, death,
and Resurrection to respond to these challenges. It
is not surprising, then, that we find many differences
among the four Gospels in the way the same incident or event is described. This does not mean that
a given event never happened, but only that various
memories of the event were handed down in various
communities.

Thus the differences in the four Gospel accounts
of the Resurrection need not stand in the way of
belief in the essential truth of the stories—that Jesus
was raised from the dead and appeared to his followers.

Evidence for the Resurrection

We cannot actually *prove* that the Resurrection took
place in the same way that a police detective can
prove what happened, say, in a burglary. Belief in the
Resurrection ultimately comes down to faith in a
reasonable possibility, not conclusive proof. And we
have reasonable evidence that Jesus was raised from
the dead. Let's look at some of that evidence.

The stories themselves. In some ways, the
inconsistencies in the Gospel accounts make the
Resurrection event more, not less, believable. If Jesus'
disciples had indeed stolen the body and then made
up the story that he was raised from the dead, they
certainly would have been more concerned about
getting the details of their story straight!

Recall a big event you
experienced, like
a wedding or a major
tournament. Think about
all the details you can
recall. Then ask someone
who was at the same
event to tell you what
they remember about
it. What was different
in your two stories?

Imagine how the story of Jesus' Resurrection would have been announced in a social media post by the Apostles if they had been trying to pull off a hoax and guarantee that people would believe their story. What would their post have been like?

Consider your thoughts and questions about Jesus' Resurrection. Does the Christian belief in Jesus' Resurrection affect your life in any way?

Another interesting feature of the Resurrection stories adds credibility to them. In all the accounts, women are the first to hear and spread the news that Jesus has been raised. We know that Jesus valued women, but that was unusual in his era and culture. In the culture of that time, women were not valued as reliable witnesses for anything. Their word was not taken seriously. If the followers of Jesus had been trying to pull a hoax, they would not have created an account of the Resurrection that so prominently features the witness and testimony of women. They certainly would have developed a more "credible" story line, with high-status witnesses.

The experience of the disciples. We know that Jesus' followers scattered in fear after his death, terrified for their own lives. Yet shortly afterward, they were boldly and joyfully professing their faith in Jesus to everyone who would listen. They seemed to have lost all fear. And this was true not for just a handful of followers but for hundreds of people who had witnessed Jesus' appearances after the Resurrection. Their conviction in Jesus' Resurrection was so deep that many of them would later die as martyrs rather than deny their belief in the Risen Jesus. This deep conviction that Jesus had been raised, and the willingness to die to defend this belief, would not likely have been the result of a mass hallucination.

The proclamation of the early church. The early church made no attempt to *explain* the Resurrection; instead, the Gospels simply and powerfully *proclaimed* it. Belief in the Resurrection was unanimous in the early Christian communities. Saint Paul, whose letters to those communities are the earliest writings in the New Testament, wrote:

> For I handed on to you as of first importance what I also received: that Christ died for our sins in accordance with the scriptures; that he was buried; that he was raised on the third day in accordance with the scriptures; that he

A mosaic mural in Greece showing Paul preaching to a group of men and women.

appeared to Cephas, then to the Twelve. . . . Therefore, whether it be I or they, so we preach and so you believed. (1 Corinthians 15:3–5,11)

Paul proclaimed the Resurrection with great confidence, as did the Gospel writers. Belief in the Resurrection, and the depth of that belief, seem most reasonably explained by an actual, not an imagined, Resurrection.

If You Believe

The implications of believing in the Resurrection of Jesus are far reaching. If there is even a possibility that the Resurrection occurred, then the things that Jesus stood for deserve a person's attention, no matter what that person's religious background or lack thereof might be. For Christians, the belief in Jesus' Resurrection leads to a total commitment—even if that commitment should lead to pain and suffering, or death. Believing that

Jesus really was raised from the dead fosters hope and trust in God. God did not abandon Jesus; God was with him in all things, even death on a cross, and God raised him from death to the glory of risen life. This is why Christians believe that this same God will never abandon them, will be with them even in death, and will raise them too. This is the great source of hope for believers.

Before leaving this important part of this discussion, remember that Christians spend a lifetime deepening their decision and convictions about the truth of their faith, making their commitment over and over again.

A person should not feel pressured into having all their questions answered once and for all. If you ask good questions now, the answers you eventually arrive at will have more substance, depth, and maturity.

Belief in the Resurrection of Jesus is central for Christians, and so we have spent some time here on the rational basis for that belief. But assuming that there truly was a Resurrection, what is resurrected life like? Where is Jesus today? What does the Resurrection mean for believers today, two thousand years later? We turn now to these intriguing issues.

For Review

1. Briefly describe the reactions of Jesus' followers at the time of his death.
2. What core belief do Christians celebrate on Easter Sunday and every Sunday?
3. What were some of the people's reactions when they encountered the resurrected Jesus?
4. Summarize the evidence that supports Jesus' Resurrection.

What Does the Resurrection Mean?

Perhaps the most significant thing about the Resurrection is what it can mean in a person's life. The Resurrection is not simply about some distant, long-ago reality that affected the earliest Christians. It points to a great mystery that is going on today, a mystery that unites many of the realities we have already talked about in this course: the Exodus, the Passover, the Eucharist, Jesus' death, and Jesus' Resurrection, which gives meaning to everything else.

The Paschal Mystery

Christians call this great unified reality the **Paschal Mystery**. *Paschal* comes from the Greek word meaning "lamb." Each year at the Passover Seder, or Paschal meal, a lamb that had been ritually slain was eaten. The Last Supper took place in the context of the Passover Seder, which is why Christians use the term *Paschal Mystery.*

The Paschal Mystery is a mystery, but not in the sense of being a tricky puzzle or something we will never understand. Rather, it is a mystery in the way that love is a mystery—

a deep reality to be lived more so than a problem to be explained.

The Paschal Mystery is the belief that Jesus has gone through death to life. This is the simple but profound truth at the heart of Christian life. It is the belief that all human beings will also experience the small and large deaths of pain, sorrow, suffering, and physical death. But life, not death, will have the last word. The Resurrection means that ultimately death will be overcome by life, despair by hope, sorrow by joy, fear by trust, hate by love. It means that all suffering can be transformed into new, abundant life. It means that people today can be united to Jesus in his suffering and death and thus in his risen life. Saint Paul tells his friend Timothy (and all of us):

This saying is trustworthy:
If we have died with him
we shall also live with him;
if we persevere
we shall also reign with him.
(2 Timothy 2:11–12)

> **Paschal Mystery** The reality that Jesus has gone through death to new life and that those who are united with him will experience the same.

Through Death to Life: One Teenager's Story

What can the Paschal Mystery mean today? This is one young man's experience:

When I was nine years old, my parents got divorced. I loved them both, but I also hated them because they were doing this to me. My mother moved out. I then lived with my dad, whom I had hardly ever talked to before the divorce.

Life was hard for me. I had only one parent, and I had lost the other one that I cared for so deeply. And to make things even worse, we moved to a new city where I literally had no friends.

Then my father remarried. This made me extremely unhappy. First, I did not like the woman he was marrying and, second, I felt that she was trying to take my mother's place. I cried and yelled at my father for doing this, and again I asked God, "Why?"

I withdrew from my parents and friends. Instead, I concentrated on school and sports. Before my father got divorced, I had Cs in school and played no sports. After my father got remarried, I became a straight A student and an all-star soccer player. Yet this did not make up for the parents I had lost.

Because of all the things that had happened to me, I had isolated myself. A day after I realized this, I called my dad at work, something I had never done before, and asked him if he could come home and talk. So he left work early and took me out to dinner.

I told him how I felt and what made me feel that way. He just sat and listened. To me, that was one of the best nights of my life.

After my father and I had this talk, we started doing a lot of things together. We became father and son and developed an extremely close relationship. He even helped me make peace with my new stepmother. I don't think any of this would have happened, however, if I had not asked him to talk that one night long ago. (Adapted from *I Know Things Now*)

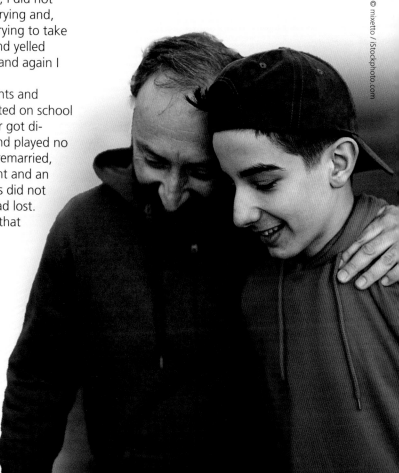

© mixetto / iStockphoto.com

In other words, the Paschal Mystery is not just about life *after* death. It is about life *now*. For Christians, entering into the Paschal Mystery by embracing the difficulties and crosses of daily life can lead to glimpses of the glorious risen life that awaits after physical death, for eternity.

Redemption: Exodus to Freedom

What do the death and Resurrection of Jesus have to do with the Exodus, the Passover, and the Eucharist? Recall the image of God freeing the Israelites from slavery in Egypt, leading them into the sea and parting the waters, bringing them to freedom on the other side. They were completely in God's hands, trusting God to bring them safely through the terror of the sea. And God did so—just as Jesus' beloved *Abba* brought Jesus through the terror of death on a cross to the risen life that awaited him. Christians believe that Jesus' death on a cross was an "exodus," the way to Redemption—freedom from sin in order to enjoy the new life of grace, a life lived in union with God. Christians call this salvation, which means being saved from sin to live with God.

The Lamb of God

The Passover, as mentioned earlier in this chapter, was the Jewish commemoration of the Exodus. And the Last Supper, the first Eucharist, took place in the context of the Passover Seder. At the Seder, a ritually slain lamb was eaten. In Christian symbolism, Jesus is the **Lamb of God**, through whose death (like the Passover lamb's) we come to freedom and salvation. Jesus, giving himself—his Body and Blood—in the Eucharist and on the cross, pours himself out for us like the lamb of the Passover. The image of Jesus as the Lamb of God is at the heart of

Think of a difficulty you face in your life. Imagine yourself embracing that difficulty with trust—taking it on and working through it—so that it leads to new life, risen life for you. What might be involved in working through this difficulty?

Lamb of God A title for Jesus Christ recalling the Passover lamb, whose death brought about freedom and salvation for the Jewish people. The title highlights the Christian belief that Jesus' death brought salvation for all people.

How would you explain the Paschal Mystery to someone who has never heard of this concept?

Think about an experience that you did not really understand until it was over. What opened your eyes to a deeper understanding, and what did you learn from it?

the Eucharist. As the Eucharistic bread is prepared to be distributed, the congregation sings or recites:

Lamb of God, you take away the sins of the world,
    have mercy on us.
Lamb of God, you take away the sins of the world,
    have mercy on us.
Lamb of God, you take away the sins of the world,
    grant us peace.

(Roman Missal)

The priest describes the consecrated bread itself using this image: "Behold the Lamb of God, behold him who takes away the sins of the world." As in the Exodus, Catholics believe they are liberated, or given a new life, every time they share in the Eucharist. In that sharing, they also unite themselves with Jesus in his death so that they may be one with him in his risen life. That is the great truth Catholics call the Paschal Mystery.

Jesus, Present in a New Way

The Resurrection of Jesus, and especially the accounts of his appearances to his disciples after the Resurrection, tell us a great deal about belief in the presence of Jesus today. An awareness of that presence is an important part of the development of Christian faith.

Jesus' resurrected body was not simply his physical body recovered to health. His body was *resurrected*, not *resuscitated*. It was a glorified body. Only people with faith, or at least an openness to faith, recognized him. Jesus had entered into an entirely new form of existence. He was still definitely Jesus, but at the same time, he was different from the physical Jesus who had walked among the people during his life. For instance, he was able to move through locked doors to be in the presence of his disciples.

The post-Resurrection appearances of Jesus are important because they are transitional moments. That is, the appearances reveal the change from Jesus' earthly physical presence two thousand years ago to his presence as Christians experience it today. Today, Jesus is no longer present in a physical way—we can no longer see or touch him. Nevertheless, Christians believe that Jesus is truly present among us. As he promised, Jesus is present through his Spirit, a Spirit who continually brings back to mind all that Jesus taught and who gives people the courage and insight to live out that message.

The appearances offer another, related insight about Jesus' risen life: Present through his Spirit in our midst, Jesus can only be recognized with eyes of faith. Even the disciples who experienced the appearances had to have faith. You may know of the story of doubting Thomas, the Apostle who refused to believe that Jesus had been raised from the dead until he could put his finger into the nail holes in Jesus' hands and put his hand into Jesus' pierced side.

The encouraging fact here, for anyone struggling to believe, is that even Jesus' disciples sometimes had difficulty recognizing and accepting him in his risen state. Some people might think that if only we could see Jesus, just like his followers could two thousand years ago when he literally walked among them, faith would then follow. The post-Resurrection appearances demonstrate that faith was required even of those who were present at those marvelous moments, that only in faith were they able to recognize Jesus in their midst. People today can also recognize him through the eyes of faith.

For **Review**

1. What is the meaning of the Paschal Mystery?
2. How are Jesus' death on the cross and his Resurrection like an exodus?
3. In Christian symbolism, why is Jesus known as the Lamb of God?
4. In the appearances after the Resurrection, how was the Risen Jesus different from how he had been before he died?

reflect

Jesus Today

One of the most touching stories in the Gospels is the account of Jesus' appearance to two of his followers in the evening after the Resurrection. These disciples were walking along on the road from Jerusalem to Emmaus. They were depressed and afraid; all they could think about was the terrible event that had just taken place in Jerusalem: the Crucifixion of their leader, Jesus. Their hopes were crushed. It appeared that everything they had believed in was crumbling. So preoccupied were they that when this stranger (the Risen Jesus) came along to walk with them, they did not recognize him.

Seeing the disciples' sadness, Jesus talked with them along the way. He encouraged them by showing them that all that had happened was not really a defeat—that it was the fulfillment of the Hebrew Scriptures. The awful suffering their leader had endured was not meaningless. His suffering was necessary to fulfill what had been prophesied by Isaiah about a suffering servant who would give his life for the people and thus save them.

Still the two disciples did not recognize that this man who accompanied them on their journey was Jesus. But their hearts were filled with joy as they talked with him. Finally, as evening came on and they reached the village, they invited their companion to come in and eat supper with them.

Here is how Luke tells the rest of the story:

> While he was with them at table, he took bread, said the blessing, broke it, and gave it to them. With that their eyes were opened and they recognized him, but he vanished from their sight. Then they said to each other, "Were not our hearts burning [within us] while he spoke to us on the way and opened the scriptures to us?" (24:30–32)

We too have our own discouragements and preoccupations as we walk along on our journey of life. But the Catholic perspective is that we are gifted in having the Risen Jesus with us—in the Eucharist and in all those moments of sharing the bread of our everyday lives with one another. We have only to open our eyes to see him "in the breaking of the bread."

chapter **6**

The Church: Gathering in the Spirit of Jesus

IN THIS CHAPTER

The Spirit Is Poured Out   157

What Is the Church?   165

The Spirit in the Church through History   173

The Spirit Is Poured Out

"I wonder what it would have been like to be one of the disciples who saw the resurrected Jesus," Susanna mused. "I mean think of it. Seeing someone you knew was dead come back to life and walking and talking with you."

"And not just any person," Devon added. "Someone who was your beloved teacher and friend, who was both strong and kind, who performed miracles, and who was brave enough to challenge the authorities. His return from death had to mean something important."

"And then Jesus left them again," Susanna replied. "Doesn't that seem strange? Why didn't he just stick around to keep leading them?"

Susanna is right in saying that the Risen Jesus did not physically stay with his followers for long. Catholics believe there was a divine reason for this. In John's Gospel account, before Jesus' death he had told his friends that he would soon be leaving them to return to the Father. But he also promised them, "I will not leave you orphans" (14:18). He told them, "The Advocate, the holy Spirit that the Father will send in my name—he will teach you everything and remind you of all that [I] told you" (14:26).

Jesus left the material world but remained spiritually present to all people through the **Holy Spirit**. This was the beginning of a new phase of humanity's relationship with God, a phase in which Jesus' followers continue his mission empowered by the Holy Spirit. The Holy Spirit is one of the three persons of the Holy Trinity, a belief about the Christian understanding of God, which is covered in depth in chapter 8. The Spirit guides people in the way of truth and gives them courage and strength to do things they never dreamed possible. Let's look at two events in the New Testament that talk about the power of the Holy Spirit: the Ascension and Pentecost.

The Ascension: Returning to the Father

The Acts of the Apostles, also referred to as Acts, is a book in the New Testament. It tells the story of the early Christian communities and how they spread from Jerusalem to the larger world.

As the Acts of the Apostles tells it, forty days after the Resurrection, Jesus left the material world and returned to his Father in heaven. But first, he left in his Apostles' hands the mission of spreading the Good News of God's Kingdom to every corner of the world. They would not have to take on this task alone, for the Spirit of Jesus would fill them with power:

> "But you will receive power when the holy Spirit comes upon you, and you will be my witnesses in Jerusalem, throughout Judea and Samaria, and to the ends of the earth." When he had said this, as they were looking on, he was lifted up, and a cloud took him from their sight. (Acts 1:8–9)

Christians call Jesus' return to the Father in heaven forty days after his Resurrection the **Ascension** (based on the word *ascend*, meaning "go up"). Its feast is celebrated by Catholics each year on Ascension Thursday, forty days after Easter Sunday.

In calling this reality the Ascension, we need to be careful that we do not misunderstand its meaning. It is not really about Jesus "going up there." When we say the word *heaven*, we automatically tend to think of a place "up there." In the meaning it seems to have in Scripture, however, heaven is a state of being in the

---

Holy Spirit One of the three persons of the Holy Trinity, along with the Father and the Son. Also called the Spirit of God and the Spirit of Jesus.

Ascension The returning to heaven of the Risen Christ forty days after his Resurrection.

presence of God, who exists everywhere, not just "up there." During earthly life, people can experience glimpses of heaven. Catholics believe that after death people can be fully with God.

So in saying that Jesus ascended into heaven, Catholics mean that he is no longer tied to one place, to one era, to talking about one thing at a time to one particular group of people. He is freed from the physical limitations of earthly existence. He is freed to be everywhere, with everyone, for all time, loving and caring and calling people into relationship with God.

Jesus' physical presence, as he walked and talked on earth with people, was only one kind of presence. We may wish we could know Jesus in that way. But Catholics believe the presence of Jesus we can experience today is even more than that. It is the personal presence of God with us, loving us totally, perfectly, and without limits of time and space. Catholics believe we can experience this presence in many ways, including in nature, through the loving presence of other people, through the quiet of our own hearts and minds, and through the sacred words and actions in worship, most especially in the Eucharist.

Pentecost: The Gift of the Holy Spirit

As Jesus had promised, he would remain with his followers through the power of the Holy Spirit poured out among them. The Acts of the Apostles describes the coming of the Holy Spirit as a dramatic, marvelous event that took place several days after the Ascension, on the Jewish Feast of Pentecost. The Apostles and some of the disciples, including Jesus' mother, Mary, were gathered in a room in Jerusalem. Here is how the event is told:

> And suddenly there came from the sky a noise like a strong driving wind, and it filled the entire house in which they were. Then there

Imagine explaining heaven to a seven-year-old. What words and ideas would you use?

Recall an experience watching a fire. What are its characteristics? If something such as the nature of God's power and love is likened to fire, what might that mean?

Think about wind, fire, and the ability to communicate in new ways as symbols for change. Have you, or has someone you know, gone through a sudden, dramatic change for the better? If so, how would you describe this change? Are wind, fire, or the ability to communicate in new ways useful symbols for describing the change?

appeared to them tongues as of fire, which parted and came to rest on each one of them. And they were all filled with the holy Spirit and began to speak in different tongues, as the Spirit enabled them to proclaim.

Now there were devout Jews from every nation under heaven staying in Jerusalem. At this sound, they gathered in a large crowd, but they were confused because each one heard them speaking in his own language. . . . They were all astounded and bewildered, and said to one another, "What does this mean?" But others said, scoffing, "They have had too much new wine." (Acts 2:2–6,12–13)

The immediate result of the presence of the Spirit was total, uninhibited joy. Bystanders thought the Apostles must be drunk. Peter, the leader of the Apostles, assured the crowd that this was not the case. Then he delivered a powerful proclamation of the Good News to the gathered crowd.

Notice the images used to describe the power of the Spirit—the rush of a mighty wind, "tongues" of fire resting on each person, the ability to speak in languages they did not even know. These are strong images. They symbolize the effect that the disciples of Jesus must have felt. It was like a forceful wind came through and swept out the old fears and clouds of doubt, bringing in the new, fresh air of confidence and clear vision. The Apostles' hearts, souls, and minds were on fire with love, zeal, and courage. They could speak boldly to anyone, even foreigners, about Jesus as the Lord and Messiah who had been raised from the dead. They felt completely transformed, made new. Jesus' Spirit indeed had been poured out among them, and they would never, ever be the same.

Christians call this coming of the Holy Spirit **Pentecost**. They celebrate this feast every year on Pentecost Sunday, fifty days after Easter. When Jesus walked the earth, he had put into place the foundations of the church by announcing the Kingdom of God and calling others to join in it. But the church did not really take off until Jesus left to go to the Father and sent his Spirit to his followers. Then the church was in their hands. For this reason, Pentecost is sometimes called the birthday of the church.

The Spirit at Work in the Early Christian Communities

The outpouring of the Spirit of Jesus continued in the early community of followers in Jerusalem and flowed beyond Jerusalem to new communities. Saint Paul is the person most responsible for spreading Jesus' message beyond Jerusalem. Before too long, Christians took on an identity distinct from Jews.

In Jerusalem

The Acts of the Apostles reports that three thousand Jews were baptized in Jerusalem in the name of Jesus after Peter preached to them on Pentecost. Here is how Acts describes the joyful new community:

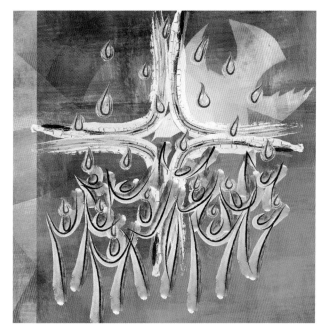

They devoted themselves to the teaching of the apostles and to the communal life, to the breaking of the bread and to the prayers. Awe came upon everyone, and many wonders and signs were done through the apostles. All who believed were together and had all things in common; they would sell their property and possessions and divide them among all according to each one's need. . . . And every day the Lord added to their number those who were being saved. (2:42–45,47)

Pentecost The descent of the Holy Spirit upon the Apostles, Mary, and the disciples gathered with them, empowering them to continue Jesus' mission.

Holy Spirit, Comforter

In a Homily given during Mass on Pentecost, Pope Francis talked about the Holy Spirit as comforter:

> All of us, particularly at times of difficulty . . . look for consolation. Often, though, we turn only to earthly comforts . . . that quickly fade. Today, Jesus offers us heavenly comfort, the Holy Spirit. . . . What is the difference? The comforts of the world are like a pain reliever: they can give momentary relief, but not cure the illness we carry deep within. They can soothe us, but not heal us at the core. They work on the surface, on the level of the senses, but hardly touch our hearts. Only someone who makes us feel loved for who we are can give peace to our hearts. The Holy Spirit, the love of God, does precisely that. (May 23, 2021)

Where have you looked for comfort and consolation in times of difficulty? Where have you found it?

Imagine you are one of the early followers of Jesus in the Jerusalem community. How would you describe the community to a friend who is curious about it? Would you encourage your friend to join the community? Why or why not?

These first Christians still considered themselves good Jews. Notice that they went to the Temple in Jerusalem every day. As followers of the Jesus movement, they also "broke bread" in their homes; that is, they shared the Eucharist in memory of Jesus. No one, not even the poorest among them, had to go without, for they put all their money and possessions together and shared them. This way of life was so attractive that people flocked to join them.

Beyond Jerusalem

Before long, the Spirit of Jesus spread beyond Jerusalem into new cities and regions—first in Palestine (Israel) and later in other parts of the Roman Empire. Inevitably, the young movement began attracting non-Jews, or Gentiles, as converts. The first community that included both Jewish *and* Gentile followers of Jesus was established in the city of Antioch. The Acts of the Apostles tells us that "it was in Antioch that the disciples were first called Christians" (11:26), because they were followers of Jesus the Christ.

With so many Gentiles being baptized, the Apostles, who were Jewish followers of Jesus, had an important decision to make: Would the Gentiles who joined the Jesus movement have to become Jewish first and keep the whole Jewish Law, including the practice of circumcision for males? At a meeting known as the Council of Jerusalem, the Apostles decided to open the doors to Gentiles without requiring them to first become Jews. After this, the movement of Jesus' followers spread like wildfire throughout the Roman Empire.

Paul, Apostle to the Gentiles

The man most responsible for spreading the Gospel beyond Jerusalem and to the Gentiles was Paul, a Jew and zealous Pharisee who had once persecuted the followers of Jesus. Paul (who was also called Saul) had been dedicated to putting an end to this new movement. He had never met Jesus during Jesus' earthly life, but

Gentile A non-Jewish person.

© Renata Sedmakova / Shutterstock.com

A stained glass depiction of the Council of Jerusalem.

Imagine that you were writing a message to someone who needed encouragement, hope, and friendly advice. Who is this person, and what would you say to them?

one day Saul had a life-changing encounter with the Risen Lord (see Acts 9:1–9). He was never the same again after this encounter. Now Paul was zealous for Christ, starting up new churches of Jesus' followers in cities and towns all over the empire. Paul is known as the Apostle to the Gentiles.

After beginning or visiting a church in a city— for instance, Corinth, Ephesus, or Philippi—Paul would write letters to the community from a distance, even from prison, where he was held a number of times for stirring people up about the Christian faith. Passionate, tender, and sometimes scolding, these letters nurtured the faith of the new churches. They were the first written documents in what would become the New Testament.

Eventually, Paul was arrested for inciting rebellion. He was taken to Rome as a prisoner where he lived for several years under house arrest. Later, Peter made his way to Rome where he led the local church. Christian tradition maintains that both of these great Apostles were martyred—killed for their faith—around AD 64–67, during a Roman persecution of Christians.

The Separation from Judaism

Once Christian communities became open to Gentile converts without insisting they strictly follow the Jewish Law, the rift between Christians and the leaders of Judaism widened. After the Jewish Temple was destroyed by the Romans in AD 70 and the Jews were driven from their homes in Jerusalem, the leaders of Judaism became even more concerned that the Jewish practices be kept strictly. Many of them no longer considered Jewish Christians to be true Jews.

Before long, Jewish Christians were no longer allowed by the Jewish leaders to worship in the town synagogues with their fellow Jews. At that point, the

This woodcut depicts Paul writing a letter to the Ephesians from prison.

Christian movement separated from Judaism and became a religion of its own: Christianity. But Christians knew their faith was built on Judaism. They continued to read and pray the Hebrew Scriptures (traditionally called the Old Testament by Christians) and still do today in worship.

For Review

1. What is meant by the Ascension of Jesus? When do Catholics celebrate the Feast of the Ascension?
2. What happened at Pentecost? When do Christians celebrate the Feast of Pentecost?
3. Describe the meaning of the three images of the Spirit's power at Pentecost.
4. What was Paul's important role in the early church?
5. Why and when did the Christian movement separate from Judaism?

What Is the Church?

The first Christian communities, established after the outpouring of the Holy Spirit at Pentecost, are the foundation of the Catholic Church today. In fact, today's Church is the continuation of those early Christian communities, but with over two thousand years of history behind it. It has grown and developed through the almost twenty centuries of its existence and has spread to every continent on earth. Today, about one-third of the world's population is Christian, and approximately half of Christians are Catholic.

Believers Who Carry on Christ's Mission

Whether we are talking about the church of the year AD 70 or the church of the year 2000 and beyond, the essence of the church is the same. It is the gathering of those who profess belief in Jesus Christ and are baptized into that faith. But it is more than that. The church is also the active presence of Jesus in the world, carrying on his mission through the power of the Holy Spirit. And what was Jesus' mission? As we have seen in earlier chapters, Jesus' mission was to proclaim and bring about the Kingdom of God through his life, sacrificial death, and Resurrection. Jesus was sent by God to overcome the power of sin, uniting humanity with God and beginning God's reign of justice and peace in the world.

The church does not exist simply for itself, to give its members comfort and support, or to educate them or help them lead holy lives. It certainly should and does do those things, but the church is intended to do more than that. It exists *for the world*—to be a beacon of light and hope, a source of healing and unity in a world troubled by division, sin, and injustice.

Think about the times when you have seen Christians being a source of healing and unity, either in your local community or in the bigger world. How would you describe what you have seen?

Christ Will Come Again

Christian belief is that one day, at the end of time as we know it, Christ will come to earth again in the second coming. He will pronounce the last judgment of the living and the dead, in which evil will be overcome once and for all and good will be victorious.

During the first decades of the church, Christians believed that Jesus' return would be soon, within their lifetime. But when decades passed and Jesus did not come back, they had to readjust their hopes, recognizing that the end of time was probably not as near as they had once believed. They committed themselves to a church that would probably be around for a long time. Two thousand years later, Christians still live with the hope of Christ's return, when God's plan will be realized for all creation.

The church is meant to bring all humanity—and even all creation—together as one. It is meant to bring about life in union with one another and God, as God intended from the beginning of the world.

Mary: Mother of God, Mother of the Church

Mary, the mother of Jesus, who carried Jesus into the world by letting God's Spirit work wonders in her, has a special place among Catholics as the model of the church. An angel proclaims that Mary is God's "favored one" (Luke 1:28). She was completely open to the Spirit. Though she did not understand exactly how God was at work in her, she agreed to bring the Son of God into the world. Mary's openness to God's will for her life can serve as a model today for how the church can be open to God and thus bring the healing, loving presence of Jesus Christ into the world.

To honor her special role, Mary has been given honorary titles. She is called the Mother of God, because she willingly gave birth to Jesus Christ, the Son of God. Being the mother of Christ, Mary is also called the Mother of the Church, and Catholics believe she continues to love and aid her son's disciples who call on her name.

Catholics believe that because of Mary's unique role among all human beings, she was united with God at the end of her life on earth without going through the corruption of death. This is called the doctrine of the **Assumption** (because Mary was taken up, or "assumed" into heaven). In a way unlike any other human being, Mary shares in the glory of Jesus' Resurrection. She gives believers hope that one day they too will share in that Resurrection.

Imagine that you could have a conversation with Mary, the mother of Jesus. What would you want to ask her about?

Assumption The doctrine that recognizes that the body of Mary, the mother of Jesus, was taken directly to heaven after her life on earth had ended.

"Church" at Different Levels

The church is the assembly, or gathering, of believers, but it exists at different levels—from a small group of Christians to the whole worldwide church. The church can mean any of these:

- a group of Christians gathered for worship
- a specific parish or congregation
- a local diocese, which is a group of many parishes or congregations led by a bishop
- the whole worldwide church

I magine that you were creating your own image of the church. What would the image be, and how would you explain it to another person?

Images of the Church

We can think of the church, whether at a small-group or worldwide level, by using three images from Scripture:

- the church as the **people of God**
- the church as the **body of Christ**
- the church as the **temple of the Holy Spirit**

These images show the Christian understanding of how the church is the work of the Trinity in human beings—the work of God the Father, Jesus Christ the Son, and the Holy Spirit. (The meaning of the Trinity is covered in more depth in chapter 8.)

People of God

Saint Peter expressed the image of the church as the people of God in his first letter to several Christian communities: "But you are 'a chosen race, a royal priesthood, a holy nation, a people of his own, so that you may announce the praises' of him who called you out of darkness into his wonderful light" (1 Peter 2:9).

Like the Israelites, chosen long ago by God to be the ones through whom God would save the world, the church is the people of God. Also like the Israelites, the church is a "pilgrim" people, on the way to the "Promised Land"—the Kingdom of God—but not there yet. Like the Israelites, the church is a chosen people but not a perfect people. It is made up of imperfect persons who sin and lose their way, and who at times even disgrace the religion of Christianity. But believers trust that the church is beloved by God and ultimately guided by God, who will never abandon it.

Body of Christ

In his first letter to the Christian community at Corinth, Paul wrote about the church as Christ's own body:

> As a body is one though it has many parts, and all the parts of the body, though many, are one body, so also Christ. For in one Spirit we were all baptized into one body, whether Jews or

Greeks, slaves or free persons, and we were all given to drink of one Spirit. (12:12–13)

Paul's message to the Corinthians (and to Christians today) is that they are the hands and feet, and the heart, mind, and soul of Christ in the world. They are Christ living in history. And though every person has different talents or contributions to make (like hands and feet do), everyone is needed and are all united as one. Everyone is meant to care for one another as members of one body and to care for the world as Christ does, to be Christ in the world. The sharing in the Eucharist expresses and brings about this unity with Christ and one another.

Temple of the Holy Spirit

Paul uses another analogy to make it clear that the Holy Spirit dwells not in a building called a church but among a people called the church. Here are two examples from his letters:

> Do you not know that you are the temple of God, and that the Spirit of God dwells in you? . . . the temple of God, which you are, is holy. (1 Corinthians 3:16–17)

> Through [Jesus Christ] the whole structure is held together and grows into a temple sacred in the Lord; in him you also are being built together into a dwelling place of God in the Spirit. (Ephesians 2:21–22)

Church Buildings

Even though the church is primarily the people of God, the building where Catholics gather to worship has an important place in Catholic life. It provides a place for the community to gather and worship. Different types of church buildings are used for different reasons.

- A house church is typically someone's home. The first Christians gathered in houses for fellowship and celebrating the Eucharist. Some Christians still gather in house churches today, especially in places where they are being persecuted.

- A parish church is the building where a community of Catholics gathers and the local priest celebrates the Mass and other sacraments.

- A cathedral is the central church in a diocese. The bishop of a diocese is officially associated with the diocese's cathedral.

- A chapel is a small building—or a room in a building, such as a school or a retreat center—that is set aside for personal or small-group prayer.

Remember that before Paul became a Christian, he was devoted to the Jewish Temple in Jerusalem, the focus of so many dreams and hopes for the Israelite people. It must have been a great insight for him to realize that the temple of the Lord is not a building but a community of people.

The people are the place where God dwells, where the Holy Spirit is alive and active. Whenever we are inclined to equate the church with a building, we should recall Paul's teaching that the church is primarily the community of Christ's disciples.

The Splits in Christianity

It is a painful reality that Christians today are divided, not united under one organized church. What should be the one body of Christ is fragmented. A variety of Christian **denominations**, which usually call themselves churches, exist today. This is because many groups have separated from the Catholic Church over the centuries. It might seem arrogant that Catholics believe they are the original church, but there is a good historical reason for this. The Catholic Church can trace its history back to the church of the Apostles through an unbroken line of bishops, who are the successors of the Apostles. The Catholic Church is also led by the **pope**, who is the successor of Saint Peter, the person Christ appointed to lead the Apostles. (Chapter 8 considers the role of the pope in Catholicism.)

The splits in Christianity occurred for many reasons—sometimes over disputes about rituals, at times over differences in beliefs. Sometimes the reasons were more senseless, having to do with political or military conflict, personal power struggles, or hurts and misunderstandings. Often a combination of all these reasons was involved.

Christian churches today include Catholics, Orthodox Christians, Protestant Christians (which include many denominations), and other small denominations. In recent decades, many Christian denominations have been working with one another to build mutual understanding and respect. This work is a movement called **ecumenism**. As a result, some Christians are discovering just how much their faith traditions have in common even though important differences still prevent them from being fully united as Jesus hoped all his followers would be. John's Gospel tells of Jesus' prayer for unity to his Father at the Last Supper, a prayer that the movement to bring about Christian unity echoes today:

> I pray not only for them, but also for those who will believe in me through their word, so that they may all be one, as you, Father, are in me and I in you, that they also may be in us, that the world may believe that you sent me. (17:20–21)

denomination A group of churches or local congregations that are united by a common creed or shared faith under a single governing structure (for example, the Episcopal Church or the Presbyterian Church).

pope The name for the leader of the Catholic Church. He is the successor of Saint Peter, the person Christ appointed to lead the Apostles.

ecumenism The movement to restore unity among all Christians, the unity to which the church is called by the Holy Spirit.

Investigate how different groups of Christians work together in your community. In many places, Christians from different denominations work together to feed the hungry, provide shelter for the homeless, or work for justice.

Talk to someone who is a member of a religion unfamiliar to you. Discover what is important to this person about their faith. Do you and this person have any beliefs in common?

Beyond the Christian Religion

Billions of people in the world are religious but not Christian—Jews, Muslims, Hindus, Buddhists, Confucians, Shintoists, members of Indigenous religions, and so on. Do they have the truth or not? How does Christianity relate to them? Are they considered saved by God?

The Catholic answer to those questions is that God is certainly revealed in non-Christian religions. In fact, many of the moral concerns and principles of Christianity are shared by all the great religions of the world.

Catholics believe, however, that the fullest revelation of God and truth has been given to humankind in Jesus Christ. It is through the church of Jesus that all humankind will ultimately be saved, though we do not know just how that will happen. The Catholic belief that non-Christians can also be saved is rooted in the conviction that Christ died for all, and that all human beings—regardless of religion or any other differences—are sons and daughters of the God who loves us all without boundaries.

For Review

1. Give a definition of the church, including its mission.
2. In what sense is Mary the Mother of the Church?
3. What is meant by the Assumption of Mary?
4. At what different levels does the church exist?
5. Describe the meaning of the images of the church as people of God, body of Christ, and temple of the Holy Spirit.
6. Why did Christianity become divided into different denominations?
7. What is Catholic teaching about whether non-Christians can be saved?

The
Spirit in the Church
through History

Catholics believe that the Spirit that was poured out on the followers of Jesus at Pentecost is the same Spirit that is with the church today, over two thousand years later. Throughout the church's history, the Spirit has been at work in the life of the church, in good times and in bad. The Spirit has been guiding its leaders, raising up new voices when the church most needed to hear them, and inspiring men and women to acts of great courage and sacrifice. The heroic lives of Christians through the ages are perhaps the best evidence we have that God has been with the church all along and is with the church today.

Meet the Saints

The church is its people. The ideal way to understand the church is to meet a few of its greatest, best-known people and to discover through them how the Spirit of God has been working in the church all through history.

Saint Perpetua: Wife, Mother, Convert, and Martyr

Perpetua lived in North Africa, which was then part of the Roman Empire, during the early days of the church. While preparing to join the church, Perpetua was arrested by Roman authorities with other catechumens (those preparing to be initiated into the church) and thrown in prison. The Roman Empire inflicted periodic persecutions on the early Christians. We know about Perpetua through the diary she kept in prison and through the eyewitness testimony of other Christians who kept diaries.

Perpetua was of noble background, and she had a servant girl named Felicity. Felicity was pregnant and had been imprisoned for being a catechumen. Perpetua was a mother also; her infant son meant everything to her. When she was finally allowed to keep him with her in prison, that dungeon became a "palace," in her words. And although Perpetua and Felicity were mistress and servant, in prison these two young women became like sisters.

Before long though, Perpetua had to give her son to her parents to raise—she and Felicity were about to be executed for refusing to sacrifice to the Roman gods. Felicity gave birth just two days before the execution, and a Christian woman came forward and agreed to raise the baby as her own.

The Christian prisoners went to their torture and execution, which was held in an amphitheater as public entertainment. Perpetua, although

hermit A person who seeks to be closer to God by living alone, apart from the world.

monasticism A way of life in which people seek holiness by living apart from the normal society, either living alone or in community.

wounded by wild animals, ran to Felicity to help her when she was attacked by the beasts. Perpetua was twenty-two years old when she was killed in AD 202, and Felicity probably younger. Perpetua's love and serenity in facing death inspired the early church to be courageous in the face of persecution. The names of Perpetua and Felicity have been included in the prayers of the Eucharist since the earliest centuries of the church.

Saints Benedict and Scholastica: A New Way of Living

Benedict and Scholastica, related to each other as brother and sister, together founded a monastic way of life in sixth-century Italy. They lived in a corrupt society that was falling apart around them. In the monastic lifestyle, men and women move away from the concerns of the world to seek holiness apart from the common world as **hermits**, or in small communities. To help people lead holy lives in community, Benedict and Scholastica began monasteries where manual work was combined with prayer and study, and where the great heritage of Christianity could be kept alive and passed on by copying the sacred books by hand.

Benedict and Scholastica developed a rule of life that became the basis for Christian **monasticism** in the western part of the Roman Empire. The monastic way of life was one of the most significant developments in the history of the church and of Western civilization because it created harmony and order in the midst of chaos, encouraged growth in holiness, and ensured that knowledge would be passed on. The sisters, brothers, and priests who follow this monastic rule are called Benedictines, and they remind us of the great gift that Benedict and Scholastica gave to the church and the world. Scholastica died in AD 543, and Benedict in AD 547.

A monastic settlement founded in Ireland in the sixth century.

Saints Francis and Clare: A Return to the Gospel

Francis and Clare of Assisi, Italy, lived in the late twelfth and early thirteenth centuries, a time when the church had become wealthy. Conflicts between Christians were common, and Christians were involved in holy wars, called the Crusades, against Muslims in the Holy Land.

Into this time of challenge for the church came Francis, a wealthy young man who had enjoyed the nightlife and had a brief career as a soldier. However, Francis's spiritual hungers eventually led him to big changes in his lifestyle. He seemed to see through all the corruption, excessive wealth, and violence around him to the heart of the Gospel—the poverty, humility, and nonviolence of Jesus. Francis began living a life of total simplicity, trusting in God's providence to care for his needs. He wandered about the countryside, preaching the love of God and serving the poor and the sick. Soon he was gathering other men around him to live this kind of life. His followers became a religious order, later called the Franciscans.

As a rich young woman of Assisi, Clare was inspired by Francis to start a similar movement of women. The

Becoming a Saint

The people in this section have been declared saints, or are in the process of being declared saints, by the Catholic Church. The Church takes this process seriously, and it takes decades or even centuries before someone can be declared a saint. Generally, the process has three stages:

Stage 1: Investigation into the person's life. Five years after the person's death, the process can begin. The diocese the person lived in, in cooperation with the pope's representatives, looks at the person's life to see if they truly lived a life of heroic virtue or died as a martyr. If at the end of this process the answer is yes, the person is given the title Venerable.

Stage 2: Beatification. Now the Church waits for a true miracle to occur after someone in need prays to the Venerable. If this happens, the miracle is thoroughly investigated and, if approved, the person is given the title Blessed. (A martyr does not need this first miracle to be declared Blessed.)

Stage 3: Canonization. After the person has been declared Blessed, another approved miracle is required. If this happens, the pope declares the person an official saint, through the process of canonization.

Poor Clares, as they later became known, followed a life of simplicity and total trust in God, but they did not leave their convent walls because of the customs of the time.

Francis and Clare, in their quiet and joyful way, inspired many in the church to take a good, hard look at their values. They called the church to be true to its own origins in Jesus. Francis is one of the most popular saints of all time because people see in him a figure who seems most like the Jesus of the Gospels—poor, trusting, nonviolent, serving, and completely in love with God. Francis died in 1226, and Clare in 1253.

Saint Catherine of Siena: Strong Advice for the Pope

Catherine of Siena, Italy, was a woman of remarkable intellect, generosity, and courage who lived in the fourteenth century. She is perhaps best known for telling the pope what he should do.

In the fourteenth century, the church was beset with a scandal involving a series of popes who moved the center of the church from Rome to Avignon, France. On the surface, that does not sound like such a terrible thing to do. But the Avignon Papacy, as that period of almost seventy years is called, was a corrupt time in the church for several reasons—excessive wealth in the Avignon palace and court, political control of the pope by the French kings, and a loss of the tradition of Peter, who died in Rome as its bishop. At the age of thirty, Catherine went to Avignon to see the pope and challenged him to move the center of the church back to Rome. In a letter, she pleaded with him to return the church to its early condition of being poor, humble, and meek. The following year, the pope brought the papacy back to Rome.

Catherine had been associated with the Dominican religious order since her teenage years. As a youth, she had a contemplative heart and stayed in her room praying much of the time. When she emerged at the age of twenty-one, it was to serve people in an incredibly active life. She cared for sick and dying people in the streets of Siena during the terrible bubonic plague, or Black Death. Recognized as a holy person with great conviction and a forceful personality, Catherine became known for her ability to mediate conflicts among powerful Italian city-states. She was also a gifted writer on the spiritual life. Her books, letters, and prayers are still studied today. She died of illness in 1380 at age thirty-three.

Saint Ignatius of Loyola: "Soldier for Christ"

Ignatius of Loyola, Spain, was a spiritual leader in the reform of the church in the sixteenth century. He founded the Society of Jesus, or the Jesuits, about fifteen years before his death in 1556. In Ignatius's lifetime, the Catholic Church was being torn apart. The **Protestant Reformation**, which had started as a reform of the Catholic Church, resulted in the breakaway of large groups of Catholics to form new denominations of Christians. The Catholic Church badly needed to have new life breathed into it, so it undertook its own reform to correct the abuses that had started the Protestants' conflicts with the church.

Imagine that you had the opportunity for a frank discussion with the current pope. What issues would you ask him to respond to or have the Catholic Church approach in a different way?

Protestant Reformation The movement that began in the early sixteenth century and sought changes to the Catholic Church. It eventually led to the formation of separate Protestant denominations.

In the midst of that crisis in the Catholic Church, Ignatius of Loyola came on the scene, ushering in a deep spiritual renewal when it was so badly needed. Ignatius had been a soldier, so he was used to war. But after his leg was severely injured in battle, he had a conversion experience. He vowed to become a "soldier for Christ," using only the weapons of prayer, learning, teaching, and preaching to convert people to the Gospel.

Soon Ignatius was gathering university students around him. He led them in a process he developed called the Spiritual Exercises. (To this day, Catholics and others use these well-known exercises of prayer and meditation to deepen their conversion to Christ.) This little band became the Society of Jesus, and they grew quickly. Ignatius gave them intense training, and the seminaries and universities founded by the Jesuits to train others raised the level of education among the clergy as a whole. The Jesuits were scholars and writers too, and their work was significant in the reform of the Catholic Church. The Jesuits also became missionaries to the continents where Christianity had not gone before, carrying the Good News to the far corners of the earth. Today, the Jesuits are known for the excellence of their Catholic universities and high schools.

Imagine talking to Saint Ignatius of Loyola about reforming the Catholic Church. What would you want to ask him?

Saint Kateri Tekakwitha: "Lily of the Mohawks"

In 1656, Kateri Tekakwitha, an Indigenous woman from the area that is present-day New York state, was born to a Christian Algonquin mother and a non-Christian Mohawk chief. When Kateri was four, smallpox killed her parents and younger brother and left her disfigured and partially blind. She was adopted by her aunt and uncle, who taught her how to make clothing from animal skins, weave baskets, and cook.

When she was seventeen, Kateri refused to accept an arranged marriage, for which she was punished by members of her family with ridicule and harsh workloads. When she met a missionary priest visiting her village, she told him her story and about her interest in Christianity. Kateri began studying the Catholic faith and was baptized a year later, on Easter Sunday. Having made a vow not to marry, she led a life of prayer, fasting, teaching, and service until her death in 1680 at the age of twenty-four.

What advice would you give a friend about keeping a positive attitude despite the challenges of their life? What advice have people given you about this?

> Kateri surely had the gifts of wisdom and courage. She once said: I am not my own; I have given myself to Jesus. He must be my only love. The state of helpless poverty that may befall me if I do not marry does not frighten me. All I need is a little food and a few pieces of clothing. With the work of my hands I shall always earn what is necessary and what is left over I'll give to my relatives and to the poor. If I should become sick and unable to work, then I shall be like the Lord on the cross. He will have mercy on me and help me, I am sure. (*Saint of the Day*, Leonard Foley and Pat McCloskey)

Kateri was the first Indigenous person to be declared a saint of the Catholic Church in 2012.

Saint Charles Lwanga and Companions

In 1879, a group of Catholic missionaries, called the White Fathers by the local people, were peacefully received into Uganda by King Mutesa. Before long, a number of young men serving the king were baptized

Statue of Saint Kateri Tekakwitha in Santa Fe, New Mexico.

© meunierd / Shutterstock.com

Investigate religious persecutions in the world today. What did you discover about the reasons behind these persecutions?

as Catholics. Unfortunately, King Mutesa died, and his corrupt and cruel son, Mwanga, came to power. King Mwanga abused the young men and boys in his court. When Joseph Mukasa, a Catholic convert and the chief page, or servant, in the king's court denounced the king's actions, King Mwanga had him executed.

Charles Lwanga, a servant in the king's court, had taken it upon himself to continue instructing the young men in the Catholic faith. He also protected them from the king's abuse. Realizing that their lives were in danger, they went to the White Fathers and were baptized. Furious over this, King Mwanga ordered the Christian pages to be separated from the rest. There were fifteen of them, between the ages of thirteen and twenty-five. When the king asked them if they were willing to keep their Christian faith, they answered together, "Until death!" The king ordered all of them to be executed by being burned alive.

After a cruel two-day walk, they arrived at their place of execution. After seven more days of imprisonment, they were again given the chance to renounce their Christian faith. They all refused to do so, after which they were executed, starting with Charles Lwanga. The year was 1886, and Charles was twenty-six years old. All in all, one hundred Christians, both Protestants and Catholics, were executed during King Mwanga's rule. Charles Lwanga is the patron saint of African Catholic Youth Action.

Chiara Badano and Carlo Acutis: Teenage Saints to Be?

Chiara Badano and Carlo Acutis are teenagers who lived ordinary but faith-filled lives. Chiara was born in 1971 and died in 1990 when she was only eighteen. She grew up in a small Italian town. At a young age, Chiara was sorting her toys into piles of old toys and new toys. She told her mother she was giving the new toys away. When asked why, she said, "I can't give my old toys to poor children!"

Chiara was deeply influenced by the Focolare movement, a Christian group whose purpose is to build a more united world in which people value and respect every person in all our diversity. She was fascinated by the Focolare commitment to live out Christ's commands in a very concrete way. However, when Chiara was only seventeen, she was diagnosed with cancer, which soon led to the paralysis of her legs. Throughout her often painful treatment, she remained peaceful and never lost faith in God's love for her. As she approached death, her words inspired many people. As she died, she said goodbye to her mother and then uttered her last words: "Be happy, because I am."

Carlo Acutis was born in 1991 and died in 2006, when he was only fifteen. Like Chiara, he lived in Italy. He was an ordinary teen in many ways. He liked movies, comics, and PlayStation games. He also took his Catholic faith very seriously, frequently attending Mass and receiving the sacrament of Reconciliation weekly. He lived out his faith in the world, defending disabled peers from bullies and doing volunteer work with the homeless after school. He also used his computer to create a website cataloging reports from around the world of miraculous phenomena involving the Eucharist. He finished this project when he was fourteen, and it is still available online today.

When Carlo developed leukemia, he offered his suffering for the pope and for the Catholic Church. He

Left: Chiara Badano.
Right: Carlo Acutis.

Think of someone who has died whom you would consider a saint according to Catholic belief. Have you been inspired by this person? How might you still be connected to them?

saint A person trying to live the Gospel of Jesus Christ, especially those who have died and who live in full union with God.

Communion of Saints The spiritual union of all those who have been saved by the grace of God, those on earth and those who have died and are with God.

hoped to go on pilgrimages to the sites of the Eucharistic miracles he had cataloged but was too sick to do so. When he was asked if he was in great pain, he drew attention to the many people who suffer more than him. Because Carlo had a strong devotion to Saint Francis, he was buried in Assisi.

Both Chiara and Carlo have been given the title Blessed, the last stage before being declared saints of the Catholic Church. Chiara was declared Blessed in 2010 and Carlo in 2020. Their lives may not be that much different from yours, which is exactly why the Church lifts them up. They help inspire us to live our ordinary lives with holiness.

The Communion of Saints

You may be wondering why two teenagers were included with the lineup of great figures that preceded them. The great figures described in that lineup are in fact canonized **saints**—officially declared to be saints by the Catholic Church.

So why are contemporary teenagers included under a topic called "Meet the Saints"? In Catholic Tradition, "the saints" can mean officially recognized, canonized saints. But the term also has a much broader meaning, as broad as the whole Church itself. "The saints" are all people who are trying to live the Gospel of Jesus, and all the faithful persons who have died and are now united with God in eternal life. Catholics believe that a special bond holds all the saints together, creating the **Communion of Saints**. That bond is God's life of love itself, which stretches across time, across space, and across the barrier that separates the living from the dead.

To be perfectly clear, Catholics believe that anyone can be a saint. Sainthood is not limited to only those who go through the official process. Your faithful grandmother or grandfather who loved you, lived by the Gospel, and passed away, leaving an empty place in your heart, can be a saint. A peasant who lived an obscure life in tenth-century Europe trying to take care of his family and be faithful to the Gospel can be a saint. And you can be a saint as well, if you love God with your whole heart and love your neighbor as yourself.

Catholics have a special love for the saints who have died. They believe that these people are still connected to them, caring about them, rejoicing with them, and pulling for them when they are in trouble. Just because these saints have died does not mean they are not part of the church anymore. So Catholic devotion to the saints is a way of saying: "We are not alone in this journey of life. Others have made the journey, and they can help us along if we let them."

For **Review**

1. Give one significant fact about each of the following people or pairs in church history:
   - Perpetua and Felicity
   - Benedict and Scholastica
   - Francis and Clare
   - Catherine of Siena
   - Ignatius of Loyola
   - Kateri Tekakwitha
   - Chiara Badano
   - Carlo Acutis
2. Define *saint*.
3. What is the Communion of Saints?

reflect
reflect

Together, We Will Make It

Monarch butterflies' life of journeying is a kind of parable of what the church is like, the communion of Jesus' followers across time and space.

Every year monarch butterflies take part
in a journey of five thousand miles,
from their ancestral home in the mountains of central Mexico
to places in Canada and the United States,
and then back home again to Mexico.

No one monarch can complete
the whole round-trip journey.
It takes several generations of butterflies
to migrate north from Mexico in spring
and then back south to their special home in fall.

How do the monarchs transmit
the instructions and route
to their children and grandchildren
that will have to carry on and finish the journey?
Scientists still do not fully understand
how this happens.

But without fail, each year
hundreds of millions of monarchs
find the distant home in Mexico
that they had never known.

And we can find our way home too.

Catholics believe that even though
we have never seen heaven, we can
find our way there. Even though
life after death remains a mystery,
we believe we are supported by those
who have gone before us, and that
we will find our way to the home
we were created for.

© Tim Herbert / Shutterstock.com

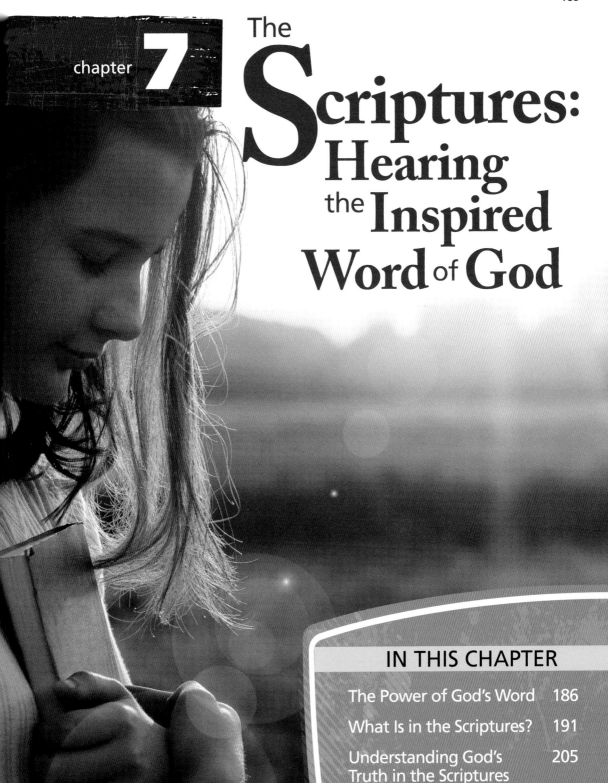

chapter **7**

The Scriptures: Hearing the Inspired Word of God

IN THIS CHAPTER

The Power of God's Word   186

What Is in the Scriptures?   191

Understanding God's   205
Truth in the Scriptures

The Power of God's Word

Picture this scene: Large crowds are following Jesus as he preaches in the towns and villages of Galilee. People are fascinated by this man who proclaims a God whose love is so wide and deep that it embraces everyone, including the lost and forsaken, the rejects of society—*everyone*.

A few of those rejects—some tax collectors and sinners—come near Jesus to better hear this Good News. Several Pharisees and scribes, who disapprove of such "riffraff," grumble about this fellow Jesus, who insists on welcoming, and even eating with, losers and outcasts. What business does he have letting "those people" think they are so important?

Hearing their grumbling, Jesus tells this story: "A man had two sons, and the younger son said to his father, 'Father, give me the share of your estate that should come to me.' So the father divided the property between them" (Luke 15:11–12).

The younger son then takes his wealth and goes to a foreign country where he foolishly spends it all on selfish pleasures. When a famine strikes, he has to take care of pigs and is so hungry that he wants to eat their food. So, he decides to return to his father and ask for forgiveness.

The return of the son who was lost to the father.

He could scarcely hope that his father would forgive him, but maybe his father would give him work as a servant so he wouldn't starve. This is what happens:

> While he was still a long way off, his father caught sight of him, and was filled with compassion. He ran to his son, embraced him and kissed him. His son said to him, "Father, I have sinned against heaven and against you; I no longer deserve to be called your son." But his father ordered his servants, "Quickly bring the finest robe and put it on him; put a ring on his finger and sandals on his feet. Take the fattened calf and slaughter it. Then let us celebrate with a feast, because this son of mine was dead, and has come to life again; he was lost, and has been found." Then the celebration began. (Luke 15:20–24)

The older son heard the celebration and was angry that his father was throwing a party for his sinful brother, especially when his father had never thrown a party for him. He refused to come inside, and when his father heard about this, he came out to talk to the older son. This is what the father said. "My son, you are here with me always; everything I have is yours. But now we must celebrate and rejoice, because your brother was dead and has come to life again; he was lost and has been found" (Luke 15:31–32).

Inheritance, Pigs, and Honor in Ancient Jewish Culture

To fully understand and appreciate the significance of some Bible stories, it helps to understand the culture at the time in which they were written. Here are some aspects of ancient middle Eastern culture that will help you better appreciate the parable of the lost son:

- Typically, the family inheritance would pass to the eldest son and only at the time of the father's death. This means the younger son's requests were inappropriate and dishonorable.

- Pigs were considered unclean, and Jews were forbidden to eat pork. Caring for pigs and eating their food was about as low as you could go in their society.

- Many of the father's actions—running in public and forgiving a son who had shamed the family, for example—would have been shocking and even seen as dishonorable. The father's willingness to do these things showed the depths of his love.

- Giving the wayward son a robe, a ring, and sandals was a sign that the son was fully accepted back into the family. By giving the son these things right away, the father saved the son from the ridicule of neighbors and family members.

- Who do you think the father in the story is meant to represent?

- Which character do you think the outcasts in Jesus' audience identified with? How do you think the story affected them?

- Which character do you think the Pharisees and scribes in Jesus' audience identified with? How do you think the story affected them?

Jesus knew the power of stories, like this one known as the parable of the lost son or prodigal son. That is why he used stories so often in his preaching and teaching. Stories touch us. They draw us in and stir up something in us—especially if we find someone in the story that we can identify with. Stories have the power to change us, or at least unsettle us. This is because they affect our heart as well as our head.

The Power of Stories

Stories are powerful. A great deal of research shows that a good story can be a greater influence in changing a person than facts and logical arguments. Why? One reason is that stories light up a part of our brain that facts and figures do not touch. Because stories often involve people and situations we identify with and care about, they are easier to understand and remember. Finally, stories often make us feel emotional, and those emotions often have a bigger impact on us than just logical arguments.

Our Story, the Word of God

The Bible is full of stories meant to touch people and make a difference in their lives. And even more, the Bible as a whole is the Story of God's

© fboudrias / Shutterstock.com

The fictional village of Hobbiton on the movie set for *The Lord of the Rings*.

people—who they are, how God has loved them and saved them, and where they are going. It is not just *a* story but *the* Story (capital *S*) that Christians live by and know themselves by.

So the Bible is the powerful Story of a people. But many stories are powerful—the *Star Wars* movies tell a powerful story, as do the *Lord of the Rings* books and movies. What is the difference between the powerful Story told in the Bible and the many other powerful stories that have been told throughout history?

Christians believe that the power of the Bible has a deeper origin than the power of a story like *The Lord of the Rings*. The Scriptures contain God's own Word, the gift of God's truth revealed to us. This is the source of their power. The Bible was written over many centuries by human beings who used their own means of expression, but the Bible's

When you hear someone say that the Bible is the Word of God, what do you think they mean?

Big Idea from the Bible

Creation Is Good

One of the great themes of Scripture is that creation is good. The beginning of the Book of Genesis says, "God looked at everything he had made, and found it very good" (1:31). The forests are good, the meadows are good, the deserts and mountains are good, the oceans are good, and everything living on them or in them is good! Human beings have been the benefactors of this goodness, and God also calls us to be its caretakers. However, for far too long we have considered ourselves masters over creation rather than living in harmony with creation. We are now seeing the costs of that: pollution, environmental destruction, and global climate change. This Bible belief calls on people to protect the goodness of creation! Some key Bible passages on this theme are Genesis, chapter 1; Psalm 104; Isaiah 24:4–6; and Romans 8:19–22.

truth is inspired by God. (We take up the meaning of "inspired by God" later in this chapter.) As God's Word, the Scriptures have a power beyond any other story we can imagine.

No Chaining the Word of God

While in prison for spreading the Gospel, Saint Paul once wrote to his friend and fellow Christian Timothy about the power of God's Word:

Remember Jesus Christ, raised from the dead, a descendant of David: such is my gospel, for which I am suffering, even to the point of chains, like a criminal. But the word of God is not chained. (2 Timothy 2:8–9)

The Scriptures are not dead words on a page. They are alive and active, full of God's power. They make a difference in people's lives. Paul says, "They may put me in chains, but nobody can chain up the Word of God!"

1. Why do stories have the power to affect people's lives?
2. What is the Christian belief about the power of the Scriptures? Where does this power come from?

What Is in the Scriptures?

This course so far has quoted various parts of the Bible to illustrate aspects of the Catholic faith and has briefly introduced the Bible. Now it is time to step back and take a deeper look at the Scriptures as a whole.

Sacred Writings

The word *scriptures* means "writings." Nearly every religion has its own set of writings that members of that religion regard as sacred and authoritative because of the connection of these writings with the divine. For instance, Muslims revere the Qur'an (also spelled Koran) as their sacred scriptures, which they believe were revealed by God to the founder of Islam, Muhammad. Hindus look to the Bhagavad Gita as a sacred book, and Confucians hold the Analects, or the teachings of Confucius, in the highest regard.

© selimaksan / Shutterstock.com

A Muslim reading the Qur'an.

Look for study aids such as book introductions, footnotes, maps, and time lines in your Bible. What study aids do you find and how might you use them?

Use a Bible to answer the following questions:

- How many pages are in the Old Testament? In the New Testament?

- How many books are in the Old Testament? In the New Testament?

- Which book in the Old Testament has the most chapters? In the New Testament?

The Bible: Jewish and Christian Origins

Jews look to their Scriptures with the greatest reverence. They call these Scriptures the Tanakh, or sometimes the Hebrew Bible (from a word meaning "book"). Christians also call their sacred Scriptures the Bible. As mentioned in a previous chapter, the Jewish Bible corresponds closely to what Christians know as the Old Testament in their own Bible. In addition to the Old Testament, the Christian Bible includes the New Testament—that is, the sacred, authoritative writings from the early Christian communities led by the Apostles.

Testament is another word for *covenant*. In the Old Testament, *covenant* refers to the sacred bond between God and the Israelites. In the New Testament, this sacred bond is renewed and extended to all humankind. This New Covenant is established by Christ's sacrificial death for all people.

The words *old* and *new* may imply that the Scriptures of the Jewish people are old-fashioned or no longer relevant, and that the Scriptures of the Christian era are a replacement for the old. This is a serious misunderstanding of these terms. The Catholic Church emphatically opposes the idea that the Old Testament is out of date. In fact, it would be more accurate to think of the Old Testament as the original covenant (rather than "old") and the New Testament as the fulfilled covenant (rather than "new").

From the days of the early Christian communities to the present, Christians have had a great reverence for the writings in the Old Testament, reading them as the Word of God at eucharistic worship, and using them as a source for understanding God and humankind. Christians often turn to the Old Testament to address God in prayer also.

Like a Library

You may have the impression that the Bible is basically one book, composed from beginning to end as a single continuous account. If that is your image, it would not be surprising, because from childhood on we see the Bible as a big, thick book on the shelf.

In fact, the Bible is not simply *a* book, nor is it just two books—the Old Testament and the New Testament. It is a collection of dozens of books, long and short, filled with many different kinds of writing. Stories abound, of course, but there are also poems, conversations, rituals, speeches, legends, letters, biographies, historical records and accounts, laws, family trees, songs and hymns, prayers, and bits and pieces of wisdom, like proverbs. So we can think of the Bible as being more like a library than a single book.

For Christians, what is special about this library of literature is that all of it was written under God's guidance, as the inspired account of God's people and God's relationship with them. Thus, there are important religious truths that run through the books of the Bible, tying them together even though they were written in different times and places. Some of these themes are highlighted in special features in this chapter. In revealing these religious truths, the Bible has a power and authority that goes way beyond that of ordinary literature.

Find an example of each of the following kinds of writing in the Bible:
- a song, poem, or prayer
- a greeting in a letter
- a historical account of an event
- a legend
- a law
- a piece of wisdom, like a proverb

The Bible is divided into two main sections: the Old Testament, which has forty-six books, and the New Testament, which has twenty-seven books.

Each of the two divisions of the Christian Bible—the Old Testament and the New Testament—has major sections within it. Let's briefly look at those sections within the Old Testament and the New Testament.

The Old Testament

Catholics group the forty-six books of the Old Testament into four major sections, in this order:

- the Pentateuch
- the historical books
- the wisdom and poetry books
- the prophetic books

While reading this material on the Old Testament, it may be helpful to refer to the time line of biblical Jewish history on page 71.

The Pentateuch

Christians refer to the first five books of the Bible as the **Pentateuch** (meaning "five books"). Jews call these books the Torah, which means "instruction" and "law." These books are the heart of the story of Israel and the most significant writings for Jews. Among these books are the accounts of the origins of the Jews as a people. In fact, Genesis, the first book, means "origin." Genesis includes the stories of Creation, of Adam and Eve, and of Noah and the flood. In addition, Genesis covers stories about the call of Abraham (around 1850 BC) and the other patriarchs and matriarchs.

The Pentateuch also contains the Book of Exodus, which includes the amazing stories of Israel's liberation

---

Pentateuch   A Greek word meaning "five books," referring to the first five books of the Old Testament.

A Jewish teenager reads the Torah.

Big Idea from the Bible

God Calls Us to Freedom!

Have you ever felt trapped and unable to be who you really are because of people's expectations or their prejudices, or even because of pressure from your family or peers? The Bible has many stories about slavery and oppression that communicate this message: God wants people to be free—free from physical slavery and oppression, of course, but also free from the ill effects of sin. Personal sins and the sins of others keep people trapped in unhealthy behaviors and attitudes. In a memorable phrase, Saint Paul says, "For freedom Christ set us free; so stand firm and do not submit again to the yoke of slavery" (Galatians 5:1). Some key Bible passages on this theme are Exodus, chapter 3; Isaiah 61:1; John 8:31–36; and Galatians 5:13–26.

from slavery and the Exodus from Egypt; of Moses and the Sinai Covenant between God and the Israelites (around 1250 BC); and of the giving of the Law, the people's part of keeping the covenant. The Pentateuch ends with the Israelites just about to enter the Promised Land, Canaan, located in modern-day Israel.

The Historical Books

The **historical books** begin with the Israelites entering Canaan around 1200 BC and proceeding to take over the land by force. Although the books are called historical, this does not mean they are all equally factual. In Joshua and Judges, for instance, a good deal of legend is mixed in with history. The purpose of these books is to bring out the religious dimension of Israelite history more than to present a complete and perfectly accurate historical account.

Most of the historical section of the Bible tells of the Israelite monarchy and their kings—like Saul, David, and Solomon, beginning around the year 1000 BC. It recounts the breakup of the kingdom of the Israelites into the two kingdoms of Israel and Judah, which was followed by centuries of corrupt kings and occasional reformer kings. The period of exile for Judah (587–537 BC) and the developments in Judaism after the Exile are also covered in the historical books. In Catholic Bibles, the historical books end with the story of the Maccabean revolt against the Greeks (167–160 BC).

historical books The section of the Old Testament that tells the story of the Israelites from the time they enter the Promised Land until the time of the Maccabean revolt. The accounts combine historical information with religious interpretation.

Big Idea from the Bible

God Keeps Promises

In the historical books, we find a cycle repeating itself over and over. It goes like this:

- God's people are at peace.
- They start to be unfaithful to their covenant with God.
- A foreign power threatens them.
- They cry out to God to rescue them.
- God hears their cry and rescues them through a judge or good king.
- The people are at peace again.

At some point, you think God would say: "I've had it with these people. Let them suffer the consequences of their choices." But the Bible reveals this is not in God's nature. God never stops loving his people and is faithful to the covenant promises—no matter how many times they turn away. Christians believe the same thing—God's love and care never cease, no matter what happens.

The Wisdom and Poetry Books

Some of the most beautiful literature the world has ever known can be found in the **wisdom and poetry books**. These seven books contain collections of wise advice and prayers for living good and holy lives. Several of the books are written in the form of Hebrew poetry, usually in two-line verses. The second line reflects the thought of the first line—or its opposite—only in different words. Here's an example from the Book of Proverbs:

My son, if you receive my words *[original thought]*
and treasure my commands, *[original thought in different words]*
Turning your ear to wisdom, *[next thought]*
inclining your heart to understanding . . . *[next thought in different words]*
Then will you understand the fear of the LORD; *[next thought]*
the knowledge of God you will find. *[next thought in different words]*

(2:1–2,5)

---

wisdom and poetry books The section of the Old Testament that contains collections of wise advice and prayers.

The most famous wisdom book is the Book of Psalms. We have already read passages from several psalms in this course. The Book of Psalms contains 150 songs, expressing a wide range of heartfelt sentiments, including gratitude and praise, anger with God, rage at enemies, grief, repentance, desperation, fear, trust, joy, and so on. Other wisdom books focus on themes such as the meaning of life and suffering, how to be good and upright in everyday life, and the joys of married love.

Choose a psalm from the Bible that expresses a feeling similar to what you have felt at one time or feel now. How might you rewrite the psalm in your own words?

The Prophetic Books

We have heard already from three of Israel's prophets in this course: Isaiah, Amos, and Jeremiah. Isaiah, Jeremiah, Ezekiel, and Daniel are called the major prophets, not because they are more important, but because their books are so much longer than the others. The other twelve are sometimes called the minor prophets because of their shorter books. Two books that are not the words of prophets, Lamentations and Baruch, are included in the prophets' section because of their close association with the prophets. And there are other prophets, such as Elijah and Elisha, who do not have their own books but whose words and actions are recorded in the historical books.

Remember that prophets were not so much predictors of future events as confronters of present evil situations. So when the people of Israel—especially their kings—failed to keep the covenant with God by worshipping idols and depriving the poor of what was due to them, the prophets went into action. Sometimes the prophets leveled blistering accusations at the wealthy and the proud. But other times they consoled the people in periods of great trial and distress, reminding them of God's great promises to Israel, and assuring them that God would never abandon them. The **prophetic books** are the records of their writings. Let's turn now to the New Testament.

prophetic books
The section of the Old Testament that contains the words of many, but not all, of Israel's prophets.

Big Idea from the Bible

God Expects Justice

If there was one thing the prophets were big on, it was that God expected his Chosen People to act with justice. "Let justice surge like waters, / and righteousness like an unfailing stream," proclaimed the prophet Amos (5:24). "Make justice your aim," proclaimed Isaiah, "redress the wronged, / hear the orphan's plea, defend the widow" (Isaiah 1:17). Orphans and widows were the most vulnerable people of the time and those most easily oppressed.

The prophets demanded justice because it was part of God's covenant with the people. Here's one example of a justice-themed covenant law: "You shall not oppress or afflict a resident alien. . . . You shall not wrong any widow or orphan. If ever you wrong them and they cry out to me, I will surely listen to their cry" (Exodus 22:20–21).

Jesus continues the prophetic tradition of calling for justice. In the Sermon on the Mount, he calls his followers to love their enemies and to treat people justly (see Matthew 5:38–48). Many of his parables challenge people to share their wealth with the poor (see Luke 16:19–31). How does the Catholic Church work for justice in today's world?

> **Evangelist** From a Greek word meaning "messenger of good news," the title given to the authors of the Gospels of Matthew, Mark, Luke, and John.

The New Testament

The twenty-seven books that make up the New Testament are grouped in these major sections:

- the Gospels
- the Acts of the Apostles
- the Letters
- the Book of Revelation

The Gospels

The accounts of Jesus' life, death, and Resurrection are found in the four Gospels—the books of Matthew, Mark, Luke, and John, which are probably the most familiar parts of the Bible to Christians. Matthew, Mark, Luke, and John—the four **Evangelists**—are traditionally accepted as the writers of the Gospels, but parts of the Gospels may have been written by other disciples in the name of the Evangelist whose name is on the Gospel. (The word *evangelist* comes from a Greek word meaning "good news" or "gospel.")

Each Gospel, or proclamation of the Good News, offers a distinctive portrait of Jesus and a different emphasis on his message. The Gospels are not biographies in the sense of providing exact dates, locations, and factual details about Jesus' life. Because each of the Gospels was written within a certain Christian community and with a particular audience in mind, each gives a somewhat different perspective on Jesus and his message. A comparison may help:

In trying to photograph a mountain, it takes many different views to get a full picture of the mountain on film—from each side, from the top, from the bottom, and so on. With six or eight camera angles, we get a sense of the whole mountain. The Gospels are somewhat like that. Each portrait adds to the understanding we have of the mystery of Jesus and the Good News he preached.

The Gospels of Matthew, Mark, and Luke are often referred to as the synoptic Gospels. This means that when they are read side by side, parallels in structure and content can easily be seen. According to scholars, these parallels came about because the writers of Matthew and Luke used Mark, the earliest Gospel, as a source. Let's take a closer look at these Gospels.

Matthew. This Gospel is named for Matthew, a tax collector, who was one of Jesus' Apostles. The Gospel was most likely written for a primarily Jewish audience. It emphasized to the Jews that Jesus was clearly the Messiah they had been waiting for, and that Jesus' whole life was the fulfillment of all the ancient promises made by God to Israel. Matthew's Gospel shows Jesus as a great teacher, the "New Moses." For example, this is the Gospel

Imagine being a Gospel writer today, writing to an audience of young people in US society. What aspect of Jesus and his message would you focus on?

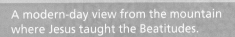

A modern-day view from the mountain where Jesus taught the Beatitudes.

Big Idea from the Bible

Unlimited Forgiveness

Many people struggle with forgiveness, whether it be forgiving others, forgiving themselves, or even accepting that there is a God who forgives. Perhaps this is why the Bible's messages about forgiveness are profound for many people. The emphasis on forgiveness is touched on in some Old Testament books, like the prophet Isaiah: "It is I (God), I, who wipe out, / for my own sake, your offenses; / your sins I remember no more" (43:25).

Jesus, however, really drives home the depth of God's forgiveness, especially in the parables about the lost sheep (see Luke 15:4–7) and the lost or prodigal son (see 15:11–32). Jesus tells Peter that we must forgive another person's sin "not seven times but seventy-seven times" (Matthew 18:22). Jesus himself is a model of forgiveness, even forgiving the soldiers who crucified him (see Luke 23:34).

One more important thing: Jesus teaches that people must be willing to forgive in order to experience God's forgiveness. This concept is even in the Lord's Prayer: "Forgive us our trespasses as we forgive those who trespass against us."

containing the Sermon on the Mount, a passage where Jesus delivered his moral teachings, including the Beatitudes, from a mountain. Recall that Moses brought God's Law to the Chosen People from a mountaintop. Matthew's Gospel was written between the years AD 80 and 100.

Mark. The Gospel of Mark is generally accepted as the first Gospel written (around the years AD 65 to 70). It is also the shortest. It was apparently addressed primarily to Gentile (non-Jewish) Christians in Rome. The church was undergoing persecution at the time; Saints Peter and Paul were probably martyred during this persecution. Mark's Gospel is full of references to the trials and persecution that Jesus' followers might expect, and it highlights the suffering and death of Jesus. This theme encouraged the early Christians by letting them know they were suffering just as Christ suffered, and because of this they would one day also be glorified with him.

Jesus comes through as very human, full of strong emotion, in Mark's Gospel. Reading it is a good introduction to the story of Jesus.

Luke. The Gospel of Luke, written around the year AD 85, is the first volume of Luke's two-volume history of early Christianity. His second volume is the Acts of the Apostles.

Gospel Portraits of Jesus	
Matthew	Jesus is a great teacher, the "New Moses."
Mark	Jesus is a suffering servant.
Luke	Jesus brings God's forgiveness and justice.
John	Jesus is the divine Son of God.

A portrait of Jesus as compassionate savior and healer emerges from Luke's Gospel. The Gospel is named for Luke, a physician and traveling companion of Saint Paul. The Gospel portrays Jesus healing people through physical miracles and the forgiveness of sins. Luke is addressed primarily to Gentile Christians, many of whom were well educated and wealthy. This Gospel emphasizes the image of Jesus embracing poor people and outcasts of society. As Luke conveyed it, the Christian message is for *everyone*—rich and poor, men and women, Jews and Gentiles.

John. John's Gospel comes out of a Jewish Christian community most likely led by the Apostle John. It is quite different from the synoptic Gospels, both in structure and in the way it tells about the words and actions of Jesus. From the beginning, the Gospel emphasizes Jesus' divinity and relationship with God: "And the Word [Jesus] became flesh / and made his dwelling among us, / and we saw his glory, / the glory as of the Father's only Son, / full of grace and truth" (1:14). This Gospel communicates a deepened understanding of Jesus as the divine Son of God, perhaps because it was the last Gospel to be written (between AD 90 and 100).

It is full of symbolic language and reflections on the nature of God. Its beautiful discourses and teachings of Jesus make it a wonderful source for personal and communal prayer.

The Acts of the Apostles

The continuation of Luke's Gospel is the Acts of the Apostles, or simply, Acts. Luke wanted to show how the Holy Spirit was alive and active in the early church after Jesus' departure from earthly life. Thus, Acts is sometimes called the Gospel of the Holy Spirit.

The first half of Acts tells the story of the early church community in Jerusalem from the time of the Ascension and Pentecost. Peter figures prominently in the first half of the book. The second half follows Paul's journeys as he establishes new Christian communities throughout the Roman Empire. Acts is full of high drama and action-packed stories of courage and faith.

The Letters

This section of the Bible consists of twenty-one letters written to various Christian communities or individuals in the early church. The letters respond to a wide variety of problems and needs, but they also teach and encourage the communities of believers. Some of the letters offer deep, profound reflections on the Christian message. The best-known letters are those of Paul, a few of which you have heard from in this course.

Paul's thirteen letters were written between the years AD 50 and 65, whereas the others were written after the year AD 80. The letters are organized in the Bible in the following order and are traditionally assumed to have been written by the following authors (although in some cases their disciples may have written the letters in their name):

- thirteen letters written by Paul to various communities
- one letter, the Letter to the Hebrews, whose author is unknown
- one letter by James
- two letters by Peter
- three letters by John
- one letter by Jude

Review the Letter of James and find a piece of advice or a teaching that if followed would help make your school a better community.

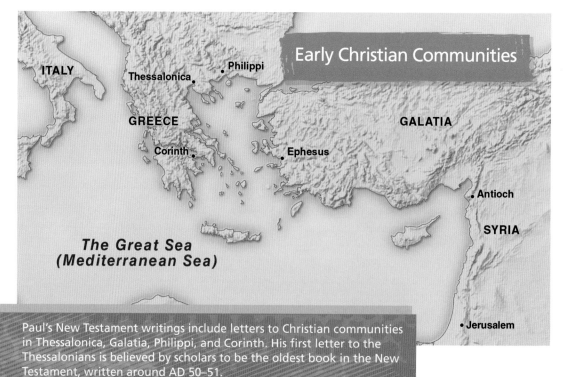

Paul's New Testament writings include letters to Christian communities in Thessalonica, Galatia, Philippi, and Corinth. His first letter to the Thessalonians is believed by scholars to be the oldest book in the New Testament, written around AD 50–51.

Big Idea from the Bible

Idolatry Has Many Forms

The Bible consistently teaches that idolatry—putting something at the center of your life that isn't God—is bad. The very first commandment condemns it: "I am the LORD your God. . . . You shall not have other gods beside me" (Exodus 20:2–3). Here are a few of the various forms of idolatry that have been criticized in the Bible:

- In the historical books and the prophets, idolatry was literally the worship of other gods, primarily the god Baal and the goddess Asherah (see Judges 3:7–8, Micah 5:12–13).
- Making wooden or stone statues to represent gods and goddesses was ridiculed by the prophets and the wisdom authors (see Isaiah 44:9–20, Wisdom 14:7–14).
- Jesus taught on several occasions about the foolishness of worshipping wealth as an idol: "You cannot serve God and mammon [wealth]" (Luke 16:13).

In the Bible, idolatry is not just worshipping other gods and goddesses, it is putting anything in the center of your life that isn't God.

The Book of Revelation

The last book of the New Testament is the Book of Revelation. Its author is identified in the book as John, but he was most likely not the Evangelist John, the man associated with the Gospel of John.

The Book of Revelation is full of strange and powerful symbols of the end time. This is when Christ will come again and bring to the world the final victory of God over sin and death. Probably written at the end of the first century, Revelation was meant to give hope and courage to Christians who were enduring another ruthless persecution by the Roman authorities.

Catholic Scripture scholars today agree that Revelation's symbolic language is not to be taken literally. Its repetition of certain numbers, its strange beasts, and even its image of Christ as a lamb with seven horns and seven eyes can be very confusing to the typical reader. Christians of some denominations try to use the images in Revelation to predict when the end of the world will come. They even see signs from the book that the end is very near. In Catholic

Read the symbolic description of Jesus Christ in glory in Revelation 1:12–16. What do you think the gold sash, white hair, feet like polished brass, voice like rushing water, two-edged sword coming from his mouth, and face shining like the sun each symbolize? If your Bible has footnotes, read them to see if they help explain the meaning of these symbols.

teaching, however, careful attention is paid to the symbolic meanings of the images and numbers to discover the real intent of the book. Revelation's underlying message, according to Catholic interpretation, is a call to Christians to be faithful, even in the face of persecution, and to trust that God will finally be victorious.

Why *These* Books?

Why did any particular writing become part of the Bible? In any religion, many writings are circulated that could be seen as conveying beliefs or teachings about that religion. This was certainly true with the Jews and the early Christians, who had many sources from which to select in composing their official, authoritative list, or **canon**, of sacred Scriptures. Why then are some books canonical (that is, included in the canon) and some are not?

The answer to that question is complex and incomplete. Many of the choices were made in the earliest centuries of the church, and we do not have enough information about the reasons behind the choices to understand them fully. The faith answer, however, is that God guided the pope and bishops who made the final decisions about which books belonged in the canon. They believed that certain books expressed the truth of God's message in a way that others did

not—that these books were inspired by God and that others lacked such divine authority. Other human factors and motives no doubt entered in, but even those can be seen as part of God's way of guiding the process of selection.

All Christians—Protestant, Catholic, and Orthodox—agree on the canon of the New Testament, the twenty-seven books shown in the Bible bookshelf graphic on page 193. The canon was largely settled on by the year 400.

However, Catholics and Protestants differ in what they include in the canon of the Old Testament. Catholics include the forty-six books also shown on page 193. Protestants, following the canon set by Jewish authorities in AD 90, include just thirty-nine. The seven books or parts of books in the Catholic canon that are not in the Protestant or Jewish canons were written late in Jewish history, in the two hundred years before Christ. They were also preserved in Greek, not in the original Jewish languages of Hebrew and Aramaic. (In some Protestant Bibles, the seven noncanonical books are given at the end of the Old Testament, under the section Apocrypha, meaning "unknown" or "of doubtful origin.") Now that we have an overview of what is included in the Scriptures, let's consider how to understand what they convey.

---

canon The official list of books included in the Bible.

1. In what sense is the Bible like a library? How many books are in each of the two major divisions of the Catholic Bible?
2. List the four major sections of the Old Testament, and briefly describe what is in each.
3. List the four major sections of the New Testament, and briefly describe what is in each.
4. Explain a distinctive characteristic found in each of the four Gospels.
5. What is meant by the canon of the Bible? Why were certain books chosen to be part of the canon?

Understanding God's Truth in the Scriptures

As previously mentioned, the Bible was not composed from front to back as a single book, or even as two books—the Old Testament and the New Testament; rather, it is a library of many kinds of books and different types of literature developed over a span of more than a thousand years. Because of this, we cannot just read the Bible as we would read other books. We must put in effort and follow guidelines to understand the meaning and significance of biblical passages. This effort is sometimes called **biblical interpretation**. For Catholics and all those who venerate the Bible as the inspired Word of God, this interpretation includes special attention to what God is revealing through the words of the human authors.

> **biblical interpretation** The process and guidelines used to correctly understand the meaning and significance of the Bible.

Big Idea from the Bible

The Human Authors and the Divine Author

Catholics apply a two-step process in reading and interpreting the Bible. The first step is considering what the human authors intended to communicate. This step requires keeping in mind the author's literary style, historical situation, and cultural background. For example, for Jewish people at the time the Gospels were written, nothing was more important than loyalty to your family. So, when Jesus stretches out his hand over his followers and says, "Here are my mother and my brothers" (Matthew 12:49), the human author is communicating that Jesus is making a break with this tradition.

The second step in the process is understanding what the divine author, God, is revealing through the human author's words. Among other things, this means considering how a particular passage fits into the Bible's overall message and considering the church's teaching about the passage. Going back to the example of Matthew 12:49, the second step of Catholic interpretation leads to the idea that God is revealing that God's family is not based on family of origin; rather, it includes all those who accept God's Word and faithfully live it out in their lives.

The Development of the Scriptures

To appreciate the Catholic understanding of how God's truth is revealed in the Scriptures, it will help to gain a sense of how the books of the Bible were developed. We'll review the five-step process and then discuss God's role in the process.

The Process

In general, the development of the Scriptures—both the Old Testament and the New Testament—followed a five-step process:

Step 1: Events. People had intense spiritual experiences through which they encountered God. God revealed God's own self through these experiences, even though the people experiencing them might not have understood the full meaning at the time. A couple examples of some concrete experiences include the Israelites escaping from slavery in Egypt, led by a great leader, Moses, and the Apostles following Jesus in his ministry for three years and witnessing his death and then his risen glory.

Step 2: Oral tradition. Over a period of years (sometimes centuries, sometimes decades), people talked about their experiences. They came to see how God was present in those events. They told stories about the events and passed them on from one generation to the next. Different communities may have developed their own versions of the same events.

A modern depiction of the "Song of Miriam" from the Book of Exodus.

Step 3: Written pieces. Parts of the oral tradition were gradually written down—like songs, riddles, and stories about heroes. For instance, the "Song of Miriam" is a beautiful song of joy about how God freed the Israelites from slavery. It appears in the Book of Exodus after the account of the Israelites crossing the sea on dry land to escape Pharaoh's army. Miriam's song is perhaps the oldest piece of writing in the Old Testament, written down long before the full story of the escape was recorded.

These writings usually evolved over time. Matthew's and Luke's Gospels provide other examples. As noted earlier, it is quite likely both writers of

Recall an event in your life or your family's life that was significant to you and your development. It may have happened years ago. Reflecting now on that event, can you see how God may have been present in the event?

these Gospels had Mark's Gospel as a source. But it is likely that both also drew from an earlier written collection of Jesus' sayings. This collection, based on the oral tradition among the early Christians, has never been found.

Step 4: Edited books. At some point, people collected and put together in one written document the various oral and written traditions about a particular event like the escape from slavery. The pieces were edited, and sometimes several versions of the same event were integrated into the written account. For example, two versions of the "Song of Miriam" appear in Exodus, one long and one short. (The ancients were not as concerned about being consistent as we are today!) These edited pieces came together in what we call a book. However, people of ancient times did not have books with pages as we know them. Their "books" were scrolls of parchment or animal skin.

During and after the Exile in Babylon, the Jews edited many of their oral and written traditions into the books we have today in the Old Testament. The Jewish people were refugees in a strange land that was hostile to their religion. Imagine how important it was for them, while in exile, to have these sacred writings collected and preserved. They passed

Caves near the Dead Sea in present-day Palestine, where the oldest known scrolls of the Hebrew Scriptures were discovered in 1947.

them around and treasured them like letters from their ancestors. They read, studied, and prayed over them to remind themselves of who they were and how to stay faithful to their God.

An editing process also took place with the Gospels in the New Testament. A community—say, of the Evangelist John's disciples—put together all the materials they had from their teacher and edited them into the Gospel of John.

Step 5: Canonical status. Some of the edited works are recognized by the community of faith as inspired by God, revealing God's truth, because these pieces faithfully reflect the people's experience and belief. These books entered the official canon of the Scriptures. Not all the written and edited works of the early Christians achieved canonical status, however. Works such as the Gospel of Thomas, the Gospel of Peter, and the Apocalypse of Peter were widely used among the early Christians, but for a variety of reasons they were not added to the official canon of the New Testament.

Not all the books of the Scriptures followed this exact process of development. For example, the Creation stories in Genesis are not based on people's memories of actual events; they are more like legends or myths. And the letters known to be written or dictated by Paul did not pass through a stage of oral tradition. They were written, possibly edited to a degree, and sent as letters. They became so well known and loved that it was obvious to the early church that they belonged in the canon of the Scriptures.

God's Role in the Process

If we reflect on this rather complex process, we may marvel at how the Bible came to be. Rather than God "dictating" words or truths to one or a few writers, God entered into a long process with thousands of people over centuries. God was present in their storytelling around campfires, their

Have you ever treasured a certain book, song, poem, or movie because it connected with an important part of your life? What did that connection mean to you?

gatherings around teachers, their writers carefully putting words on parchment and paper.

The process was not neat. It was "messy," with all kinds of human factors influencing what was told, what was kept, what was discarded or adapted a bit to suit an audience's needs. But God breathed life into and guided the whole process. In that sense, we can say the Scriptures were inspired by God (a word that means "to breathe into"). And we can understand the Bible as a work truly of both divine and human origins.

Religious Truth in the Scriptures: The Catholic Insight

By now it must be fairly clear that when we interpret the Bible's meaning, we cannot look to the Scriptures for scientific explanations or historical accounts that are accurate and factual in all respects. The Bible gives us something much greater and more profound than scientific or historical facts. It gives us religious truth, a people's understanding of the inner truth of God. For example, the accounts in Genesis are not meant to be a diary of Creation but, rather, the assurance that all creation comes from God and is good.

The Catholic insight into interpreting the Scriptures is that we can find that religious truth by first of all understanding what the writer of any given passage intended to communicate. Who was the audience? What problems or concerns of the community influenced what was written or edited into the passage? What form of literature is the passage? (Some writings were intended as fiction pieces or as exaggerated heroic tales; others were meant to be more historical, factual accounts.) If there are two versions of a story in the Bible, we need not be troubled over differing details in them. Rather, we need to try to understand the inner truth behind the story, and it is often the differing details that can shed light on that truth for us.

For instance, Matthew's version of the birth of Jesus has astrologers, also called Wise Men or Magi, coming from the East (indicating they were Gentiles, not Jews) to see the newborn child. Luke's version makes no mention of the Wise Men but depicts shepherds coming from

the neighboring hillside to adore Jesus. Matthew, writing for a Jewish audience, wanted to make the religious point that Jesus came not only for the Jews but for the whole world—the Gentile world as well as the Jewish world. And Luke, writing for a fairly well-to-do Gentile audience, wanted to make a religious point that Jesus came not just for privileged people like themselves but for poor and outcast people, like the shepherds, who were close to the bottom rung of society. The differing details are not contradictory; in fact, the differences between the Nativity stories tell us more about what Jesus means for the world than either version alone.

This brief look at the stories of Jesus' birth can help us make another significant point about interpreting the Bible: It is best to study the Bible with guidance. To understand the differences between Matthew's and Luke's versions, we need to know about the Christian communities for whom the authors were writing. Were they primarily Jews or Gentiles? Were they poor or rich? Were they under persecution? The answers to such questions are important in the study of the Scriptures, but the answers cannot always be found within the Scriptures themselves.

Inspired by God

Christians believe that the Bible is inspired by God, just as Jews view the Hebrew Scriptures as being inspired by God. **Biblical inspiration** does not mean that every word in the Bible is scientifically and historically correct; rather, it means that God inspired and guided the whole process of developing the Scriptures. Thus the sacred writers included every truth needed for our salvation, and all the books that contained that truth were chosen for the canon. The writers communicated the truth using their own powers and abilities, even their cultural limitations

Notice that the image on page 210 combines details from two Gospels. What do you see? Why might the artist have done this?

Why would God choose to let the human authors of the Bible use their own creativity and knowledge in communicating his truths to us, despite their human limitations? Why wouldn't God just dictate those truths to someone who would then record them word for word?

biblical inspiration The divine assistance guiding the authors of the books of the Bible so the authors could write in human words the truths God wanted to reveal.

and at times their narrow images of God. (These images broadened over centuries of experiencing God's love for all people. But we may be shocked to read some of the deeds or attitudes attributed to God by the early writers of the Old Testament!)

God entrusted the communication of truth to limited human beings who expressed that truth in their own way, using the tools and concepts available to them at the time. Many marvel at a God who trusts human beings so much and works so intimately with them to reveal divine truth.

The Heart of the Bible's Message

What is the Catholic understanding of the underlying truth that God has revealed in the Scriptures? No one can fully capture that truth in words, but here are a few statements that attempt to summarize the Bible's underlying message:

- God is the source of all goodness, all life, and all creation.
- God made human beings in the divine image, out of love, and God wants to be in loving relationship with people.
- By giving people freedom, God gave them the ability to choose between good and evil. Sin and its terrible effects on relationships came into the world when human beings first chose evil.

Describe in three words what the Bible's message might be for you after reading these summary statements.

© Keep Smiling Photography / Shutterstock.com

- God will never abandon people. When they sin and fail, God is ready to forgive them. When they are oppressed, God wants them to be free.

- The whole purpose and meaning of life is to love—to love God, our neighbor, ourselves, and creation.

- By proclaiming and living out the Reign of God, Jesus, the Son of God made flesh as a human being, showed people the way to live in God's love. He called his followers to a new life centered on love of God and neighbor.

- In Jesus' death and Resurrection, human beings are saved. His dying and rising become the pattern for people's lives. If people give their lives in love to others and to God, they find new life and growth.

- Through the power of the Holy Spirit, the church of Jesus Christ carries on Jesus' mission to bring about the Kingdom of God in the world. God's Spirit will be with the church for all time, until Jesus returns to bring all creation to fulfillment.

The Word of God cannot be chained up or controlled; it has been speaking powerfully to human beings and making a difference in their lives for thousands of years.

For Review

1. What is the five-step process of development that most of the books of the Bible went through? Describe each step in a sentence or two.

2. What was God's role in the development of the Scriptures?

3. What is the Catholic approach to interpreting the Bible? Offer an example from the versions of the stories of Jesus' birth given by Matthew and by Luke.

4. What does it mean to say that the Bible is inspired by God?

reflect

The Bible, A Love Letter

Catholics hear the Bible proclaimed every Sunday at Mass. They read from it during community prayer services. They study it in small groups. Many read from it daily or weekly as part of personal prayer. Why do Catholics have this devotion? Let's consider two informal ways some Catholics describe the Bible's importance.

Some Catholics describe the Bible as God's love letter to humanity. In a love letter, you tell the person you love just how much they mean to you, how much you want to be with them, how you want the very best for them, and how you would give everything you have for their happiness. And Catholics believe that's what the Bible does. It reveals God's great love for humanity as a whole and God's love for each person as a unique human being.

Another way some Catholics describe the Bible is with this phrase: Basic Instruction Before Leaving Earth. (Get it? Notice what the first letters in the phrase spell out.) This is a clever way of saying that God wants people to become their best selves and gives them the Bible to guide and inspire them on that journey. Catholics believe the Bible also reminds them that this life is not the end, but the beginning of a new and glorious eternal life with God.

Ultimately, Catholics believe that the fullness of God's Revelation has been given to humankind in Jesus Christ. Jesus is the one source of Revelation, the truth that God wants to communicate to people.

The Catholic faith holds that people come to know the one truth revealed in and by Jesus, God's Revelation, through two means: the Scriptures (both the Old Testament and the New Testament) and what is called the church's Tradition. Chapter 2 introduced Tradition briefly, and the next chapter explores it in more depth.

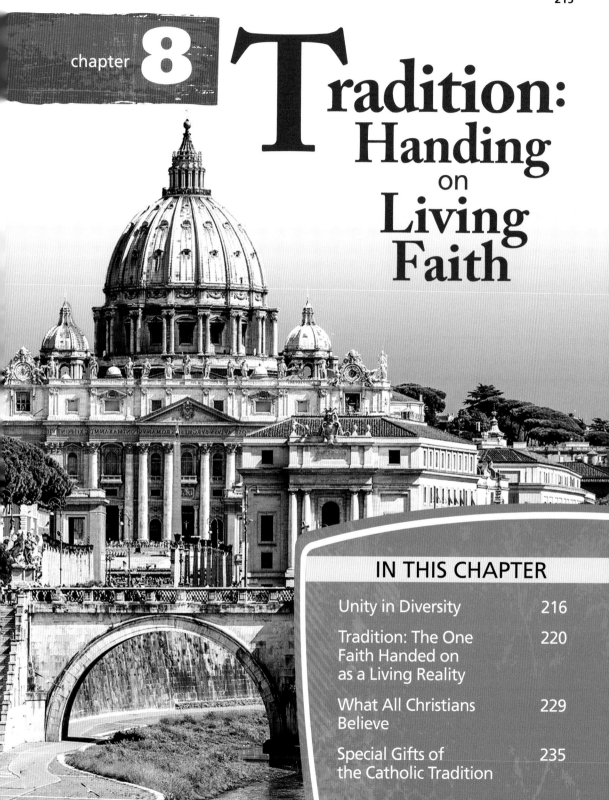

chapter **8**

Tradition:
Handing on Living Faith

IN THIS CHAPTER

Unity in Diversity   216

Tradition: The One   220
Faith Handed on
as a Living Reality

What All Christians   229
Believe

Special Gifts of   235
the Catholic Tradition

Unity in Diversity

Twenty students from Saint Francis High School were at the end of their two-week summer program abroad. They had spent the entire time in Italy studying religious art and architecture. Their leader, Dr. Lin, asked them to share their favorite moments from the program.

"Definitely the time we spent in Florence," responded Inez. "The art there was so amazing! Seeing Michelangelo's *David* in person . . . I just have no words for it. To think of those artists' imaginations for

depicting their faith in paintings and mosaics and sculpture—it's pretty incredible."

"And speaking of incredible, how about our two days at the Vatican Museum?" said Rafe. All those works of art from so many different cultures and time periods. It really gave me a sense of the impact of the Catholic faith all around the world."

"For me it was our time in Assisi," said Gayle. "The countryside and the churches were so beautiful! It was just so peaceful and serene. I could really

Pope Francis greets people outside of Saint Peter's Basilica.

see how Francis and Clare found God there."

"I think it had to be the audience we had with Pope Francis at the Vatican," added Jerome. "I know it wasn't art, although Saint Peter's Basilica is the most impressive work of architecture I have ever seen. It was just seeing people from so many different countries gathered in Saint Peter's Square. I counted twenty-eight different flags from almost every continent. And those sisters from Nigeria singing, laughing, and dancing in their habits were so cool!"

Dr. Lin smiled. "I'm so pleased with your answers," he told the group. You have really entered this experience with open hearts and minds. I believe you are truly grasping the theme of our program: unity in diversity. Let's talk about how the Catholic Church has cultivated unity among so many different cultures and time periods."

Pope Francis on Unity and Diversity

In his homilies on the Feast of Pentecost, Pope Francis often speaks about how the Holy Spirit builds unity from the diversity within the Church. Here is one example:

> The Holy Spirit does not bring only harmony *within* us but also *among us*. He makes us Church, building different parts into one harmonious edifice. Saint Paul explains this well when, speaking of the Church, he often repeats a single word, "variety": *varieties* of gifts, *varieties* of services, *varieties* of activities (1 Cor 12:4–6). We differ in the variety of our qualities and gifts. . . . On the basis of this variety, he (the Holy Spirit) builds unity. . . . He is the creator of this diversity and, at the same time, the one who brings harmony and gives unity to diversity. He alone can do these two things. (June 9, 2019)

In your religious or spiritual life, where do you see diversity? How does diversity lead to unity?

---

pilgrim A person who travels to a sacred place for a religious purpose.

The Catholic Church Is Diverse

During their program in Italy, the students discovered the great diversity that exists in the Catholic Church. Even though they traveled in only one country, they saw how Catholicism has been lived out as a global religion with a two-thousand-year history. By seeing religious art from around the world at the Vatican Museum, they recognized how people from different cultures lived out their faith with unique customs and practices. And even how the same culture had different customs and practices in different historical periods.

Even more, at the audience with Pope Francis, they witnessed a diversity of religious customs while all the gathered **pilgrims** waited for him to speak. Sisters from Nigeria danced native African dances. Pilgrims from Mexico held banners of Our Lady of Guadalupe while singing her praises in Spanish. Pilgrims from Thailand bowed their heads in silent prayer with lighted incense. Some of these pilgrims came from countries in which Catholicism was the dominant faith, and others came from countries with few people who are Catholic. Some pilgrims came from wealthy, developed countries, and others came from underdeveloped, economically struggling countries.

Rather than seeing these different expressions of faith as a source of division, the students experienced this diversity as positive. The differences seemed to say to them that the Catholic faith is alive around the world in beautiful and diverse ways. They saw a great richness in all these various expressions of living faith.

The Catholic Church Is One

Despite the diversity in customs and practices the students witnessed, they also experienced the unity that marks the Catholic Church. They saw Jesus and the saints depicted with different skin tones and clothing, depending on the artist's culture. Yet despite these differences, the art focused on how Jesus' mission continued through the work of the Church. As the pope's message was delivered and translated into several languages, hundreds of people from different cultures were nodding their heads in agreement. When the pope later passed through the crowd giving his blessing, the pilgrims smiled and shouted their joyous affirmation. For them, the pope was the living symbol of the unity of their faith.

The Catholic Church embraces an amazing variety of cultures, races, languages, philosophies, patterns of thinking, customs, and ways of expressing the faith. Recognizing and affirming variety enriches Catholicism and helps people see a united church that embraces many different cultures. This unity in diversity can bring a great sense of joy, belonging, and even awe to people when they experience it firsthand. The Church's unity is no accident, however. Catholics experience this unity through the leadership of their bishop and the pope. And they know this unity because of their common faith in God's revealed truth, communicated through Scripture and Tradition.

Have you ever seen a religion lived out in different cultures? Or do you know someone who has had that experience? What things were different? What things were the same?

What is your experience of cultural diversity? How many different racial and ethnic groups are present in your school or community? Are there students from different countries? How does this diversity enrich your school or community?

This does not mean that Catholics agree on everything. There are differences of opinion, of belief, of how best to respond to certain moral questions. If people focus on these differences, they might think there is disunity in the Catholic Church. However, most Catholics experience a fundamental unity through their common faith in Jesus Christ.

For **Review**

1. How is diversity present in the Catholic Church?
2. Why is diversity important?
3. Name two things that unify the Catholic Church.

Tradition: The One Faith Handed on as a Living Reality

How does the Catholic Church unify such a diverse membership? The answer lies at least partly in the Catholic belief that the truth of Christ is passed on not only through the Scriptures but also through Tradition. To understand how this is so, let's explore what *Tradition* means.

Tradition versus traditions

To start, note that we are talking about *Tradition* with a capital *T.*

This is different from the ordinary meaning of the word *tradition* (lowercase *t*). Ordinary tradition is a customary practice, like having a turkey dinner for the whole family on Thanksgiving, opening presents on Christmas Eve, or lighting the menorah during Hanukkah.

The Catholic Church has many traditions (lowercase *t*)—like blessing oneself with holy water, genuflecting in front of the tabernacle, or starting prayer with the Sign of the Cross.

tradition A religious practice, often rooted in a specific culture, that can change or even disappear over time.

A tribe in Ethiopia celebrates Mass.

These traditional practices are valuable and important in their own time and place, but they are not essential parts of the faith. Other examples of Catholic traditions (lowercase *t*) are cultural traditions. Different cultures within Catholicism may have particular traditions that other cultures do not have. For instance, countries like Italy, Mexico, Spain, and El Salvador have processions in the streets to honor certain saints; and in Ethiopia, Kenya, or South Africa, Mass may include African dancing and drumming. Such traditions are part of the diversity that is so enriching to the whole Catholic Church; in no way do they harm the unity of the Church.

That meaning of *tradition* is not the same as *Tradition* with a capital *T*. For Catholics, Tradition is the process by which the Catholic Church reflects on, deepens its understanding of, cherishes, and hands on to every generation the teachings and practices that are essential to the faith. Christ revealed the fullness of God's truth to the Apostles, who passed it on to their successors, the bishops of the first Christian communities, to teach and protect. Likewise, they passed it on to the next generation of bishops and so on to the present day. (The word *tradition* comes from a Latin word meaning "to hand over.")

Talk with someone who has experienced Catholicism in a culture different from your own—for instance, in a Mexican, Filipino, Nigerian, Italian, or Vietnamese culture. Find out about one religious tradition of that culture that is different from your own.

Tradition The process by which the Catholic Church reflects on, deepens its understanding of, cherishes, and hands on to every generation the teachings and practices that are essential to the faith, as interpreted by the Magisterium under the guidance of the Holy Spirit.

God's truth, which was fully revealed in the person of Jesus Christ, does not change. But human beings are limited creatures who do not understand God's truth perfectly or express it perfectly. By reflecting on and living this truth over many centuries, the Catholic Church has come to a deeper understanding of God's truth under the guidance of the Holy Spirit. Tradition is like the household treasures of a family that has been living and growing for generations, rather than the artifacts of an ancient culture enshrined in a museum and marveled at by visitors.

A "Scripture and Tradition" Approach

Many Christian denominations do not have the same belief in Tradition that Catholics do. They see Scripture as the *one* way God has revealed sacred truth. Catholics, however, see both Scripture *and* Tradition as the two ways of handing on the fullness of God's Revelation in Christ.

A "Scripture Only" Approach

A "Scripture only" approach, held by some Christians, is that God has given divine truth in the Bible alone. Christians with this perspective believe they will find in the Bible whatever they need to know about life, about God, and about how to be a follower of Jesus. In thinking about any moral or religious question, they believe the best answer will be found by going directly to the Bible for insight.

Why Scripture and Tradition?

However, a "Scripture and Tradition" approach, which is the Catholic approach, says that God has made divine truth available to us not in just the Bible. Tradition was first given by Jesus to the Apostles. The Catholic Church has grown in understanding the full meaning of Tradition through years and even centuries of living with and reflecting on the truth that was first revealed to the Apostles. Because the Holy Spirit is present in the Church, guiding it in the path of truth, Catholics believe that the experiences and reflections of the Church over time, throughout its history, are inspired just as surely as the Scriptures were inspired by God.

Tradition Came First

Tradition began before the New Testament existed. This is because the first Christian communities predate the development of the books of the New Testament. Think about how the New Testament developed in the early church. As discussed in chapter 7, first came the community's experience of certain events like Jesus' healings and the coming of the Holy Spirit at Pentecost. Then followed a period of reflecting on and talking about the experience, and sharing stories in an oral tradition. Only later were the stories written down, edited into the Gospels, and finally accepted officially as the books we know as the New Testament. The church did not grow out of the New Testament; rather, the New Testament grew out of the Tradition of the early church. Tradition came first.

An Interwoven Process

Since the beginning of the Catholic Church, Scripture and Tradition have been woven together. They are not two separate sources of God's truth; rather, they are two interwoven means that God uses to communicate the truth. The Holy Spirit acts within that whole process to inspire the Church to arrive at a deeper understanding of Jesus Christ and his message. Tradition can never contradict the Bible, and the Bible can never contradict Tradition; rather the two means of passing on God's revealed truth support and shed light on each other.

Imagine a religious community with tradition but no sacred scriptures or one with scriptures but no teaching tradition. Why might a religious community be stronger because of the belief in both?

Trusting Tradition

"Why should I trust what the Catholic Church teaches when there are so many differing opinions on what's true?" This is a legitimate question that many sincere people ask. Here are some responses to this question, adapted from interviews with people who have joined the Catholic Church.

- "One of the most wonderful things about becoming Catholic was coming face-to-face with the truths hammered out by the Church under the Holy Spirit. The experience I had with learning the doctrine of the Church was like coming home and coming into truth."

- "Accepting the teaching of the Church was like accepting the teaching of a loving father. I had a loving, caring father, and God the Father shares his truth with us just like my dad did with me."

- "Having the teaching of the Church actually set me free to be in tune with the Spirit and to become my best self. Without the guidelines and truths of the Church, I was just fumbling around in the dark, trying to discover what has already freely been given to us."

The Church's Teaching Voice

The process of formulating and expressing the Catholic Church's Tradition is more involved than simply going to the Scriptures for answers to life's questions. It takes time, prayerful discernment, and patience with the complex process for the Church to arrive at the teachings it embraces as part of its Tradition. And further, think of what would happen if every individual had the authority and power to determine what the Church's Tradition is—what is essential to the faith. A great deal of confusion and probably complete lack of unity would result. We would have millions of versions of "the truth." If the "one body in Christ" is to have any unity of faith, the task of discerning what is true cannot simply be left to individuals to decide for themselves.

So who has the job of interpreting and preserving the truths revealed in Scripture and Tradition? Catholics see this authority as belonging to the official teaching voice of the Catholic Church, called the **Magisterium** (from a Latin word meaning "to teach"). The Magisterium consists of the pope, believed by Catholics to be the suc-

> **Magisterium** The Catholic Church's official teaching voice, which consists of all bishops in communion with the pope. The Magisterium interprets and preserves the truths revealed in Scripture and Tradition.

cessor of Saint Peter, and the Catholic bishops of the world, the successors of the Apostles. The pope and the bishops are responsible for discerning what is essential to the faith based on the experience of the Church's members and on the work of theologians and Scripture scholars, all under the guidance of the Holy Spirit.

Forms of Church Teaching

How does the Magisterium fulfill its teaching responsibility? The pope and bishops often teach in speeches and homilies. But when they want their teaching to reach a wide audience, it is usually done in a written form. Here are some of the written forms used by the Magisterium:

- a pastoral letter written by a bishop for his own diocese

- a statement or pastoral letter by national or regional conferences of bishops, such as the United States Conference of Catholic Bishops

- a major teaching document prepared with the advice of the world's bishops, such as the *Catechism of the Catholic Church*, issued in English by the Vatican in 1994

- a document written by a gathering of all the world's bishops (called an ecumenical, or worldwide, council, like Vatican Council II, which took place from 1962 to 1965); or by a representative group of the world's bishops who meet about a particular topic, like global justice or the role of the laity in the Church (this is called a worldwide synod)

- a post-synodal apostolic exhortation, which is a paper written by a pope after a worldwide synod, presenting his conclusions and recommendations for action

- a papal encyclical, which is a letter from a pope to the worldwide church or an official declaration from the pope

How would you explain the role of the Magisterium of the Catholic Church to someone who has never heard of it?

Imagine writing a letter to the whole world about something you thought everyone needed to hear. What would you write about? What are two or three key points you would want to communicate?

Dear Young People: Make a Ruckus!

In his post-synodal apostolic exhortation "Christ Is Alive" ("Christus Vivit"), Pope Francis has many encouraging words for young people. In this paragraph, he tells young people to make the most of their youth:

> Dear young people, make the most of these years of your youth. Don't observe life from a balcony. Don't confuse happiness with an armchair, or live your life behind a screen. Whatever you do, do not become the sorry sight of an abandoned vehicle! . . . Take risks, even if it means making mistakes. . . . Make a ruckus! Cast out the fears that paralyze you, so that you don't become young mummies. Live! Give yourselves over to the best of life! Open the door of the cage, go out and fly! Please, don't take early retirement. (143)

What keeps you from living your life to the fullest? What are the fears that paralyze you? How will you give yourself over to "the best of life"?

Doctrines and Dogmas

Official Catholic Church teachings, expressed by the Magisterium, are called **doctrines**. The Church's teaching on Original Sin is an example of a doctrine. Although the fundamental truth of a given doctrine does not change over time, the Church's understanding of the doctrine can always grow and develop.

Doctrines taught under the fullest seriousness and authority of the Catholic Church are identified by a distinctive name—**dogmas**. Dogmas are central to the life of the Catholic Church. Examples are the Trinity (God is Father, Son, and Holy Spirit), the Incarnation (God became human in Jesus), and the Resurrection (Jesus was raised from the dead and lives

doctrine An official, authoritative teaching of the Catholic Church based on the Revelation of God.

dogma A doctrine recognized as most central to the life of the Catholic Church; it is defined by the Magisterium and considered definitive and authoritative.

in glory). Virtually all Christians believe in these dogmas. Two doctrines about Mary, held by Catholics and defined as dogma by papal declarations, were discussed earlier in this course: the Immaculate Conception (Mary was conceived free from Original Sin) and the Assumption (Mary was assumed body and soul into glory with God). All dogmas are doctrines and may be correctly referred to by either name; however, not all doctrines are dogmas.

Infallibility

An important doctrine related to the teaching voice of the Catholic Church is infallibility. According to this doctrine, when the Church makes a solemn declaration on matters of faith and morals, the Church is free from the possibility of error. Catholics do not believe that the members of the Magisterium are unusually smart or never wrong; rather, they believe that the Holy Spirit will protect the Church from error when it comes to religious truths that are important for union with God.

Infallibility can be officially exercised by the Magisterium in only two ways. When the pope defines a matter regarding faith or morals and speaks as the head of the Catholic Church with the clear purpose of uniting the Church, he is empowered by the Holy Spirit to speak infallibly. Also, the world's bishops, as a group, can teach infallibly in communion with the pope under certain circumstances. In neither case are the human beings involved considered to be infallible. It is Christ's infallibility that is given to the Church.

The Catholic Church's understanding of dogmas that have been defined infallibly can evolve as the pope and bishops apply the truths they express to new situations. For example, Catholic dogma states that all human life is sacred, even the lives of sinners and criminals. However, the Church had reluctantly permitted the death penalty as a legitimate way to protect innocent life against violent criminals. This

changed in 2018 when Pope Francis issued new Church law calling for an end to the death penalty. He recognized that in the modern world, all countries now have the police protection and jails to imprison even the most violent criminals for the rest of their lives. This is one example of how infallible dogmas continue to be reflected on, refined, and communicated in new ways so that the truth behind them can be more deeply grasped.

The teaching authority of the pope with the bishops is one important way the Catholic Church has been able to keep unity in the midst of diverse conditions, customs, and ways of thinking among Catholic people around the world. The young people on their study tour in Italy sensed how powerful it is to belong to a Church that is united in its faith yet diverse in its ways of expression.

Identify a time when you have felt a sense of unity or oneness in a group of people. What words or experiences contributed to that feeling?

For **Review**

1. What is the meaning of *Tradition* (capital *T*)? How does it differ from *traditions* (small *t*)?
2. What is the Catholic understanding of a "Scripture and Tradition" approach to knowing God's truth?
3. What is the Magisterium? Why is it needed?
4. Give three examples of ways the Catholic Church's teaching may be expressed by the Magisterium.
5. What are doctrines? What are dogmas? Give three examples of dogmas from the text.
6. What is meant by infallibility? Why is it important?

What All Christians Believe

The three major divisions of Christianity—Catholic, Protestant, and Orthodox—share essential beliefs that are at the core of their faith. Let's look at beliefs they hold in common before we consider some characteristics or gifts that Catholicism in particular has to offer.

The Apostles' Creed

A creed is an official profession, or statement, of the beliefs of a particular faith. The Latin word *credo* (meaning "I believe") is the source of the word *creed*. *Credo* is the combination of two other Latin words, meaning "heart" and "set," so the root meaning of *credo* is, "I set my heart on." Thus a creed is best understood as a statement of heartfelt, active belief that is more than just intellectual acceptance.

The Apostles' Creed is a very early statement of the Christian faith. It is based on a creed used in the second century, close to the era of the Apostles themselves. All Christians can claim faith in the beliefs expressed in the Apostles' Creed, although interpretations of those beliefs may differ slightly.

This course is intended to introduce, or more deeply explain, the Catholic Christian faith to you. While reading the Apostles' Creed, take note

of the chapters of this book that deal with the contents of the creed. (In the chart on the next page, the chapter numbers and titles are given across from the section of the creed they pertain to. Chapter 7, on the Scriptures, pertains to the whole creed.) You will notice, you have already been studying in this course much of what is contained in the Apostles' Creed, and other sections of the creed are the focus of later chapters.

The Beliefs of the Apostles' Creed	Chapters That Explore These Beliefs
I believe in God, the Father almighty, creator of heaven and earth.	• Chapter 2: Revelation and Faith: Knowing and Responding to God • Chapter 3: Judaism: Christianity's Religious Roots
I believe in Jesus Christ, his only Son, our Lord. He was conceived by the power of the Holy Spirit and born of the Virgin Mary.	• Chapter 4: Jesus: Son of the Living God
He suffered under Pontius Pilate, was crucified, died, and was buried. He descended into hell. On the third day he rose again.	• Chapter 5: Jesus' Death and Resurrection: Experiencing New Life
He ascended into heaven and is seated at the right hand of the Father. He will come again to judge the living and the dead.	• Chapter 6: The Church: Gathering in the Spirit of Jesus
I believe in the Holy Spirit, the holy catholic Church, the communion of saints	• Chapter 6: The Church: Gathering in the Spirit of Jesus • Chapter 8: Tradition: Handing on Living Faith
the forgiveness of sins,	• Chapter 9: The Sacraments: Celebrating the Grace of God
the resurrection of the body,	• Chapter 5: Jesus' Death and Resurrection: Experiencing New Life • Chapter 6: The Church: Gathering in the Spirit of Jesus • Chapter 11: Christian Morality: Living in the Spirit of Jesus
and the life everlasting.	• Chapter 5: Jesus' Death and Resurrection: Experiencing New Life • Chapter 11: Christian Morality: Living in the Spirit of Jesus
Amen.	

Notice that the Apostles' Creed follows a structure that highlights belief in the Trinity—in God as Father, Son, and Holy Spirit. The Nicene Creed, the creed Catholics recite at Mass on most Sundays, follows this same trinitarian structure, but with somewhat more complex language. Both of these creeds represent the essence of the Christian faith, which above all is a faith in the Trinity.

The Trinity: Bringing Us into the Divine Life of Love

Every belief in the Christian faith goes back to the Trinity. Everything else in Christianity is related to this truth of who God is and how God relates to us.

Father, Son, and Holy Spirit

The "simple" explanation of the **Trinity** is that there are three divine persons—the Father, the Son, and the Holy Spirit—in one God. There is one divine nature, but three persons. This is simple to state, perhaps, but not as simple to understand.

Review the Apostles' Creed and write a list of questions you may have about it. Keep track of these questions and make notes on the answers you discover in your future religion classes.

Trinity The central Christian mystery and dogma that there is one God in three divine persons: Father, Son, and Holy Spirit.

An icon depicting the Trinity.

The understanding of God as Trinity is rooted in the New Testament, where God is revealed as Father, Son, and Holy Spirit. God is one; there is only one God. But God is at the same time a loving union of persons—the Father, the Son, and the Holy Spirit. This is puzzling, so do not be surprised if you feel confused. When theologians and church leaders formulated this understanding of God into the dogma of the Trinity back in the fourth century, they knew they were trying to put into words a reality that is beyond human beings' limited abilities of understanding and expression.

You may be wondering what the dogma of the Trinity has to do with us human beings and our lives. Let's consider what Catholics believe about how God relates to us as Trinity.

God Is Personal and Relational

The first lesson Christians take from the doctrine of the Trinity is that God is personal, and being personal, God is also relational. The persons of the Trinity are in loving relationship, or communion, with one another. And for Christians, they are also in relationship with *us*. God is calling human beings to share in God's own life of love. This is why Catholics believe they have a built-in longing for God. Human beings are made in God's image,

Name three things of value to you that you get out of being part of a community. That community could be family, friends, a religious community, a sports team, a club or organization, or something else.

© Monkey Business Images / Shutterstock.com

and so, like God, are yearning for loving relationships. Human salvation is to participate in the life of God's love.

The Trinity Saves

Salvation, the new life of grace lived in union with God, is brought about by the whole Trinity, not just one person of the Trinity. For Catholics, it is not enough to say, "Jesus saves," because it is believed that *God* saves, *through* Jesus, *in* the Holy Spirit. A more detailed explanation would be this: God the Father, the source of all love, pours out that love into the Son, who became one with humanity as a human, Jesus Christ, and who died and rose from the dead for us. The love of the Father and the Son flows out to all through the power of the Holy Spirit. The Spirit—God present and active everywhere—transforms humanity and all creation and unites human beings with the Source of love so that they can live, now and forever, in union with God and one another. This understanding of how the Trinity saves is evident in a phrase Catholics often use in their public worship, praying to "God the Father, through Jesus Christ his Son, in the Holy Spirit," or a similar formula.

Images of the Trinity

All this may seem quite abstract, so let's look at a few metaphors, or images, of the Trinity. These come from a theologian, Tertullian, who wrote during the second century, in the early years of the church.

Tertullian compared God as Father, Son, and Holy Spirit to a river. Every river has a source, which we can think of as God the Father, source of all goodness. The river flowing out from its source can be likened to Jesus Christ, the Son of God, who comes forth from the Father. The river irrigates the land and helps crops and other plants grow, which is like the Holy Spirit acting in our life to change us, renew us, and bring forth good growth.

Another image of how the Father, Son, and Holy Spirit relate to us, Tertullian said it, the sun in the heavens (the Father), the sunbeam coming to earth (Christ), and the point where

Think of an image that could describe the Trinity besides those given in the text. Can you draw a picture of it or explain the image in writing?

the sun hits the earth and brings us warmth and light (the Spirit). Saint Augustine used a similar metaphor, relating the Trinity to a fire source (the Father), shining its rays (the Son) into the darkness, and making everything around it warm (the Holy Spirit).

All these images of the Trinity include a source (the Father), a way that source is communicated or given out (the Son), and a means by which the source brings forth good effects (the Holy Spirit). God is saving us every day, trying to bring us into loving communion with God, one another, and all of creation. God saves us through the loving activity of the Trinity, reaching out to us, transforming us, and uniting us with our divine source.

Signs of a Living Faith

Baptism in a South African Village

Ramona Miller, a Franciscan sister from Minnesota, gives this account of the celebration of Baptism in a small South African Catholic parish:

Like most village churches in South Africa, this community does not have a resident priest. The people are enormously proud that they constructed the church themselves, which took two years. While they were building the church, they decided to hold off on having Baptisms until the church was completed. Then they could celebrate in grand style, baptizing over one hundred children and adults.

The liturgy lasted four and a half hours. I was so hungry, but the people did not even seem to notice the time passing or their own hunger. One by one, the many candidates for Baptism came forward. Each one was plunged into the refreshing, cool water three times by the priest:

I baptize you in the name of the Father (plunge),

and of the Son (plunge),

and of the Holy Spirit (plunge).

Amen.

After the liturgy, there was a buffet party that lasted into the night. A group of ten men dressed in colorful shirts entertained us for seven hours straight with their unbelievably beautiful singing. It was a celebration unlike any I have witnessed before.

Christians believe that through Baptism their relationship with the Holy Trinity is strengthened, allowing them to more deeply experience and share God's love.

© Sr. Ramona Miller

1. What is the Apostles' Creed? What structure does it follow?
2. Give the "simple" explanation of the Trinity.
3. Describe the first lesson Christians take from the doctrine of the Trinity.
4. Offer one image or metaphor of the Trinity from the text and tell how it corresponds with the Father, the Son, and the Holy Spirit.

Special Gifts of the Catholic Tradition

The faith that unites Christians of all denominations is far greater than that which separates them. The faith of the Apostles' Creed, with its belief in the Trinity, is central to all Christianity. However, the emphasis that is placed on certain dimensions of Christian faith helps distinguish Christian denominations from one another.

The following four dimensions of the Christian faith are especially emphasized in the Catholic Church. Certainly, these dimensions are present in lesser degrees in other Christian denominations and the Jewish religion as well. Yet, the emphasis by Catholics helps make up the special character of Catholicism. They might be considered the special gifts or insights that Catholics offer to the world.

- *A sense of the sacramental.* A sense that God and the sacred are encountered in the ordinary things and events of everyday life.

- *An emphasis on the communal.* A recognition that the church, as a community, is essential to individual salvation and the life of faith.

- *A commitment to both faith and reason.* A reliance on both human intelligence and faith in God to understand what God intends.

- *Love for the saints.* A relationship with those who have died who were especially close to God and now are models and helpers for those still living.

Think of a time and place in which you experienced something awesome or in which you were filled with peace. How might this have been a sacramental experience?

sacramental
The sense that God and the sacred are encountered in the ordinary things and events of everyday life.

sacrament A visible sign of God's saving love, instituted by Christ, by which spiritual gifts are given.

A Sacramental Sense

In the Catholic vision of reality, all the world is sacred because it is created by God and filled with the presence of God. God is not "out there" but is "with us" in every aspect of our experience. People only have to open their eyes in a new way to see how God is present in their lives and in the world around them. This awareness is a sense of the **sacramental** quality of reality—a sense that God and the sacred are encountered in the ordinary things and events of everyday life.

Symbols and Symbolic Actions

God can be experienced in a meal, a refreshing drink of water, a hug from a friend, and an enduring marriage. Catholics try to recognize God as "visible" by finding ways to celebrate God's presence in the ordinary material world.

That is why Catholics have traditionally appreciated symbols such as holy water, incense, candles, rosary beads, religious medals, statues of saints and angels, and beautifully decorated churches. Catholics find God's power present in certain symbolic words and actions called sacraments. For Catholics, material objects, visible actions, and sacred words symbolize spiritual realities, and they offer a "window" into the sacred.

The Seven Sacraments

In the seven official **sacraments** that Catholics celebrate, certain materials and actions from everyday life symbolize and help bring about the gift of God's saving love in people's lives—breaking and sharing bread, pouring and sharing wine, anointing with oil, pouring water, placing hands on a person's head or shoulder, making a promise, and so on. The Eucharist, one of those sacraments, is at the center of Catholic life and worship. Chapter 9 considers in more depth the sacramental sense, the seven sacraments of the Catholic Church, and the church's liturgical year, which is its annual cycle of feasts and sacred seasons.

An Emphasis on the Communal

Catholics believe that God is working in the world through communities of people, not just through individuals. Because human beings are relational—made for relationships and community—God saves people through community, in particular the community of Christians throughout the world. The Catholic Church, in particular, is extremely important in the faith life of Catholics.

One way Catholics live out the emphasis on the communal is by participating in the Eucharist. People need the guidance and wisdom of a community—a community that loves God and that loves them—if they are to figure out what is right and true. And they need all the grace and support that the sacraments can give them. So the Catholic Church strongly encourages that where possible, its members participate in the Eucharist each weekend on Saturday evening or on Sunday to stay connected with the community's life of faith and be nourished by it.

The emphasis on the communal in Catholicism means that there is great importance placed on keeping Catholics united in their beliefs, rather than allowing groups within the Catholic Church to hold different beliefs. The pope and the bishops are servants of the whole Church who are responsible for guarding and keeping the faith so that the community is united around its shared beliefs.

The emphasis on the communal also means that at times the pope and the bishops explain how the Scriptures and Tradition can be applied to current social issues. These teachings

Signs of a Living Faith

Students Serving Those in Need

Students from Holy Family Catholic High School in Victoria, Minnesota, have been serving breakfast to overnight guests at the Simpson House for many years. It all started with one student who launched the program in his junior year. When he graduated, he passed the leadership on to other students who have kept the tradition going. This student-led ministry serves forty-five to fifty guests fifteen to eighteen mornings each year.

Student Gracie Lund said this about the program: "I think it is important for Holy Family to continue this service tradition and make sure it is student-led. It gives students a chance to take leadership, organize, and get kids together so they can see how they have an impact on others."

that promote justice in society are called **Catholic social teaching**. Chapter 11 looks at Catholic social teaching as an important theme of Catholic moral teaching.

A Commitment to Both Faith and Reason

In learning about God, the meaning of life, and how to live, is it reasonable to ask if human beings should trust their own intelligence—their own power of reasoning? Or should human beings rely on faith, trusting that God will enlighten us as to what we need to know? The Catholic answer is that human beings need both faith and reason. In other words, people can use their own intelligence to look for evidence of God's existence in the world and in their own life, and to determine what is right and wrong. But they also need faith to know God fully and to understand how God wants them to live.

One example of the commitment to both faith and reason can be found in the Catholic approach to the Scriptures. To understand what God is communicating in the Bible, a person needs to have faith that it is indeed God's Word, God's self-revelation. But the person also needs to use intelligence to interpret the Scriptures. Scripture scholars use the tools of science and archeology, knowledge of history and ancient languages, and appreciation of the many forms of literature used in the Bible. These tools enable scholars to reason out the intent of the original human author in a given passage.

For Catholics, no contradiction exists between what can be known by intelligence and what can be known by faith: faith sheds light on what their reason tells them, and reason helps them understand and articulate their faith more clearly.

List some ways that both faith and reason are valued at your school.

Catholic social teaching The teachings of the Catholic Church that address social issues and promote justice.

The school you are attending is another example of Catholic respect for both faith and reason. The Catholic Church has put much emphasis on education. It has a long tradition of support for study (the first universities were part of the cathedrals of the Middle Ages). Faith and reason are highly valued in your school and in the great Catholic high schools, colleges, and universities around the world. Some of the greatest intellectuals in history have been saints of the Catholic Church, like Augustine of Hippo, Thomas Aquinas, and Teresa of Ávila. In them, we can see the union of reason and faith at its best.

Love for the Saints

In chapter 6, we met a number of saints from the Catholic Church's history, and we discussed the Communion of Saints, the bond among all faithful Christians, both living and dead.

This focus on the saints and the Communion of Saints is characteristic of Catholicism. Sometimes it is misunderstood as an attempt to substitute the saints for God, giving honor and glory to human beings that should be given to God alone.

A healthy love for the saints is a beautiful and consoling part of Catholicism that does not at all threaten the love that is due to God. The **devotion** to saints is really just an aspect of two other dimensions of Catholicism already discussed—the sacramental sense and the communal sense. Saints are like sacraments of God; they were flesh-and-blood people who today are still pointing others to God through the example of their lives. They are full of God's love and are honored for that. Catholics see the saints as family, caring about them and helping them. Catholics also recognize the saints as still part of the body of Christ.

Saint Teresa of Ávila.

Research the life of one saint who interests you. What can you learn from that saint's life, and what do you most admire about them?

devotion The love and admiration held for a holy person, especially the saints; the prayer to an angel or saint asking for their help.

The Letter to the Hebrews speaks of all those brave and faithful men and women who have gone before us in the faith: "We are surrounded by so great a cloud of witnesses" (12:1). For Catholics, who are so aware of the presence of the saints, the "great cloud of witnesses" can seem very near and very inspiring.

Mary, Mother of God, deserves special honor. Many people around the world are devoted to Mary, as they are to their own mother. They relate to Mary as their protector and advocate.

She is the focus of festivals, pilgrimages to shrines, special holy days, and processions. One of the most beloved prayers in Catholicism is the Rosary, the prayer in which the "Hail Mary" is repeated many times while a person meditates on the mysteries of Jesus' and Mary's lives.

Sacramental, communal, committed to reason as well as faith, and devoted to the saints—these characteristics represent the special gift that Catholicism offers to all of Christianity and to the whole world.

© Adam Jan Figel / Shutterstock.com

Signs of a Living Faith

Pilgrims to the Guadalupe Shrine

In 1531, the Blessed Virgin Mary appeared as an Aztec native woman to Juan Diego, a poor peasant, and spoke to him in an Aztec language. In one of her appearances, the Virgin sent Juan Diego off with amazing winter-blooming roses wrapped up in his cloak. This was to be a sign to the bishop that the Virgin Mary wished a shrine to be built on that spot. When Juan Diego showed the roses to the bishop, they tumbled out of his cloak. But there on the rough cloak was an even more miraculous sign—an image of Mary herself, the Virgin of Guadalupe.

The Indigenous peoples of the Americas have interpreted this visit to a poor native by the Virgin of Guadalupe as a sign that God is with them. A great church was built on the spot and the miraculous image of the Virgin on Juan Diego's cloak is on display for all to see. In almost five hundred years, this image and the rough cloth it is on have not deteriorated. At the shrine, millions of pilgrims have raised their voices in prayer—asking for Mary's help in their lives and thanking her for favors received.

For **Review**

1. What is meant by a sense of the sacramental?
2. What is meant by the Catholic Church's emphasis on the communal? Name three ways this emphasis is shown in Catholicism.
3. Describe the Catholic understanding of how reason and faith are both needed to know God, the meaning of life, and how to live.
4. Briefly explain why Catholicism includes devotion to the saints.

A Living Tradition

The Catholic faith is a great heritage handed on from generation to generation. In that process, the teaching authority of the Catholic Church has helped people understand the faith and live it out in response to the needs and challenges of every age. Thus our understanding of the Church's Tradition is deepened and passed on.

The process of living out the Tradition over centuries has not always been smooth. There have been great and noble moments; heroic leaders; and courageous, good, ordinary people living the faith from day to day. But sin has also entered the process. The Catholic Church has been affected by occasional violent disagreements, even wars, over theological issues. Human factors such as greed, lust for power, and pride have sometimes played a role in the process. At times, leaders have acted in shameful and unchristian ways.

To say that the Spirit is with the Catholic Church, protecting it from error, does not mean that the Church's members are free from sin. And there have been, and continue to be, legitimate disagreements in the Church over various issues. Even in the midst

Think of an example of a disagreement that was resolved peacefully, and a disagreement that led to violence, hurt, or resentment. What was different in how the two disagreements were handled?

of disagreements, the Spirit is at work in people's sincere attempts to resolve conflicts and arrive at the truth peacefully, with charity toward one another.

Despite the "messiness" of the process, Catholics believe that the Spirit of Jesus has been with the Church all along. The Holy Spirit has been guiding the Church on the path of truth through all the dangers along the way. The Spirit will never abandon the Church. Through God's grace, the unity of faith has been and will be preserved until the end of time.

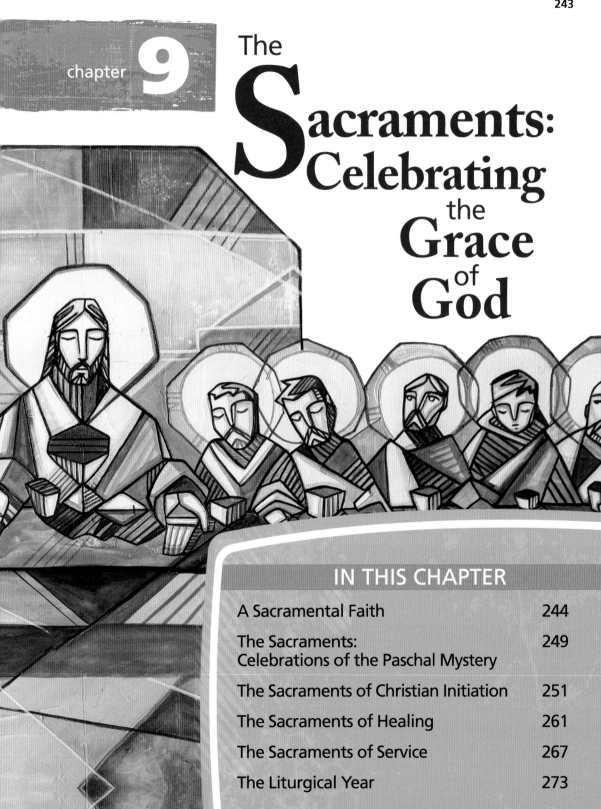

chapter **9**

The Sacraments: Celebrating the Grace of God

IN THIS CHAPTER

A Sacramental Faith	244
The Sacraments: Celebrations of the Paschal Mystery	249
The Sacraments of Christian Initiation	251
The Sacraments of Healing	261
The Sacraments of Service	267
The Liturgical Year	273

A Sacramental Faith

Catholics have a certain way of looking at the world, often referred to as a sacramental worldview, as discussed in chapter 8. This sacramental sense is an awareness that the world is full of God's presence. The underlying belief is that if one has the eyes to see, they will find God revealed in the people, places, things, and events of everyday life. The Catholic use of seemingly ordinary things such as water, oil, incense, bread, wine, and fire in community prayer reflects this sacramental sense.

Catholics take the Incarnation—the belief that God became one of us, a human, in Jesus—seriously. Based on belief in the Incarnation, Catholics understand that everything human, and all creation, can reveal God. The world is good not only because God created it but also because God united with the world in Jesus. And God remains with the world through Jesus' Spirit, which is poured out for all people and for all time.

Grace: God's Love All around Us

Catholics believe that grace—God's loving, active presence in the world—is all around us, among us, and within us. They believe that God constantly

offers to touch people's lives, trying to reach each person through the people, events, and material things of everyday life:

- a special, close conversation with a friend

- a loss or failure that causes us to think hard about what is important in life

- a meal shared with people we love

- a teacher's caring about how we're doing in school

- an incident of admitting we were wrong and receiving forgiveness

- a warm hug from a loved one

- the beauty of a crisp, sunny day

If people are open to them, such experiences are moments of grace. In these moments, God truly comes to people, and through these experiences helps them grow into the people they are meant to be. Moments of grace transform us—sometimes a little, sometimes a lot. And even if people are not consciously aware of God's presence in these moments, grace can still help them grow into fullness of life.

Symbols: Snapshots of Meaning

We have already mentioned some familiar symbols in Catholicism. Let's stop and consider what any symbol, not just a sacred symbol, actually is. Here is one definition: A **symbol** is "a tangible (able to be perceived with the senses), physical reality that represents an invisible reality." A symbol is a "snapshot of meaning." For instance, a wedding ring represents the love and faithfulness involved in the marriage covenant. A flag stands for a country's identity and can be a sign of pride in one's country. A person like Adolf Hitler stands as a symbol of great evil for many people, whereas Saint Mother Teresa of Kolkata (Calcutta) symbolizes compassion and goodness.

L ook through the bulleted list of experiences that might be recognized as filled with grace. Which of these have you experienced recently? How did the experience affect you?

symbol A tangible, physical reality that represents an invisible reality.

Call to mind experiences you or others you know have had with water, bread, and light. Consider how each thing might symbolize something you know about Catholic Christianity's beliefs or practices.

Symbols are fascinating in that any one symbol can be interpreted with several different meanings. For instance, fire may represent warmth but also destruction; an ocean may represent mystery but also loneliness. Symbols reach us at different levels of our awareness. They may touch several emotions at once and charge our imagination. They may surface in us great dreams or a sense of defeat, hope or fear, love or emptiness. Symbols can be rich, powerful ways of expressing meaning.

Rituals: Symbolic Actions

Rituals are concrete, visible actions—often combined with words—that have symbolic meaning for a group or community. They are done in a similar way every time they are performed. Think, for instance, of a graduation ceremony with the customary speeches and awarding of diplomas. Consider a birthday party with the singing of "Happy Birthday," the cutting of the cake, and the opening of presents. A school pep rally with cheers before a big game is also a ritual.

ritual Words and actions that have symbolic meaning for a group or community.

All these actions communicate meaning and have real power to affect us if we put our heart into them. However, because rituals are repeated actions, those who participate in them may be tempted to do them routinely and without paying attention. Think of a pep rally in which the cheerleaders do their cheers very well and the captain of the team gives an inspiring speech, but the audience members just yawn and look away, not caring about what is going on or the outcome of the game. The intended effect of the pep rally—to charge up everyone's spirit for the game—is lost.

In the Catholic faith, symbolic actions are drawn from experiences of everyday life. The rituals that make up the seven sacraments are full of such words and actions. For instance, the pouring of water suggests refreshing or cleansing. The rubbing of oil on the body suggests being healed or strengthened. The lighting and holding of a candle suggests that truth and hope will overcome the darkness of ignorance and despair. The blessing of bread calls to mind the idea that spiritual nourishment is as important as physical nourishment.

What does eating cake together at a birthday party symbolize?

As with rituals like pep rallies and graduation ceremonies, people have to put themselves—body, mind, and spirit—into the rituals of faith if they are to fully touch and transform them.

Catholics believe that God is present and active as grace in a special, intense way in the official rituals of the Catholic Church called the seven sacraments.

The World Is Full of God's Presence

Shh, be quiet.
Sit still, and you can hear God.
Open your mind,
let your eyes wander,
focus on the world around you.
Let the sounds pour freely into your ears.
Do you hear the song of that bird?
That is God singing.
Do you hear the children laughing?
That is God laughing.
Do you smell the spring flowers?
That is God beckoning.
God is everywhere.
When you are in despair,
God is with you.
Look outside your window,
   and God will appear.
Abstract yet present,
God is not hard to see,
a light full of color,
magnificent hues.
From black to white,
God sees no boundaries.
God is in everything.
Everything is in God.

(Adapted from Michael Elmer Bulleri,
      in *More Dreams Alive*)

For Review

1. What is the understanding about humanness and creation that comes from the doctrine of the Incarnation?
2. Give three examples of how someone might experience a moment of grace.
3. What is a symbol? Give two examples from the text of how a symbol can have different meanings.
4. What is a ritual? Give two examples of ritual actions from your experience.

The Sacraments: Celebrations of the Paschal Mystery

Before we consider the seven sacraments, let's consider how Jesus and the church can also be described as sacraments. Recall from chapter 8 that a sacrament is a visible sign of God's love, through which spiritual gifts are given to us. In Christian belief, the most visible sign of God's love is the person of Jesus Christ. Through the life and teachings of Jesus Christ, God has given the gift of his immense love to human beings in a tangible way. In Jesus' life of love poured out for all people, he showed humanity what God is like and how God wants us to be. In that sense, Christians can say that Jesus is the original sacrament of God.

Now Jesus is present in the world through the Holy Spirit who works inside and outside the church. Catholics believe that the Spirit works in a special way to sustain, make holy, and enable all those who commit to following Jesus to be Jesus in the world. The followers are not perfect at showing Jesus to the world, but with the Spirit's help, they continually strive to be Jesus for others.

If Jesus is the original sacrament of God, then the church and its members are sometimes called "the sacrament of Jesus." This is a way of saying that the church is the way people can see and touch and experience Jesus concretely in the world today.

Through the church's members, people experience the gift of God's love. For members of the church, being the presence of Jesus as a community is an awesome responsibility.

The Seven Sacraments

You may be wondering how the seven sacraments of the Catholic Church fit in with Jesus as the sacrament of God and the church as the sacrament of Jesus. First, let's identify the seven sacraments:

Baptism, Confirmation, and the Eucharist are called Sacraments of Christian Initiation because they bring people, or initiate them, into the life of the Catholic Church. The sacraments of Penance and Reconciliation and the Anointing of the Sick are called the Sacraments of Healing because they bring healing, comfort, and strength when people need forgiveness or when they are ill. Holy Orders and Matrimony are called Sacraments of Service because they bring people into

The Sacraments of Christian Initiation

Baptism

Confirmation

Eucharist

The Sacraments of Healing

Penance
and Reconciliation

Anointing
of the Sick

The Sacraments of Service

Holy Orders

Matrimony

particular ministries in the Church, as ordained clergy or as married people.

Through the seven sacraments, the Catholic Church carries on the life of Christ in the world. The sacraments are rituals carried out by communities that celebrate the saving moments of grace that happen for people in every-day life. They are special, intense moments when God's grace, the lov-ing life of the Trinity, is particularly focused and given to people, bearing fruit in them if they are open to it. For Catholics, the sacraments not only signify the saving change going on in the believer but also help bring about the change they celebrate.

For Review

1. What does it mean to say that Jesus is the original sacrament of God?
2. What does it mean to say that the church is the sacrament of Jesus?
3. List the seven sacraments according to the categories given in the text.

The Sacraments of Christian Initiation

The next three sections consider the deeper meaning of each sacrament. Rather than simply describe the ritual of each sacrament, the text tries to show the meaning that is "under-neath" the sacrament, by way of a story of a saving moment from the life of a young person. Read the story as a kind of parable of what happens to a person in that sacrament. Each story will lead into a brief description of what the sacrament is and what it does for those who enter into it with an open spirit.

Baptism: Celebrating New Life and Community

Paige remembered her first day at the new school. She'd been especially nervous because it seemed like so much was at stake in changing schools—like her whole future. What if she didn't fit in?

She recalled that within fifteen minutes of setting foot in Gibbons High, she had met seven kids who were really friendly. A girl named Brianna had been assigned to take her around to classes and introduce her to everybody. Within a few weeks, Brianna was one of her best friends.

But Paige had had a problem with shoplifting. Before coming to Gibbons, she had been caught shoplifting at a mall. She was questioned by police, had to go to court, and was put on probation. It had been a wake-up call that things were going in the wrong direction. It had also been a signal to her mom and dad that Paige needed help to change. They decided she needed a fresh start with new friends who would not drag her down.

Now, having been at the school for six months, Paige was feeling great relief. Her new friends weren't perfect, but they were headed in the right direction. She had turned away from the trouble she'd been in, was doing well in school, and had a part in the school play. She felt like she really belonged at Gibbons.

Identify a time when you had a fresh start. What made the fresh start possible?

Baptism The first of the seven sacraments, by which one becomes a member of the Catholic Church through new life in Jesus Christ.

The Sacrament

Paige's story gives us some idea of the meaning underlying the sacrament of Baptism. **Baptism** is about being welcomed into a new life in the community of Jesus Christ. The sacrament celebrates leaving behind an old life of being a slave to sin and embracing the freedom and responsibility of life in the community of Christ, the church. It is "dying" to an old self in order to be raised up to a new self—somewhat like Paige's experience.

You may be most familiar with Baptism for babies. But in the early centuries of the church, Baptism was mostly for adults. These adults were often Gentiles, and by being baptized they were changing their lives in a significant and sometimes dangerous way. They were rejecting the Roman state religion, in which the emperor was given godlike status, to follow Jesus, who they believed was the true Son of God. They rejected the moral values of Roman culture, which were centered around wealth, power, and personal pleasure, to embrace the nearly opposite moral values of Jesus.

Today, when babies are baptized, their parents want to bring them into the community of Jesus Christ, so they profess their own faith on the child's behalf. Godparents, chosen by the parents, participate in the Baptism and are responsible for supporting the parents in helping the young Christian "grow into" Christian life. The entire community welcomes the child as well and pledges to support the parents and the child as they grow in the life of Christ.

The sacrament uses water to ritualize coming into this new life. The priest (or deacon, or, in case of necessity, a baptized layperson) pours water on the person being baptized three times, or immerses the person in water three times, while saying,

Recall some memorable experiences you've had that involved water. Have you had any frightening experiences with water? Have you had fun experiences with water? Why is water a sign of both death and life?

"I baptize you in the name of the Father, and of the Son, and of the Holy Spirit" (*The Order of Baptism of Children*, 23). The water symbolizes and brings about the cleansing and purifying action of the Holy Spirit in the person. It also recalls how God saved the Israelites in the waters of the sea by bringing them out of slavery in Egypt to freedom on the other side of the sea—just as God is saving us today. Other symbolic actions—anointing with oil, lighting a candle, and wearing a new white garment—also convey meaning in the ritual. But the water rite is essential.

Adults who want to be baptized prepare and come into the community in a step-by-step process that can last a year or longer. Through this process, called the Rite of Christian Initiation of Adults (RCIA), candidates for Baptism, called catechumens, are accompanied by a sponsor as they learn about the Catholic faith. The high point of the pro-

Water: The Perfect Symbol for Baptism

Consider these questions about water:

- Can you recall a moment you experienced refreshing cold water after an outdoor activity on a hot day?
- Would you believe that the average person's body is made up of 60 percent water (although it can vary from 45 percent to 75 percent)? It's true!
- Did you know that if you consume no food and water, you will die from lack of water (three to five days) long before you die from lack of food (two to three weeks)?
- Have you ever been pulled underwater suddenly and didn't know which way to swim to get to the surface?

Water is a symbol of both life and death. A large part of our body is comprised of water, and we constantly need to drink fluids to survive. But water can be destructive. Think of floods and drowning. This is what makes water such a perfect symbol for Baptism. Baptism symbolizes the death of the old self, the self that lived spiritually separated from God, but at the same time gives birth to a new life, lived in spiritual union with God.

cess takes place in a ceremony at the Easter Vigil, where candidates for Baptism celebrate all three Sacraments of Christian Initiation—Baptism, Confirmation, and the Eucharist—in one great community ritual.

Confirmation: Celebrating the Grace of the Spirit's Gifts

Every day after school, Lucas went to an apartment in his building to look after nine-year-old D. J., whose parents would come home after five o'clock. It was an okay way to make some spending money, and, he had to admit, it could even be fun.

The fun came to a halt one day though, when D. J.'s parents decided to separate. Lucas found out about it from D. J., who was grimly kicking up grass in front of the apartment building when Lucas arrived after school. "My stupid parents—they hate each other! My Dad's moving out tonight."

Lucas murmured, "Wow, that's tough. I'm sorry." But the little boy just kept kicking up grass and scowling. Lucas's attempts to be funny and his suggestion to play some video games or throw a football fell flat. D. J. was not interested, period. Several afternoons went by like this. Heavy gloom hung over everything.

Confirmation The sacrament by which Christians who have been baptized become more fully initiated into the Catholic Church through an outpouring of the Holy Spirit. Confirmation strengthens people to better be like Jesus in the world.

Gifts of the Holy Spirit The seven gifts received at Baptism and strengthened through Confirmation to help people live as followers of Jesus Christ.

One night when Lucas was home, stretched out on his bed listening to music, he thought about D. J. and how powerless he felt to do anything for this kid. Almost without being aware of it, he sighed a little prayer: "God, I don't know what to do. Just help me out with D. J., okay?"

The next afternoon, D. J. was waiting for Lucas with his now familiar cold stare. Instead of suggesting fun things that D. J. would turn down, this time Lucas said: "You know, D. J., you look like you've got so much going on inside you. I know if I were you right now, I'd be feeling lots of awful stuff." D. J. softened his hard expression a bit, giving Lucas an opening to ask, "You want to talk about it?"

With that, D. J. burst into tears. Lucas put his arm around him, and the little boy sobbed. For half an hour, D. J. poured out his heart, which was full of anger at his parents, fear for the future, self-blame (Did his parents break up because of him?), and loss. After that flood of feelings, D. J. seemed relieved; the weight on him felt lighter. Lucas remembered his prayer from the night before, thinking to himself: "Hey, I guess God helped me know what to do. Pretty amazing."

The Sacrament

For Catholics, the sacrament called **Confirmation** recognizes that once someone has entered the new life of Baptism, their attempt to be like Jesus in the world has just begun. Confirmation strengthens the graces received in Baptism so that a person can better be like Jesus in the world. In Confirmation, a person is "sealed in the Spirit," reminded that the Spirit given to them in Baptism is always with them to inspire, lead, and give them strength.

The **Gifts of the Holy Spirit**, given in Baptism, are the ways the Spirit acts within a person's life. Confirmation strengthens these gifts, which are wisdom, courage, understanding, right judgment, knowledge, reverence, and wonder and awe in God's presence. Which of the seven Gifts of the Holy Spirit do you think Lucas was responding to in the story?

In the early centuries of the church, Confirmation and Baptism were celebrated in the same community gathering, just as is done today at the Easter Vigil with catechumens being initiated into the Catholic Church. Today, most Catholics are baptized as infants. So Confirmation is usually celebrated years later, when a young person can understand the power of the Holy Spirit and be more aware of, and responsive to, the Spirit's activity in their life. The bishop usually presides at the celebrations of Confirmation for young people. The essential rite of the sacrament is the bishop's anointing of the candidate's forehead with sacred oil (a symbol of strengthening, cleansing, healing, and joy) while saying the words, "Be sealed with the Gift of the Holy Spirit" (*The Order of Confirmation*, 9).

Review the list of the seven Gifts of the Holy Spirit. Which ones seem most needed today by people your age?

Sacred Oil

The sacred oil used in Baptism and Confirmation is called chrism. It is perfumed olive oil that has been blessed by a bishop. In biblical times, olive oil was precious and was used for many purposes. Oil was used for light and cooking. It was used to clean and soothe wounds (see Luke 10:34). It was used to anoint someone who was dedicated to a special role in the community, especially kings and prophets (see Exodus 29:7 and 1 Samuel 16:13). And oil was also used to clean and protect dead bodies from rapid decomposition (see Mark 16:1).

All these purposes of oil can be applied symbolically to Jesus. He is a healer. He is a prophet and king. Jesus being anointed by one or more women before his death (see Matthew 26:6–13, Mark 14:3–9, Luke 7:36–50, and John 12:1–8) reminds us of these meanings. They are why Jesus is given the title Christ, which literally means "anointed one." As the sacraments prepare Christians to share in the mission of Jesus, it makes sense that anointing is part of the sacramental rituals.

Eucharist: Celebrating the Grace of Giving Ourselves

After thirteen years on the move with her mother, Tess, now seventeen, was weary of it all. Would she ever have solid friends, a consistent school to go to, or a place to call home? It was hard spending her life in shelters, every so often getting into a city she and her mom thought might be the answer—only to have it all fall apart and then hitting the road again.

Now here they were in another shelter in a small Midwestern city. This was different from a lot of the other shelters though. This one was more like a home, with people living there who cared about them and called them their "guests." That sounded funny, but they said it was all part of being a Catholic Worker house.

Tess's mother was so happy in this place that she started singing again. Pretty soon she was in the kitchen, bustling around and helping out like she loved to do. Because everyone was like family in this house, people could pitch in however they wanted. The day her mother started baking, Tess knew things were looking up. Soon her mother's fabulous cinnamon rolls were coming out of the oven every morning, followed later by fragrant loaves of bread, and then several kinds of pies.

Tess herself caught the spirit of her mother's generosity, and she began painting a mural of color-ful cartoon characters on the walls of the basement, where the children who were guests would play with the house toys.

It was quite remarkable—the change in the mother and the daughter who had come to the shelter in fear and despair. Tess and her mother felt a sense of joyful hope they had not felt for a long time.

Tess and her mother shared a broken, poor life; yet they had gifts to offer. Tess's mother had her love of baking and her great skills in the kitchen. Tess had artistic talent and a spirit of fun with children. They found a community where they could share their gifts with others, including those who were home-less like them. God's grace was at work, transform-ing Tess's offerings and her mother's offerings into life for themselves and all those around them.

Think about a time someone offered their gifts in service to you. How would you describe how that felt?

The Sacrament

The Eucharist is the central saving act for Catholics, the core of their life in Jesus Christ. In the Eucha-rist, simple gifts of bread and wine, which are the fruit of the earth and vine and the work of human hands, are offered to God by the priest on behalf of the people. Then those gifts are transformed by God into nourishment for the people's spirit—Jesus himself, his Body and Blood given back to them and shared as food and drink for the journey of life.

The Mass, another name for the Eucharist, celebrates Jesus' sacrificial gift of himself to all humankind by dying on the cross so long ago. Catholics believe the sacrificial Mass makes the power of Jesus' dying and rising present today. It brings Jesus' death and Resurrection into the midst of the gathered community and enables the members to live out this Paschal Mystery in their daily lives—as Tess and her mother were living it in their gifts of themselves and their talents to those at the Catholic Worker house.

The ritual of the Eucharist has two essential parts: the Liturgy of the Word and the Liturgy of the Eucharist. In the Liturgy of the Word, the Scriptures are proclaimed and reflected on as spiritual nourishment. In the Liturgy of the Eucharist, with a priest as presider, the bread and wine are offered to God. Then they are transformed into the Body and Blood of Jesus Christ by the power of the Holy Spirit and shared by the people as food for their life's journey. Not only are the gifts of bread and wine changed in the Eucharist; those who participate are changed as well.

For Review

1. What does Baptism celebrate? What ritual action and words symbolize what happens to a person in Baptism?
2. When infants are baptized, who professes faith for them?
3. What is the meaning of Confirmation? What happens for individuals in this sacrament?
4. What is the essential rite for Confirmation?
5. What does the Mass, or the Eucharist, recall and make present today?
6. What are the two essential parts of the Eucharist? What happens in each part?

The Sacraments of Healing

Reconciliation: Celebrating the Grace of Forgiveness

Tomás was bored and wanted to get out of the house. It bugged him that Greg said he would rather stay home and watch television than go to the gym to work out. Over the phone, Tomás let Greg know how disgusted he was with him: "If you'd stop being such a couch potato, maybe you'd have some friends."

When Tomás saw Greg the next day at school, Greg's face turned red, and he looked the other way. Tomás remembered the cutting remark he had made to Greg, and he felt bad about it. He gathered his courage, caught up with Greg down the hall, looked him in the eye, and said: "Hey, Greg. That was a dumb thing I said yesterday. I wish I hadn't said it. You think you can forgive me?"

Think about a relationship in your life that needs healing—for example, a relationship with a family member, friend, or teacher. How might you best seek forgiveness and reconciliation?

Greg broke into a broad grin. "Yeah, if you can put up with me, I can put up with you." They went off together talking nonstop about the game the day before on television.

When we hurt someone, we need to acknowledge what we have done. The wound of sin is real, and we need to ask for forgiveness to heal the wound and be reconciled (brought back together) with that person. We also need to do so for ourselves, for we are hurt by our own sin. Tomás found that out in a saving moment of asking and receiving forgiveness.

Sacraments and Healing

A Young Person's Reflection

Demetrios, a student from Our Lady of the Hills College Preparatory School, wrote this reflection on the sacraments of healing:

> We are healed by the sacraments in many astounding ways, especially in Penance and Reconciliation. In this sacrament, we are healed in a sense by our own admission of guilt and sin. The realization that we are fallen and the ability to choose to amend our ways are the first part of our journey of healing. The encouragement and absolution Christ gives us through this sacrament heals my soul. The penance I do afterward helps me begin to change my life and find my way back to Christ. All have had suffering or failure in our lives, and we should all find healing in the sacraments as they are springs of grace.

The Sacrament

The sacrament of **Penance and Reconciliation** is the only Catholic sacrament with two names, which describe the effects of the sacrament. Asking for and receiving forgiveness for a sin, with the intention to not repeat the sin, is called **penance**. The process of restoring broken relationships with God, the faith community, and those hurt by one's sin is called **reconciliation**. This often requires additional words and actions, such as returning something that was stolen or making amends with a family member or friend.

The sacramental ritual includes the confession of one's sins to a priest, the expression of one's sorrow for sin and intention to turn the behavior

Penance and Reconciliation The sacrament that celebrates God's forgiveness of sin, through which the sinner is reconciled with both God and the Catholic Church.

penance Asking for and receiving forgiveness for sin, with the intention to not repeat the sin.

reconciliation The process of restoring broken relationships with God, the faith community, and those hurt by one's sin.

around, and the words of forgiveness (absolution) given by the priest. The priest may also suggest some actions the person can take to repair the damage caused by their sin. Through these words and actions, the person is reconciled to God, to themselves, and to the whole community.

When someone sins, they hurt not just themselves or another person, they harm the entire community. So they need to be reconciled with God and the whole community. That is why Catholics confess their sins to a priest in the sacrament. When the priest raises a hand in blessing over the person or lays a hand on the person's shoulder and says the words of forgiveness, he offers that forgiveness on behalf of God and the whole Christian community.

Anointing of the Sick: Celebrating the Grace of Healing Life's Hurts

As a child, Mariel had struggled with a learning disability. She often could not recognize words or even individual letters. By fifth grade, this issue cleared enough for Mariel to become an avid, though slow, reader. By high school, she was still a marginal student, taking twice as much time on homework and tests as her classmates.

Ms. Totino, the social studies teacher, asked to see Mariel after she got a D on a Friday quiz. "Why bother?" thought Mariel. She saw her education ending next year, after she graduated from high school. College was out of the question, and she just hoped to land a good paying job in a local restaurant.

At their meeting, Ms. Totino commented on the test briefly and then asked Mariel what she liked to do outside of school. Mariel sensed genuine interest and was soon talking excitedly about the books she loved and, more shyly, about the journal she had

I magine or recall confessing a sin or wrongdoing to a priest or some other person. Does confession seem like it is easy or hard for people? Why?

kept for years. "You'd enjoy my creative spellings," Mariel chuckled. After that, Mariel began stopping by after class for chats. Ms. Totino talked with her like an adult, once telling Mariel that she herself had not been a great student in school. In college, she used to say that a C stood for "Celebrate!"

Mariel began to feel better about herself. She even surprised herself by getting curious about local two-year colleges and vocational training. Ms. Totino visited Mariel's parents and talked encouragingly about her opportunities. At the end of the semester, Mariel sent Ms. Totino a card thanking her for "the best year I've had in school."

Sometimes life deals us a blow that leaves us wounded and shaky. The suffering happens not because we have done anything wrong, but simply because life inevitably brings such hurts—an illness, whether physical or psychological; an accident; a disability; or just a gradually weakened state that comes with getting older.

When Ms. Totino took a genuine interest in Mariel, the hurt in Mariel gradually healed. She grew stronger, more confident, and more trusting

Think of a time you needed support and love because you were feeling wounded and shaky. Were you able to get that support, and if so, how did it come to you?

about the future. Through the saving moment of Ms. Totino's concern, Mariel was being healed.

The Sacrament

Anointing of the Sick is about healing the hurts of life, especially when the hurts involve physical or mental illness, a serious injury, or a condition that makes a person weak and vulnerable to more hurt or even death. Mariel's situation and the help her teacher gave her are a kind of parable to show us what the sacrament basically is all about—receiving the love of God as a healing touch from our community when we are laid low by the hurts of life.

The main symbolic actions of the sacrament are the laying on of hands and anointing with oil by the priest, along with the prayers that ask for God's healing. These actions, done on behalf of the whole community, convey God's care, strengthening power, and healing. In some cases, physical healing may actually take place after the sacrament. But whether a physical recovery happens, the sacrament brings about healing of

Anointing of the Sick   The sacrament in which a seriously ill, aging, or dying person is anointed by a priest and prayed over by him and others gathered with them. One need not be dying to receive the sacrament.

a person's spirit at a time when that is needed as much as a physical cure.

Anyone who is seriously ill (either physically or emotionally), injured, or suffering from the increasing frailty of old age can celebrate this sacrament. When a person is near death, special prayers entrusting the dying person to God are included, and the dying person receives the Eucharist for the last time as a kind of "food for the journey" back to God.

For Review

1. What is the purpose of Penance and Reconciliation, and what does it celebrate?
2. What does the ritual of Penance and Reconciliation include?
3. Why do Catholics confess their sins to a priest instead of asking forgiveness from God privately?
4. What is Anointing of the Sick concerned with?
5. What are the ritual actions of Anointing of the Sick, and what do they convey?
6. Who can receive Anointing of the Sick?

The Sacraments of Service

Holy Orders: Celebrating the Grace of Leading as a Servant

Mateo's job as class president was to get everyone moving on the ninth-grade class project. By March they had raised five thousand dollars, enough to give them a fabulous overnight trip to a huge theme park, with time still left to raise more money and plan the trip.

But Mateo began to wonder if they should really spend that much money on themselves. As part of his Catholic school's outreach program, many of his classmates had been helping provide meals at their city's overnight shelters. The shelter's mattresses were old and uncomfortable, but they did not have the funds to purchase new ones. So Mateo proposed an idea to his classmates.

"What if we use half the money we've raised to help the shelter with new beds?" he asked. "That's half the money they need. Then we could issue a community challenge to pay for the other half." After much discussion, they put it to a vote. Mateo's proposal was approved by a narrow margin.

The local paper ran the story with their challenge. Amazingly, not only did they get the needed donations for new mattresses, their next fundraisers were so successful that their trip was covered too. "It's so great to see this community support," Mateo said afterward. "I'm so proud of our class for coming together to help the shelter."

Give an example of someone who has been able to lead as a servant from your experience, the news, or history. What were this person's qualities of leadership and service?

Through his concern about the homeless people in his community, Mateo sensed he was following Jesus' call to help those in need. As a natural leader, Mateo moved people's hearts and got them excited about the dream. He was a leader who knew how to bring the community together in service to others, and that is the kind of leader Jesus was.

The Sacrament

Holy Orders is a sacrament that celebrates a permanent ministry, or service, in the Catholic Church—the calling, or vocation, of those who are entrusted with official leadership as deacons, priests, and bishops. Because the sacraments are so central to Catholicism, these ordained leaders have a crucial role in presiding at the Church's sacraments.

Mateo was called not only to lead but also to serve. Ordained members of the Church are called to do likewise.

Holy Orders The sacrament by which baptized men are ordained as bishops, priests, or deacons for permanent ministry as leaders in the Catholic Church.

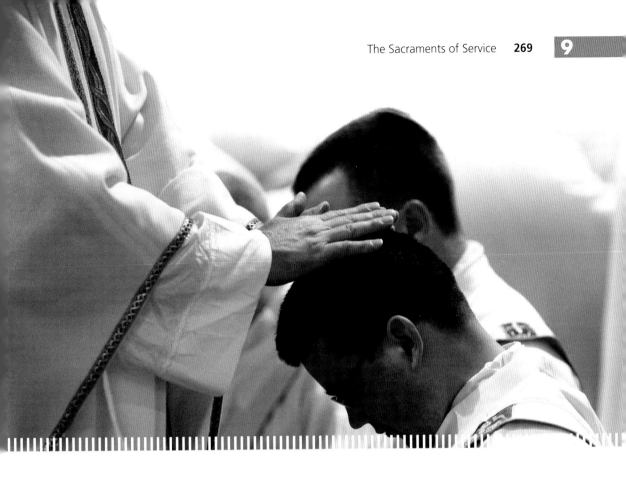

They hold out the vision of the Kingdom of God to people. They try to move people to bring about that vision by encouraging everyone to share their gifts and talents. They make sure all are welcomed and included. And they have to know how to lead others in celebrating. This is the special, challenging work of those called by God and chosen by the Catholic Church to be ordained as deacons, priests, and bishops.

In Holy Orders, the rites for ordination of a priest include the laying on of hands by the bishop, who conveys his authority from the Apostles themselves. Anointing the candidate's hands with oil is also part of the ritual, for the priest will be using his hands in many sacramental ways in his ministry—laying hands on others; using his hands to anoint others with oil; and blessing, breaking, and sharing the bread and wine of the Eucharist.

Think about the qualities of effective leaders. Which do you feel are crucial to have as an ordained deacon, priest, or bishop?

Matrimony: Celebrating the Grace of a Faithful Bond

Describe the marriage of two people you know who relate to each other as close, faithful friends.

Natanya and Cole had been through a lot together. In the same school since kindergarten, they had become best friends in third grade. From playing together as little kids, vacationing together, and working on homework together, the two were rarely apart.

Natanya and Cole's friendship grew in high school. They became best listeners to each other, best advice givers, and best encouragers. They shared all their ups and downs about their boyfriends and girlfriends with each other. They even knew how to have a good argument. Most of all, they cared about each other so much that they wanted what was best for the other one even when it didn't suit them personally.

This was becoming a deep, mature friendship. Years, geographical separations, and different life choices would never be able to destroy it. Natanya and Cole were friends for life.

Friendship—especially the kind of close, faithful, loving friendship that Natanya and Cole had—is sacred. It demonstrates something of how God loves us. God is forever faithful, seeing us through the hills and valleys of our life. God hangs in there for the long haul and calls us back with love when we have been distant and aloof, or just out of sorts. A faithful friendship mirrors that kind of faithful love in their lifelong relationship. For those who are called, marriage is the ultimate experience of friendship and love.

The Sacrament

Marriage between a man and a woman is, above all else, a deep, lifelong, faithful friendship. If the man and the woman are not friends, their marriage will not survive, or it will survive only as an empty shell without any meaning. **Matrimony** is a sacrament that celebrates the exclusive, committed love that mirrors God's love for us—a permanent covenant to always be there for the other in love and service.

Marriage has a special dimension that Natanya and Cole's friendship did not have. The bond and commitment of marriage is expressed by a woman and a man in the most intimate physical way possible—through sexual intercourse. In the union of their bodies, a woman and a man symbolize the closeness and unity of God with us. And in their physical union they also participate in God's power to create new life.

Matrimony The sacrament by which a baptized man and a baptized woman establish a lifelong partnership and commit to faithfully loving each other for life.

The essence of the sacramental ritual is simple. It consists of the exchange of vows by the couple, witnessed by a priest or deacon, who promise their commitment to each other for their whole life. Often the ceremony takes place during a celebration of Mass. Ideally, it is not a private ceremony but one where the wider community of the couple's friends and family is there to witness and support the couple in their commitment.

Questions and Answers about Catholic Weddings

Can Catholics get married at a park? A sacramental marriage almost always takes place in a church or chapel to symbolize that the couple belongs to a community of faith and that community supports them in their married life together. Special permission is required to get married in a location other than a church.

Can Catholics marry non-Catholics? Of course! If a Catholic marries another baptized Christian, it is considered a sacramental marriage. If a Catholic marries a non-Christian, it is a valid marriage but considered non-sacramental.

What are the requirements for a Catholic marriage? The Catholic Church does have requirements for sacramental marriage. Neither person can already be in a valid marriage, both must freely give their consent to marry, they must have the intention to marry for life and be faithful to each other, and they must be open to having children.

For Review

1. In what ways are ordained people in the Catholic Church intended to lead as servants?
2. What rites are involved in the ordination of priests, and what do they signify?
3. What does the sacrament of Matrimony celebrate?
4. What does the marriage ritual consist of?

The Liturgical Year

The ritual celebrations of the seven sacraments are part of the Catholic Church's **liturgy**. Liturgy is the public, communal, and official worship of the Church. Liturgy is public because it is open to everyone. It is communal because it always takes place within a community of people. It is official because it must follow the approved rites (words and actions) of the Catholic Church.

Celebrating the sacraments is one of the things that unites Catholics around the world. The Eucharist, or Mass, is the central liturgy for Catholics. In fact, in Catholic circles, if someone says "the weekend liturgy," everyone knows they are talking about Sunday (or Saturday evening) Mass. Most Catholic parishes have both weekend and weekday Masses. These Masses follow a yearly cycle, so that wherever you are in the world, every Catholic community is reading the same Bible readings and celebrating the same holy days, on the same day.

When you think of a year, the calendar year or maybe the academic year probably come to mind. But the Church has a special year, called the **liturgical year**, to mark the celebration of the liturgies. The liturgical year is built around important events in the life of Jesus, such as his birth, life, death, Resurrection, and Ascension. The liturgies in the liturgical year help people remember the power of God's love made real in those events. Yet they are not simply past events that Catholics remember. Catholics believe that Jesus' life, death, and Resurrection are happening now and saving people now. And they point to a future day when all creation will be brought into unity in the Kingdom of God.

Let's take a quick tour through the seasons of the liturgical year. The calendar on the following page can help you follow along.

liturgy The Catholic Church's official, public, communal prayer. The most important liturgy is the Eucharist, or the Mass.

liturgical year The annual cycle of holy days and seasons that celebrates the events and mysteries of Jesus' birth, life, death, Resurrection, and Ascension.

Liturgical Calendar

Advent

The liturgical year begins in late November or early December, on the fourth Sunday before Christmas. These four weeks are the liturgical season of **Advent**. Advent means "coming," and this season is a prepparation for the coming of Jesus by celebrating his birth into the world. The mood is hopeful anticipation, and the Scripture readings at Mass focus on God's promise to send a savior to deliver people from sin and death. It is a time for people to take life a little more slowly and to focus on what

Advent The season in the liturgical year during which Christians prepare for the Christmas season.

they need to do to allow God to enter their hearts more fully. Many faith communities and families mark the passing of the four weeks by lighting the candles of an Advent wreath.

Christmas

Christmas, on December 25, celebrates the birth of Jesus and the mystery of the Incarnation. God has come into the world as a human, as a child born in humble, poor circumstances. He is God with us, bringing hope and joy to the world by sharing our human condition.

Christmas Day is the start of the Christmas season, which lasts until the Baptism of the Lord, the third Sunday after Christmas Day. In days past, this was the traditional time that people would exchange gifts, go caroling, and have Christmas parties. In some cultures, gifts are still exchanged on Epiphany (January 6), which celebrates the Magi (Wise Men) who came from the east to visit Jesus.

Explain the difference between the Advent season and the Christmas season. What types of spiritual activities are most appropriate in each season?

Ordinary Time

We generally have a routine that helps us do the ordinary things that make up daily life. For example, think of the time between the end of a break and finals week at school—there's a daily routine in which you are learning and growing but not at high intensity. The liturgical year has the same balance. After the celebration of the Christmas season, a short period of Ordinary Time follows.

During Ordinary Time, the Scripture readings focus on the events of Jesus' life between his birth and his death and Resurrection. It is a time when Christians reflect on the things Jesus lived and taught so that they make their values and attitudes more like his. Ordinary Time is divided into two periods. The first period is between Christmas and Lent, and the second period is between the end of the Easter season and the next Advent.

Ordinary Time
The period in the liturgical year during which Christians reflect on the things Jesus taught and lived so that they might make their values and attitudes more like his.

Catholics burn palm leaves from the previous year's Palm Sunday celebrations to create the ashes used on Ash Wednesday.

© sterlsev / iStockphoto.com

Lent and Holy Week

Lent is a solemn, reflective season of the liturgical year that is the preparation for Easter. It begins on Ash Wednesday and lasts forty days, until Easter (the forty days do not include the Sundays during Lent). Lent recalls the forty days that Jesus spent in the desert before beginning his public ministry. During Lent, Christians are called to renew themselves through fasting, prayer, and almsgiving (giving money and service to those in need).

Holy Week begins a week before Easter Day, on Palm Sunday. During Holy Week, Catholics remember the events of the final days of Jesus' earthly life, beginning with his triumphal entry into Jerusalem on Palm Sunday. The last three days of Holy Week—from the evening of Holy Thursday to the evening of Easter Sunday—are the high point of the

Lent The forty-day period in the liturgical year that is preparation for Easter, recalling the forty days that Jesus spent in the desert in preparation for his mission.

Holy Week Beginning on Palm Sunday, the weeklong remembrance of the final days of Jesus' earthly life.

liturgical year. This period is called the **Triduum**. Following are brief descriptions of special liturgies celebrated on Thursday, Friday, and Saturday:

- **Holy Thursday.** In this liturgy, participants remember the Last Supper and Jesus' gift of himself in the Eucharist. A foot-washing ritual is part of the liturgy, reminding participants that Jesus calls them to serve one another as his followers. On this day, the people gathered also recall the institution of the priesthood.

- **Good Friday.** In this liturgy, participants remember Jesus' Passion and death. The liturgy is somber and starts and ends with a bare altar. During the liturgy, the people gathered venerate (show love and respect for) the cross in some way, in appreciation of Jesus' sacrifice.

- **Holy Saturday.** The liturgy on Holy Saturday, the Easter Vigil, is held at night. It is the greatest celebration of the liturgical year, recalling and reliving the joy of Jesus' Resurrection. The celebration incorporates rituals of darkness and light and of water blessing, and lots of Scripture reading. But the highlight is the Baptism, Confirmation, and First Communion of the catechumens, those people who have been preparing to become Catholic.

Recall that Lent is a time when many Catholics choose to practice some form of self-discipline to strengthen their spiritual life. What type of self-discipline would you most benefit from?

Triduum The last three days of Holy Week, from the evening of Holy Thursday to the evening of Easter Sunday. This period is the high point of the liturgical year.

The **Symbol** of the **Cross**

The cross has been a Christian symbol since the early days of Christianity. Christians wear it and display it because, as the instrument used for Jesus' death, it is a symbol of his sacrifice. If you think about it, wearing a cross is a little morbid, sort of like wearing a small image of an electric chair. But for those who wear the cross as a religious symbol, it serves as a reminder that Jesus willingly sacrificed his life because of his great love for us.

Catholic churches and many Catholic homes display a particular kind of cross, called a crucifix. A crucifix is a cross with Jesus body attached. It is a more graphic symbol, intended to visually remind us that Jesus Christ, the Son of God, surrendered himself to a torturous death for the salvation of the world.

Easter Season

Easter and the Easter season are the primary focus of the liturgical year. Easter celebrates the wonder and joy of Christ's Resurrection, the most holy of days and the climax of the liturgical year. The Easter season goes on for fifty days after Easter, until Pentecost. During this time, the Sunday readings focus on the appearances of the Risen Christ and on the growth of the early church (found in the Acts of the Apostles). Because of the events of Easter, Christians dare to hope for their own Resurrection and eternal life with God.

This season is marked with two special holy days. Forty days after Easter is the Ascension of the Lord. (Although this is a Thursday, it is celebrated in many dioceses on the following Sunday.) On this holy day, Christians remember how Jesus said farewell to his disciples to live in glory with his heavenly Father and to be present to all his followers without the limitations of time and space. Fifty days after Easter is the celebration of Pentecost, remembering the coming of the Holy Spirit. After Pentecost, the second period of Ordinary Time continues until another liturgical year begins on the first Sunday of Advent.

For **Review**

1. Describe what "liturgy" is.
2. What is the central liturgy of the Catholic Church?
3. What does the liturgical year celebrate, and why is it important?
4. List the main seasons within the liturgical year, and describe what they celebrate.

reflect

Living the Sacraments

In this chapter, we have tried to show that the sacraments of the Catholic Church are not some "churchy" invention separate from the rest of life; rather, the sacraments are intimately connected with the spiritual realities that are part of everyday life. Even more, Catholics believe they give unique access to God's graces—that is, the gifts that help them be more closely united to Christ and his mission.

For Catholics, sacraments bring together and celebrate the saving moments of life, the times when people are touched by God's grace and transformed in some small or large way, even when not aware that it is God who is acting within them. These might be moments of finding life new and fresh again, of responding to the Spirit's gifts, of giving oneself and being nourished and changed in the process, of forgiving another and being forgiven, of being healed by the love of our community, of being a faithful friend, or of leading others while serving them.

Catholics believe that when those saving moments are celebrated in the seven sacraments, God is present in a special, intense way. Those participating are transformed by the power of God's love to become, more and more, the marvelous people they are meant to be. And in doing so, the transforming power of the sacraments can reach the whole world. The sacraments carry on the saving life, death, and Resurrection of Christ in the world today.

chapter **10**

Spirituality and Prayer: Growing in Life with God

IN THIS CHAPTER

Spirituality: 281
Toward a Full Life with God

Prayer: Nourishing a Relationship   291
with God

Prayer and Community   306

Spirituality: Toward a Full Life with God

Catholics believe human beings are meant to be with God now in this life and forever with God after death. Experiences of God's loving presence in this life are only partial and incomplete, but rather than see that as a source of despair, Catholics see it as a source of hope. Saint Paul puts it this way: "At present we see indistinctly. . . . At present I know partially; then [in heaven] I shall know fully, as I am fully known" (1 Corinthians 13:12).

Experiences of God's presence in this life vary from person to person and can change over time. Some experience God as a deep peace untouched by life's problems. Some experience God as a close friend they can talk to about anything. Some experience God primarily in the loving words and actions of family and friends. Some experience God in the order and beauty of nature and the universe. Some do not recognize the presence of God in their experiences

at all or do so only in fleeting moments. And some experience God in "letting go" of whatever burdens them.

Catholic faith teaches that experiences of God's presence grow with focus and effort. In the first chapter, *spirituality* is defined as the ways we tend to our spiritual lives. In other words, our spirituality grows through the actions, beliefs, values, and attitudes we cultivate in our lives. These are the ways Catholics believe they become more and more identified with Jesus Christ, allowing God's love to flow into their thoughts, their actions, their worship and **prayer**, and their relationships with others.

Being Loved without Limits

Catholics believe that God loves each person, no matter who they are or what they have done. God's love is **unconditional**. It is a love that has no conditions or limits placed on it. God's love is not the kind that says, *I'll love you if you're good, and I'll love*

prayer Lifting up of one's mind and heart to God and communicating with God in a relationship of love.

unconditional Having no conditions or limits placed on it.

you even more if you're better or I'll love you if you prove what a great person you are or I'll love you as long as you don't disappoint me. Even doing really hateful or hurtful things does not stop God from loving us and wanting the best for us.

Experiencing the love other people have for us—our family, our friends, and trusted adults—is how many believers experience God's love. When someone is loved for *who they are,* not *what they do,* they get a hint of how God loves them. They feel accepted, secure, peaceful, and unthreatened. They feel like they can really be themselves without fear—like they don't have to pretend to be someone they're not. Have you ever been forgiven by someone for something bad you did that was tying you in knots of guilt? If so, you know what it feels like to be loved for who you are, not what you do. That kind of love brings healing and makes a person want to be their best self. To receive such love from others is a great and precious gift. But Catholics believe that even the most compassionate, accepting human being in the world cannot love others in the unbounded way God does—with no limits at all. God's love is grace at work in the lives of all people, renewing and transforming all who are open to it.

Knowing one is so loved by God is the beginning of wanting to grow close to God. In God's presence, people can be themselves without fear.

Describe what you think it would be like to experience unconditional love.

Being Ourselves with God

Alinda slumped into the chair in her bedroom. It was late already, and she had homework to do, but she felt so dragged down she didn't want to start it. She wasn't sick. . . . It was just another lame day. Her life seemed so pointless. It wasn't that she had such huge problems. After all, Alinda's mom or dad wasn't an alcoholic like Ellie's mom. Alinda wasn't pregnant or anything. She wasn't getting bad grades. Her parents didn't abuse her. She wasn't homeless, starving, or living through a war in a refugee camp. She didn't have any interesting, dramatic problems. So why did she feel so unhappy most of the time?

Rather than tackle *that* nauseating question, Alinda flipped open her assignment notebook. "May as well do religion first—easier than algebra." But the assignment was to respond to the writing prompt that appeared at the end of the chapter in her religion book: *Write a letter to God about whatever is going through your mind and heart right now. Don't worry. No one will see it but you and God.*

"Well, that's weird," pondered Alinda. "If no one else sees it, how will Mr. Connor know I did the homework?" However, the idea behind the assignment intrigued Alinda, and because she didn't really want to do algebra, she decided to do the religion project. It was her little way of declaring, "I'm doing this because I *want* to, not because I *have* to." Alinda was surprised at how easily the letter flowed out of her pen:

Dear God,

Hi. What's up? How are you doing? I am feeling pretty insecure. My name is Alinda, and I'm fifteen. I think I'm fat. That is my biggest hang-up. I really wish I would become anorexic or bulimic. I would stop when I reached 125 pounds. I always

look gross! I do soccer, swimming, and track, and I am bad at all of them. I am mediocre at swimming, but no matter how much I try I never excel.

I am also not very smart. I have a brother who's a lawyer and a sister at Harvard. I feel only a *little* pressure (hah!). They are naturally smart and didn't have to work hard for As. Okay, so I don't try extremely hard.

And I don't have a boyfriend. It seems as if I'll never get one! What am I doing WRONG? The worst is I always hang out with friends who make me jealous. Kyra, my friend, excels at all the things I'm bad at. She's an awesome soccer player and a track star. She gets good grades, is pretty, skinny, and has a ton of friends without even trying. I really like her but hate this feeling of jealousy. I feel like she is going to ditch me any minute. She appears comfortable in any circumstance and has no problems whatsoever. Makes me ill.

And I just recently found out that my mother, who I truly respect and love, was a total party animal before she met my dad—like booze, drugs, and sex! I wasn't supposed to know, and I wish I didn't. Now I'm feeling ashamed of her, and I hate it.

Okay, no big deal. I am just a regular screwed-up girl, no big problems, nothing much to say except I wish I accepted myself, or turned skinny really QUICK.

Alinda

Alinda stared at what she had written. "Oh, my God! That's the first time I've said any of that stuff to anyone!" Then she realized, "Oh, my God, it's because it *is* God! God's the only one I can be totally myself with." Then she almost tore the letter up, but stopped at the last second.

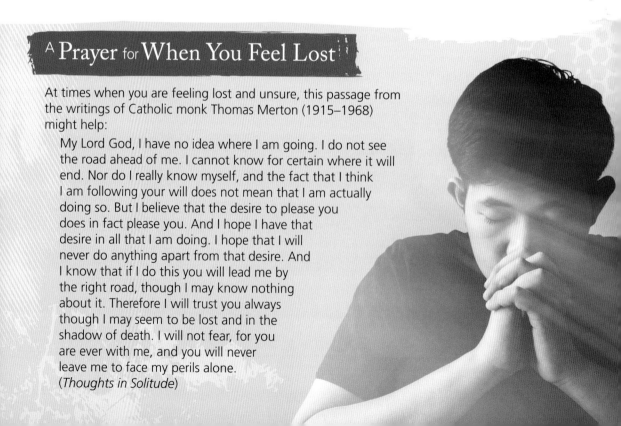

A Prayer for When You Feel Lost

At times when you are feeling lost and unsure, this passage from the writings of Catholic monk Thomas Merton (1915–1968) might help:

My Lord God, I have no idea where I am going. I do not see the road ahead of me. I cannot know for certain where it will end. Nor do I really know myself, and the fact that I think I am following your will does not mean that I am actually doing so. But I believe that the desire to please you does in fact please you. And I hope I have that desire in all that I am doing. I hope that I will never do anything apart from that desire. And I know that if I do this you will lead me by the right road, though I may know nothing about it. Therefore I will trust you always though I may seem to be lost and in the shadow of death. I will not fear, for you are ever with me, and you will never leave me to face my perils alone. (*Thoughts in Solitude*)

"There must be *some* other person I can talk to about this stuff," she thought. She hid the letter under her sweaters in the farthest corner of her bottom drawer, saving it for a time she might be able to share it with someone.

Alinda didn't do her algebra that night. She decided to go to bed and get a good night's sleep, setting the alarm for 6:00 a.m. to finish her homework. And she slept that night—a deep, peaceful sleep.

Alinda didn't immediately solve her problems of insecurity and feeling terribly let down by her mom. She didn't wake up skinny. And she didn't get a boyfriend right away. But she did discover something wonderful—that she could be herself with God, and God would not reject her. Perhaps over time, encouraged by God's acceptance, Alinda will come to accept and like herself. Maybe she will even develop deep friendships of give-and-take, where she does not feel inferior. And maybe she'll be able to forgive her mother for being less than perfect.

Growing in Trust

Like Alinda, many people have fears—of failure, rejection, lack of popularity, physical or emotional violence, pressures to do things that are harmful and wrong, not meeting others' expectations, being used or taken advantage of, poverty, disaster. Perhaps our fear is not anything specific— just an overall dread, a feeling that life could fall apart on us and we would not be able to cope.

Imagine writing a letter in which you share something significant about your inner life. Consider addressing your letter to God or to someone close to you. What would you share?

A Prayer of "Being Yourself"

Dear God,
I don't know who my friends are. I don't know who to trust. I've been betrayed by so many. Yet, you want me to forgive. If you love me, why would you want to hurt me? Do believe me when I say I want to believe in you. But how can I believe in something that I don't even know is there? Will you help me to understand and help me to believe in you?

(Megan O'Malley,
in *More Dreams Alive*)

© Stepanych / Shutterstock.com

What are your top three fears, the things you are most afraid of or worried about?

Imagine yourself in a situation where you are threatened by one of your top fears. Would you call on God? Why or why not?

Jesus' Response to Fears

When Jesus lived on earth as a human being, he felt the same fears we feel. He responded to his fears by trusting more deeply in his beloved Father. Even as Jesus prayed in great anguish over the terrible death that awaited him, he entrusted himself into his Father's hands: "'Father, if you are willing, take this cup away from me; still, not my will but yours be done'" (Luke 22:42). Later, as Jesus hung on the cross, he cried out to God, "Father, into your hands I commend my spirit'" (23:46). Jesus feared, but he also trusted.

Learning to Trust God

People who grow in trusting God work at it. Here are two simple spiritual practices that some people find helpful. The first is often simply called "turning

A sculpture of Jesus praying in anguish to the Father in the garden at Gethsemane.

it over to God." People do this when experiencing a negative feeling, such as fear, anxiety, or jealousy. The first step is to decide to give the feeling to God to carry. The next is to say a short prayer, such as: "God, I cannot handle this fear any longer. Help me turn it over to you." A person might do this many times. But little by little, the negative feeling will lose its power.

The second spiritual practice is similar. People call it "let go and let (or trust) God." A person might do this when they find themselves obsessing over something, going over it again and again in their head. It involves saying a short prayer, such as: "God, I want to be done worrying about how I did on that test. Help me give it over to you and trust that you will help me through whatever happens." Many people find it helpful to repeat the prayer. Gradually, the power of the obsession will weaken.

Learning to trust God does not mean that Christians are naive or that they let others walk all over them. They take precautions; they act reasonably; they get help when they need it. But they do not allow fear to rule them; they do not let their fears overtake them and crush them. Why? Because they firmly believe they are in God's hands. They are loved totally by God, and God is with them everywhere, in all ways, even in the worst situations.

The Lord Is My Shepherd

Psalm 23 is a good prayer for anxious times. Here's an excerpt:

The LORD is my shepherd;
there is nothing I lack.
In green pastures he makes me lie down;
to still waters he leads me;
he restores my soul.
He guides me along right paths
for the sake of his name.
Even though I walk through the valley of the shadow of death,
I will fear no evil, for you are with me.
(Verses 1–4)

Christians know that suffering and death are inescapable parts of life. But they also believe that not even suffering and death can destroy them. Jesus' Resurrection is the foundation of Christian trust and hope in God. And if people are open to the Spirit's work, God will raise them up too, turning their "little deaths" (rejections, failures, losses) into new life within and around them. When physical death comes, God will give them new life, life in union with God, beyond anything they could ever dream of.

"Please, God, Help Me!"

Here is an example of a teenager who was struggling with fear but also reaching out to God in trust. Like Alinda, this young person addressed God in a letter:

> Dear God,
>
> I'm the kind of person who is always happy and trying to solve my friends' problems, but when it comes to me having a problem, I always find myself alone with no one to talk to.
>
> I also have this fear of being put down. I usually don't ask people for favors or help because I'm afraid they might say no. I usually solve my problems by turning to drugs or alcohol. I know that doesn't solve much, but right now I don't know what else to do.
>
> I really want to stop, but I don't know how I can face my problems without pot or alcohol. Too many people have let me down before.
>
> Please, God, help me!
>
> (Anonymous)

This young person desperately needs help from a caring adult. But reaching out to God in trust may be the crucial first step before being able to reach out in trust to a human being who can help. On the other hand, for some people, taking the step of trusting a human being can enable them to trust God for the first time. Trust opens up possibilities for people that they did not even know were there, because they were too afraid to look beyond their fear. Trust in God helps people see themselves and the world with hope instead of despair.

Spirituality and the Good Times

Up to this point, we have looked at examples of people turning to God in times of trouble—when self-esteem is weak or fear is strong. During such times, a person's spirituality can bring comfort and transform their life in remarkable and dramatic ways. But what about the good times—when someone feels confident and strong, untroubled by fear? Does spirituality have a purpose when everything seems just right?

The answer is yes. Spirituality means becoming fully alive and, for Catholics and other believers, it means growing toward God, in good times as well as bad. Spirituality may not seem as necessary in the good times as it does in the hard times, but it remains valuable. Consider the following prayer, written by a high school student. This young woman's words describe a desire to grow closer to God and others when life is going well:

> God,
>
> Thank you for the life I live. Please help me to live this life with a positive outlook each day. Help me to develop into the person I'd like to be: an honest, giving, and healthy individual. Please grant me the courage to stand up against society and peer pressure as I draw up my own set of values. As I grow through my teenage

Imagine a conversation with a friend who calls out to God only when they are in trouble, but never thinks of God when things are going okay. What message from Catholicism could you offer this person?

Consider the idea that true Christian spirituality makes a person more free, courageous, and joyful. Why are some Christians fearful, judgmental, or unhappy?

A Prayer of Complete Dedication

When he was a young man, Saint Ignatius of Loyola was completely dedicated to power, fame, and wealth. But a serious injury on the battlefield led him to examine his life's purpose. He completely dedicated himself to God as a result. This is his prayer:

Take, Lord, and receive
all my liberty,
my memory, my understanding,
and my entire will,
all that I have and possess.
You have given all to me.
To you, Lord, I return it.
All is yours.
Dispose of it
wholly according to your will.
Give me your love and your grace.
That is enough for me.

(Elisabeth Meier Tetlow,
*The Spiritual Exercises of
Saint Ignatius Loyola*)

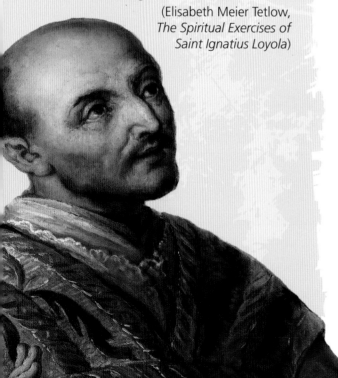

years, help me to form a special relationship with you that I will be able to build on. Teach me to respect myself, as well as others, and to treat them in a way I would like to be treated. Most of all, help me to develop your gift of love so that it may affect others in a special way—just like the way your love for me has had a great impact in my life.

(Kaitlyn Pratt,
in *More Dreams Alive*)

When Spirituality Is Genuine

Catholics believe that to grow spiritually is to become who God created them to be—the very best version of themselves. And that version is free, courageous, and joyful. In a wonderful verse in the Gospel of John, Jesus says, "I came so that they [his followers] might have life and have it more abundantly" (10:10). Avoiding the world or having a distaste for ordinary life is not part of a healthy spirituality. With genuine spirituality, a person opens their heart to let Jesus into the midst of everyday life. By living out the values and attitudes taught by Jesus, a person develops a way of life in which true happiness can be found. We have touched on some of those values and attitudes, and chapter 11 focuses on more of them.

Jesus Christ is at the center of Christian spirituality. He teaches about how to grow spiritually amid everyday joys and sorrows. He shows that spirituality touches all parts of human life, that God does not want to be confined to one day or one hour of a person's life. Catholics believe that God wants to flow into everyone's work, dreams, struggles, and relationships with others. God wants to bring self-respect, love, honesty, strength, healing, and trust into every area of human life. That is what happens, little by little, as a person grows in genuine spirituality.

For **Review**

1. With what kind of love does God love each person? How does that kind of love affect a person who is open to it?
2. How did Jesus respond to his own fears?
3. Describe two spiritual practices you can use to grow in trusting God.
4. What Christian belief is the foundation of trust and hope in God?
5. Describe how genuine spirituality can affect a person's whole life.

Prayer: Nourishing a Relationship with God

Toby and Cecilia became friends during their freshman year. They both played French horn, and they both had study hall after band, which gave them time to talk and get to know each other. They made each other laugh, and they both worked hard in school and band. In their sophomore year, they started dating and went to the homecoming dance together. They soon realized that while they cared about each other a lot, neither was ready for a steady relationship. So they stopped dating but stayed best friends. Toby felt loved and accepted for who he was around Cecilia and trusted her completely.

Then, in the summer after their junior year, Cecilia just kind of disappeared from the relationship. She didn't return Toby's texts and was always busy when he tried to get together with her. When Toby finally confronted her about it, she said: "Toby, you know that I really care about you. I just don't have time for you between my job and Blake (her new boyfriend). I'm sorry."

How do you think Toby felt after hearing that? How would you feel if a good friend just gradually stopped spending time with you? Sounds like a pretty strange friendship, right? Sounds like it may gradually dry up and wither away.

Yet Cecilia's friendship with Toby is the kind of "friendship" many people have with God. They know God loves them. They may have even felt God's love for them at some point. But they never spend any time with God. They take their relationship with God for granted. God does not enter their awareness, except maybe once in a while during a liturgy.

A friendship takes time and energy. A personal relationship with God is similar. It requires one's intentional presence—one way we might think of prayer—if it is to survive and grow.

Lifting Our Heart to God

For people of faith, prayer is the awareness of God and the heart's response to God in all areas of life. It is *paying attention* to God and communicating with God in a relationship of love. Prayer nourishes a person's relationship with God, like the time and energy we'd give to someone whose friendship we treasure. Spirituality, the process of becoming a fully alive person while growing closer to God, depends on prayer.

One saint, Thérèse of Lisieux, a young Carmelite nun who lived about a hundred years ago, described prayer this way: "For me, prayer means launching out of the heart towards God; it means lifting up one's eyes, quite simply, to heaven, a cry of grateful love, from the crest of joy or the trough of despair" (Ronald Knox, *Autobiography of St. Thérèse of Lisieux*).

Thérèse emphasized the simplicity of prayer, that it is more a matter of lifting up the heart to God than of using fancy words or saying just the right thing. A person can pray out of joy or out of discouragement. What matters in Christian prayer is turning to God.

Different Forms of Prayer

Think of all the different ways we relate to our friends: We share whatever is happening in our lives. We talk over problems and ask for help and advice. We do fun things together like listening to music, going for a walk, going to the beach, shopping, and dancing. If a friend does something nice or helpful for us, we usually say thanks. We let friends know when we think they're great, and also when we're mad at them or disappointed in them.

Recall a time when you were in a one-sided friendship— that is, a friendship in which either you or your friend did most of the work or in which one of you frequently cancelled or didn't show up. What was that experience like?

Consider the different types of prayer in this list. Which ones are you most interested in? Why?

Like the different ways we relate to our friends, Catholics believe relationships with God through prayer can take a variety of forms:

- **prayers of conversation:** sharing with God whatever is happening in one's life, thoughts, and feelings

- **prayers of petition:** asking God for help for oneself or others

- **prayers of thanks and praise:** expressing gratitude for God's gifts and telling God how wonderful God is

- **prayers of meditation:** focusing attention on God and the mysteries of God through thinking, feeling, and imagining

- **formal prayers:** praying in the special words provided by a particular religious tradition

Prayers of Conversation

Perhaps the most ordinary, familiar way people pray is by "talking to God"—usually in the quiet of their own mind and heart. They say whatever is going on inside them—such as the details of their day; their worries; the things they are happy, sad, or angry about; or their concerns about the future. Such talks with God are prayers of conversation.

Think about your typical morning. What is on your mind when you first wake up? Could your thoughts be the basis for a prayer to God? Why or why not?

Getting out of bed in the morning or going to sleep at night are typical times when a person might talk to God. For instance:

- Oh, God, I wish I didn't have to get up today. I'm so tired of school. I can't wait for summer. And I've got two tests today. Help!

- Things turned out sort of mixed today, God. The biology test wasn't too bad. History was kind of hard though—wish I'd studied more. . . . Oh, I found out I made the softball team! That'll be cool to travel with the team.

Such prayers are like the typical stream of thoughts and reactions a person has in a day, but they are shared with God. God is invited into the person's life through this type of prayer, and the person becomes increasingly aware that the ordinary activities of life are blessed by the presence and concern of God.

Conversational prayer can also be about deeper feelings and problems, like the prayers by students quoted on pages 283–284, 285, and 289–290.

In those instances, the prayers were not just inner thoughts; they were written down, as letters to God. Expressing things in writing to God helps many people because they can get their thoughts and feelings out on the page instead of just letting those thoughts and feelings rumble around inside them and make them anxious. Keeping a journal for recording one's private thoughts, feelings, and experiences can be a way of conversing with God.

Today I Commit

This is a simple conversational prayer
for use at the start of a day:

> Lord,
> Today I commit to do the good
> You created me to do,
> To see the good
> You created me to see,
> To be the good
> You created me to be.
> Amen.

Prayers of Petition

In Matthew's Gospel, Jesus says this about asking God for help: "Ask and it will be given to you; seek and you will find; knock and the door will be opened to you" (7:7).

Catholics believe that God wants to hear our every concern and need. These pleas for God's help are called prayers of **petition**; they express how much we depend on God for everything in our lives. At times, prayers of petition can be part of a conversational prayer, as in some of the previous examples.

What do people pray for? Just about anything. For instance:

- Please help me do well on the test, God.

- I'm in bad shape with drugs, God. I need your help.

- God, forgive me for being mean to my brother tonight. Help us understand each other so we don't fight so much.

- God, my grandma is sick again. Help her feel better.

- Please, God, bless all the homeless people, and make our society more compassionate to them.

- God, help me understand your will in my life. I want to serve you better. Please show me how.

Prayers of petition range from relatively small concerns to the huge ones, from personal needs to the needs of the whole world. This should not be surprising, because in every prayer of petition the person praying recognizes that God is there and that they have a relationship with God— and that God desires this relationship too.

That does not mean someone will always, or even usually, get exactly what they ask for in prayer. How God answers prayers is mysterious, not obvious. But Jesus tells us to go ahead and ask, trusting that God will care for us and those we are praying for, often in ways we do not expect or imagine. Praying petitions for ourselves, for people we love, and for people we do not even know, can

---

petition A form of prayer asking God for help for oneself or others.

^A Prayer for Help

Dear God,
Be with me when my parents are pushing me to go so far.
Be with me when school has me stressed out.
Be with me when my team is losing.
Be with me when a family member is close to death.
Be with me when the troubles of the world all seem to be on my back.
Through all the times of my life, O God, please be with me.

(Anonymous, in *More Dreams Alive*)

deepen our trust in God. When someone asks God for help with all their needs, they place their life in God's hands. When they come from a heart that is truly trusting God, prayers of petition are prayers for God's will—the coming of God's Kingdom on earth.

Prayer of Thanks and Praise

Sometimes people have a deep sense of gratitude—for their life, their family, their friends, the opportunities they have, the beauties of creation. The psalms in the Old Testament are full of prayers of thanks and praise for God's wonderful gifts and deeds. Here is one example:

> Shout joyfully to the LORD, all you lands;
>   serve the LORD with gladness;
>   come before him with joyful song.
>
> . . . .
>
> Enter his gates with thanksgiving,
>   his courts with praise.
>
> (Psalm 100:1–2,4)

Think of a big concern on your mind. Write it down, and then write a petition related to the concern. Is this something you'd ask God about in prayer? Why or why not?

^A Prayer of Simple Thanks

For all the times
you sent
a perfect light
a perfect note
a perfect word
a perfect look
thank you.
Your simple gifts
make me happy.

(Anonymous,
in *More Dreams Alive*)

Keep a gratitude list for one week. At the end of each day, write down three or four people or experiences you are grateful for that day. Give thanks in whatever way is appropriate to your spiritual beliefs.

Most people who make a daily list of all the things they are grateful for usually have many things to record, even on bad days. Many people see gratitude as the sign of a heart that is close to God or that is open to something bigger than themselves. Writing to one of the early Christian communities, Saint Paul encouraged gratitude for everything: "Rejoice always. Pray without ceasing. In all circumstances give thanks, for this is the will of God for you in Christ Jesus" (1 Thessalonians 5:16–18).

You may wonder about Paul's message: Be thankful "in *all* circumstances." Even when things go badly for us? Even when we are sad or lonely or defeated? Yes, there is something to thank God for even in a situation of suffering. For instance:

Lord, you know how bad I'm hurting. I've cried myself to sleep every night since Dad died. When will I ever feel normal again?

I don't know why this happened to us, God, and I don't know how we'll make it without Dad. But I know you are with us, Lord, even in this terrible time. You've even made some good things come out of this, like all the support from our family and friends. Thank you for loving us.

This kind of prayer of gratitude does not come easily; it comes through deep, patient trust in God,

which develops slowly in a person. The ability to thank and praise God from the heart even in difficult times characterizes those who have drawn very close to God.

Meditation

Today's contemporary, fast-paced society makes most people restless. When faced with a quiet time, most of us fidget or do something like scroll through social media. We let thoughts race through our mind like cars on a speedway. We prefer noise over silence, motion over stillness, being scattered over being focused. Many of us desperately need to slow down and get ourselves together.

Meditation is an inner quieting that helps a person slow down and focus attention on something. You may have heard of mindfulness or meditation as a way for athletes to boost their performance, or for business executives to refresh their mind amid a hectic workday.

Doctors even recommend meditation to patients as a way to reduce stress and lower blood pressure.

Those are all good uses of meditation. However, as a form of prayer, Christian **meditation** has a different purpose. Its goal is to focus on God and the mystery of God's love given to the world in Jesus, using thoughts, feelings, and imagination. That kind of focus requires inner quieting, much like the mindfulness techniques that people might use to reduce stress and improve their work performance. But Christian meditation aims to clear "inner space" to make room for God in one's heart. It is not primarily about achieving something like health or success but about consciously opening oneself up to God.

A passage in the Old Testament describes well what it means to meditate, "'Be still, and know that I am God!'" (Psalm 46:11). If you have ever tried to empty your mind of thoughts, you know how difficult being still can be. It takes self-discipline, practice, and patience to learn how to meditate.

The first step is to calm the body by consciously relaxing the muscles and breathing deeply and rhythmically. The next step is to introduce some way of focusing attention. A method might be as simple as the slow mental repetition of a sacred word, like *Jesus* or *love* (see the sidebar "The Jesus Prayer"). Or one might read a Bible passage and reflect on it by zeroing in on just one line in a passage, or putting oneself into a Gospel story

© Andrey_Kuzmin / Shutterstock.com

meditation A form of prayer that focuses a person's attention on God and the mysteries of God with their thoughts, feelings, and imagination.

The Jesus Prayer

The Jesus Prayer is an ancient one-line prayer that people slowly repeat as a meditation. It can be done anytime or anywhere. It goes like this: Lord Jesus Christ, Son of God, have mercy on me, a sinner.

The phrase "have mercy on me," does not necessarily mean "have pity on me." You can think of it as meaning "look upon me with compassion and kindness." People adapt this prayer, sometimes leaving off "a sinner" or simplifying it to "Jesus, have mercy on me."

as one of the characters and imagining one's feelings and reactions toward Jesus. A book of daily meditations or about the lives of the saints can provide material for meditation as well.

In another method, called guided meditation, a leader reads a script that takes participants through an imaginary event in which they encounter Jesus or a symbol of God or the sacred. During the process, the participants mentally fill in their own reactions and responses to what the leader is reading. The purpose of such an exercise, of course, is not for the person to create a fabulous imaginary drama but simply to be with God and to experience whatever it is that the person needs from the encounter—love, healing, strength, wisdom, challenge, or courage.

Sometimes meditation is so deep that it is purely an experience of the heart—no thoughts or words at all, just the sense of being in union with God. This type of meditation is called contemplation.

Formal Prayers

Most of the types of prayer discussed so far involve relating to God with *one's own* words or thoughts—"making up" prayers in the moment. Perhaps you are more familiar with what are called formal prayers. These are the special wordings and formulas provided by a religious tradition to help its members express their relationship to God. Formal prayers can be prayers of petition, thanks, and praise, as well as statements of belief, such as the Apostles' Creed.

Why use formal prayers? Because they say just what many people need to say on occasions when they may not be able to think of their own words. Also, these prayers unify people from all over the world who belong to the same religion and pray the same prayers in their own language. Catholicism has many such formal prayers that unite Catholics everywhere.

Try out a meditation method that appeals to you. Afterward, reflect on your experience and describe it to a classmate or friend.

contemplation
A form of meditation that is so deep that it is purely an experience of being in union with God, without any thoughts or words at all.

Reflect on one phrase from the Lord's Prayer that is meaningful to you and why that phrase is especially important.

A Formal Prayer of Sorrow

Sometimes it is hard to find the words to say, "I'm sorry," to God. This prayer, often used in the sacrament of Penance and Reconciliation, can be helpful during those times:

O my God,
I am sorry and repent
    with all my heart
for all the wrong I have
    done
and for the good I have
    failed to do,
because by sinning I
    have offended you,
who are all good and
    worthy
    to be loved above all
        things.
I firmly resolve,
    with the help of your
        grace,
to do penance,
to sin no more,
and to avoid the
    occasions of sin.
Through the merits of
    the Passion
    of our Savior Jesus
        Christ,
Lord, have mercy.

(*Order of Penance*, 45)

The Lord's Prayer. An important formal prayer is the Lord's Prayer, or the Our Father. Catholics pray it together at every Mass, for example.

Our Father who art in heaven,
hallowed be thy name.
Thy kingdom come.
Thy will be done on earth, as it is in heaven.
Give us this day our daily bread,
and forgive us our trespasses,
    as we forgive those who trespass against us,
and lead us not into temptation,
but deliver us from evil.
For the kingdom, the power, and the glory
    are yours,
now and forever.
Amen.

Taught by Jesus to his followers when they asked him how they should pray, the Lord's Prayer is rich with meaning in every line. It is derived from the Gospels, where there is a short version in Luke and a longer one in Matthew. The longer version is used most often.

The Hail Mary. A formal prayer familiar to many Catholics is the Hail Mary (known also by its Latin name, Ave Maria). It is addressed to Mary as Mother of God.

Hail, Mary, full of grace, the Lord is with you.
Blessed are you among women,
    and blessed is the fruit of your womb, Jesus.
Holy Mary, Mother of God, pray for us sinners,
    now and at the hour of our death.
Amen.

The first three lines of this prayer are from Luke's Gospel at the time Mary learned she was pregnant with Jesus. The Hail Mary is the basic prayer recited

© PhilipYb Studio / Shutterstock.com

The Mass is a formal prayer, but, as previously discussed, it is also much more than that. It is the center of the life of the Church. As a community celebration, the Mass consists of common elements that remain the same throughout the world. Some of the prayers the priest says change from day to day, but all the prayers said by the people stay the same and are often memorized. These prayers add up to an act of worship that is at the core of Catholic life.

For people of many faiths, memorizing certain formal prayers is a helpful practice because then these prayers will always be there when they need them—when their own words are not enough, or when they want to pray in unity with other believers who pray the same thoughts and words.

Putting Your Body into Prayer

Catholics believe that every person is a perfect union of body and soul from the moment of conception. Each of us is physically, emotionally, intellectually, and spiritually all wrapped up in one whole person. Sometimes prayer or meditation can seem just like a mental or emotional exercise, but that is not—or should not—be the case. This is why Catholics use their bodies in different ways during

many times in the **Rosary**, a Catholic devotional prayer that honors Mary and helps people meditate on Christ's life and mission.

The liturgy. The entire liturgy of the Catholic Church—its sacraments and rituals, including the Mass—is formal prayer. Many prayers in the Scriptures, like the Psalms, are formal prayers as well, intended to be prayed in union with others.

Rosary A devotional prayer that honors the Virgin Mary and helps people meditate on Christ's life and mission.

the Mass, sometimes standing, sometimes sitting, sometimes kneeling. Each of these postures reflects an interior attitude. Standing reflects an attitude of attention, when we are focused on hearing or interacting with something important. It is why Catholics stand when the Gospel is being read. Sitting reflects an attitude of reflection, which is why Catholics sit after the Gospel is read to meditate on its meaning while listening to the homily. And kneeling reflects an inner attitude of reverence, of special respect for someone or something, which is why Catholics kneel during the Eucharistic prayer, when they remember Jesus Christ's great sacrifice and gift of himself.

In a similar way, we can include our bodies in our personal prayer. We can let our bodies reflect our inner intention while we are praying or meditating. Here are some possibilities for integrating physical movement into personal prayer and meditation:

A Walking Prayer or Meditation

Take a walk in nature and notice everything you see—colorful leaves, spiderwebs, frost-covered bushes, puddles—as a gift. Offer thanks for each thing you see. Or walk in your neighborhood past houses and stores where you know some of the people and what they are going through in life. As you walk, lift up in your own way each of those persons and their needs.

A Musical Prayer or Meditation

Listen to a song that expresses what you are feeling or thinking and move with the music. Let the experience be a "prayer of being yourself." If you play an instrument, play your favorite piece of music with all your heart and skill. Sing a much-loved song. Music is a good way to praise God.

Recall any times you've used physical movement as a way to express yourself. What was that experience like? How might it translate into a way of prayer or meditation?

An Artistic Prayer or Meditation

Use your head, hands, and senses to create a drawing, a painting, a mobile, a sculpture, a collage, or a photo. As you work at it, be aware of the creative energy within you.

A Moving Prayer or Meditation

Pray or meditate with gestures. Open your arms up wide to say with your whole being, "God (or Life), I'm open to your love." Join hands with others when you pray or meditate to convey, "We are not alone; we are all in this together." Or if you are holding on to a lot of anger about something, try punching a pillow while asking for help: "Please, God, let me get rid of all this anger." Don't just think it; move it.

A Written Prayer

Write a letter to God or keep a journal in which you write your experiences and reflections. In the journal, try writing an imaginary conversation about an issue you need help with.

For **Review**

1. What is prayer? How is it related to spirituality?
2. Briefly describe five different forms of prayer.
3. Describe how a person might enter into meditation.
4. Give two reasons formal prayers are important to Catholics.
5. Give three ways a person could integrate physical movement into prayer or meditation.

Prayer and Community

Prayer Unites People

People of most faiths believe that genuine prayer unites them with one another and with God. They believe that if we are truly drawing closer to God, we will draw closer to other people, even when we pray privately. For Christians, this is the reality of the body of Christ: What one person does affects all the rest because all are united in Christ.

The First Letter of John in the New Testament makes the point that prayer helps people love others because of God's love for them and within them: "We love because he first loved us. If anyone says, 'I love God,' but hates his brother, he is a liar; for whoever does not love a brother whom he has seen cannot love God whom he hasnot seen. This is the commandment we have from him: whoever loves God must also love his brother" (4:19–21).

So Catholics believe that even private prayer, done in the solitude of one's heart, connects the praying person with other people. Likewise, other people are connected to the person through *their own* prayer. Whenever prayer seems impossible because a person is feeling drained or discouraged, it helps Catholics to know that the whole body of Christ is supporting them, holding them up. Prayers of others, even those they do not know or have never seen, can make up for their own lack by carrying them through times of weakness and doubt. And they too can offer

ᴬ Prayer for Being a Source of Goodness

In this prayer, Saint Francis of Assisi asks for God's
love to flow through him to others:

> Lord, make me an instrument of your peace;
> Where there is hatred, let me sow love;
> Where there is injury, pardon;
> Where there is doubt, faith;
> Where there is despair, hope;
> Where there is darkness, light;
> Where there is sadness, joy.
>
> O Divine Master,
> grant that I may not so much seek
> to be consoled, as to console;
> to be understood, as to understand;
> to be loved, as to love;
> for it is in giving that we receive,
> it is in pardoning that we are pardoned,
> it is in dying that we are born
> to eternal life.
>
> (In *The Fire of Peace*,
> Mary Lou Kownacki, OSB)

prayers when others cannot, making up for whatever
is lacking in them. The Communion of Saints, living
and dead, is always there to support one another.

Praying Together

Many of the prayer forms discussed in this chapter
can be prayed in private, but they can also be prayed
together with others. Besides private prayer, Catholics believe they need such community prayer,
occasions when they express their connections with
others by praying with a group or faith community.

Recall an experience
that was difficult
for you. Did anyone tell
you they had you in their
thoughts and prayers?
If so, what was that
experience like?

Celebrations of Mass and the other sacraments are times of community prayer. They always involve at least two people, and typically many more than that.

People of faith have many opportunities to join with others for prayer—a family grace or blessing before meals, a prayer at the beginning of a class period, a prayer service for a school or youth group.

Community prayer can take some surprising forms. For example, in many cities, people of different faiths gather on Thanksgiving to give thanks in prayer, each according to their own tradition. In some areas, all the faith communities hold a food drive or a building project on a given weekend. The drive might end with a prayer service and block party to celebrate. Often, during natural catastrophes or when a great injustice or act of violence occurs, people of faith will gather at a public vigil to prayerfully support the victims.

In what ways are you involved in community prayer or some other form of communal reflection or meditation—at home, at school, at a community gathering, or with a community of faith? What are your reactions to these occasions of prayer?

© Bill Wittman / wpwittman.com

Prayer for Peace

Popes have offered many public prayers for peace. Here is an excerpt from a prayer Pope Francis offers people of all faiths to pray with him:

> Lord God of peace, hear our prayer!
>
> We have tried . . . to resolve our conflicts by our own powers. . . . How many moments of hostility and darkness have we experienced; how much blood has been shed; how many lives have been shattered. . . . But our efforts have been in vain.
>
> Now, Lord, come to our aid! Grant us peace, teach us peace. . . . Open our eyes and our hearts, and give us the courage to say: "Never again war!" . . . . Give us the strength daily to be instruments of peace. . . .
>
> Keep alive within us the flame of hope, so that with patience and perseverance we may opt for dialogue and reconciliation. . . . Renew our hearts and minds, so that . . . our way of life will always be that of: Shalom, Peace, Salaam!
>
> Amen.
>
> ("Invocation for Peace," June 8, 2014)

Some people join a prayer group specifically to share their prayers with others. As Saint Paul encouraged the community of Christians at Ephesus: "Be filled with the Spirit, addressing one another [in] psalms and hymns and spiritual songs, singing and playing to the Lord in your hearts, giving thanks always and for everything in the name of our Lord Jesus Christ to God the Father" (Ephesians 5:18–20).

Members of a prayer group may build a strong bond of caring because they share their concerns and their reliance on God with one another. They understand part of what is in one another's hearts.

For **Review**

1. How does all prayer, even private prayer, unite us with others?
2. Why do people of faith feel it is important to pray or meditate with others?
3. Give three examples of communal prayer or meditation.

The Fruits of Spirituality and Prayer

How might someone recognize growth in their spiritual or religious life? How might someone know if their spirituality is genuine and leading them to become their best self?

One cannot evaluate their spirituality by how well-spoken their prayers are. Jesus taught that God is not interested in this. People of faith believe that God looks at their hearts, and a prayer they cannot even find words for may be more real and true than anything they could articulate. Even when someone is unable to pray, as Saint Paul says, the Holy Spirit prays within them: "For we do not know how to pray as we ought, but the Spirit itself intercedes with inexpressible groanings" (Romans 8:26).

Instead of looking for awesome spiritual experiences as a sign of growing toward God, people of faith need to look at the effects of spirituality and prayer in their lives. Paul describes these effects as fruits of the Holy Spirit: "love, joy, peace, patience, kindness, generosity, faithfulness, gentleness, self-control" (Galatians 5:22–23).

People can reflect on their spirituality with questions like these:

- Am I trusting God more fully?
- Am I more loving toward others?
- Am I more honest and peaceful?
- Do I have a grateful heart?
- Are my behaviors and actions rooted in moral truth, such as the moral teaching of Jesus?

A person can know if they are growing closer to God by looking for the fruits of their relationship with God. The next chapter, on morality, looks at what it means to live in the Spirit of Jesus.

chapter 11

Christian Morality: Living in the Spirit of Jesus

IN THIS CHAPTER

A Life of Love: 312
The *Why* of Christian Morality

The Law of Love: 318
The *What* of Christian Morality

Freedom and Grace: 328
The *How* of Christian Morality

Virtue and Character: 335
The *Who* of Christian Morality

Our Final Destiny   339

A Life of Love: The *Why* of Christian Morality

Near the end of Matthew's Gospel, just before Jesus was arrested and crucified, he told a powerful story about a "Son of Man" judging people at the end of time:

> He will sit upon his glorious throne, and all the nations will be assembled before him. And he will separate them one from another, as a shepherd separates the sheep from the goats. He will place the sheep on his right and the goats on his left. Then [he] will say to those on his right, "Come, you who are blessed by my Father. Inherit the kingdom prepared for you from the foundation of the world. For I was hungry and you gave me food, I was thirsty and you gave me drink, a stranger and you welcomed me, naked and you clothed me, ill and you cared for me, in prison and you visited me." (25:31–36)

When those on the right, the ones called blessed, asked the Son of Man when they had done these good actions, he replied that they did them whenever they cared for someone in

need who would otherwise be overlooked. Jesus continues the story with the Son of Man addressing those gathered on the left:

> Depart from me, you accursed, into the eternal fire prepared for the devil and his angels. For I was hungry and you gave me no food, I was thirsty and you gave me no drink, a stranger and you gave me no welcome, naked and you gave me no clothing, ill and in prison, and you did not care for me. (25:41–43)

When these people asked when they had failed to do these things, the Son of Man replied that they failed to do them whenever they overlooked someone in need, especially the "least ones." What is the difference between the behavior of those on the right and the behavior of those on the left? What point is Jesus making with this story?

What Is Morality?

Some biblical background helps interpret this story. First, the Son of Man is a title the early church applied to Jesus. So, the judge in the story is the resurrected Jesus Christ, who Christians believe is divine, the second person of the Holy Trinity. This makes the passage a story about God's judgment of the human race at the end of time. The people who are hungry, thirsty, naked, ill, or in prison are all categories of people from the Bible who are oppressed, in need, or living on the fringes of society. Today, we can extend these categories to include anyone who is oppressed or in need—physically, emotionally, or spiritually. Jesus' story makes it clear that how we treat these people is very important in the eyes of God. Helping someone in need is good, and turning away from someone in need when you can help is bad.

Morality relates to the way we live our lives—all parts of our lives. The principles of morality help us define right and wrong behavior with the goal of

How do you decide between right and wrong? Who or what are the biggest moral influences in your life?

morality A system of principles guiding how we live our lives. Christian morality helps define what is right and wrong with the goal of motivating people to choose what is right.

choosing what is right. Morality applies to how we treat our family and friends. It applies to how we respond to people in need. It has to do with how we spend our time and money. It applies to how we respond to important social issues such as racism, care for the unborn and the elderly, economic injustice, and conflict between nations. It applies to how you take care of yourself. Everyone—Christian or non-Christian, believer in God or nonbeliever—has a morality, even if they do not realize it or call it by that name. Whether it leads them to good or to evil, a morality of some kind is part of everyone's life.

The Commandment of Love

Christian morality, the ideal that Jesus presents, is summed up in the word *love.* In the Gospels, someone once asked Jesus which commandment of the law was the greatest. He answered with the **Great Commandment**, a law rooted in the Jewish tradition—a twofold yet single commandment of love: "You shall love the Lord, your God, with all your heart, with all your soul, and with all your mind. This is the greatest and the first commandment. The second is like it: You shall love your neighbor as yourself" (Matthew 22:37–39). Jesus ties love for God, love for others, and love for ourselves together in a way that cannot be separated.

Great Commandment Jesus' summary of the entire moral law as the love of God and the love of neighbor.

The Golden Rule

Hinduism
This is the sum of duty:
do not do to others what would
cause pain if done to you
Mahabharata 5:1517

Buddhism
Treat not others in ways
that you yourself would
find hurtful
The Buddha, Udana-Varga 5.18

Confucianism
One word which sums up the
basis of all good conduct...
loving-kindness.
Do not do to
others what
you do not
want done
to yourself
Confucius, Analects 15.23

Baha'i Faith
Lay not on any soul a load
that you would not wish to
be laid upon you, and
desire not for
anyone the
things you
would not
desire for
yourself
Baha'u'llah, Gleanings

Islam
Not one of you truly believes
until you wish for others what
you wish for yourself
The Prophet Muhammad, Hadith

Taoism
Regard your neighbour's gain
as your own gain, and your
neighbour's loss as your own loss
Lao Tzu, T'ai Shang Kan Ying P'ien, 213-218

The command to love
your neighbor as yourself
is sometimes called "The
Golden Rule." Most world
religions have some ver-
sion of this rule, as shown
in this chart.

Judaism
What is hateful to you,
do not do to your neighbour.
This is the whole Torah;
all the rest is commentary
Hillel, Talmud, Shabbat 31a

Sikhism
I am a stranger to no one;
and no one is a stranger
to me. Indeed, I am
a friend to all
Guru Granth Sahib, p. 1299

Jainism
One should treat all
creatures in the world
as one would like
to be treated
Mahavira, Sutrakritanga

Zoroastrianism
Do not do unto others
whatever is injurious
to yourself
Shayast-na-Shayast 13.29

Native
Spirituality
We are as much alive
as we keep the earth alive
Chief Dan George

Unitarianism
We affirm and promote respect
for the interdependent
web of all existence
of which we are a part
Unitarian principle

Christianity
In everything, do to others
as you would have them
do to you; for this is the
law and the prophets
Jesus, Matthew 7:12

Published by Paul McKenna
Copyright © Paul McKenna 2000
interfaithgold@gmail.com

Is deciding the most loving thing to do in a given situation easy or hard to do? Defend your answer.

On another occasion, Jesus said to his disciples, "'This is my commandment: love one another as I love you'" (John 15:12). Love—freely given and for the good of others—is the core of the morality that Jesus taught. So, on the one hand, Christian morality is easy. A person needs to ask only, "What is the most loving thing to do in this situation?" On the other hand, it can be difficult to know what the most loving choice is, and sometimes even harder to live it out. This is why the Catholic Church has a tradition of moral teachings to help guide people.

God's Love: Open or Closed to It?

Why should we love others and love ourselves? For believers, the answer is straightforward: because God loves us. The New Testament expresses this truth in a well-known passage: "Beloved, let us love one another, because love is of God; everyone who loves is begotten by God and knows God. Whoever is without love does not know God, for God is love" (1 John 4:7–8).

Christian morality means living out the love God has already given to human beings. The Christian vision is that people lead moral lives of love not to gain God's love or favor; rather, they love because God loved them first. A core Catholic belief is that God created all human beings in the divine image as God's beloved sons and daughters. The Son of God, Jesus Christ, loved them so much that he became one of them and gave his life for them.

Reflect on a time when you witnessed someone being open to goodness, truth, or beauty. Do you believe that through this experience the person was opening up to love, to God? Why or why not?

As previously mentioned, a core belief common to most religions is that every person is precious to God. Truly believing that human beings are precious to God gives religious people the true basis for self-esteem: they can love themselves because the source of all love already loves them and believes in them. If people are open to love—like a cup that has a wide mouth—God's love fills them up and spills over into their thoughts, words, and actions.

Food
Donations

On the other hand, if people are closed to love—like a cup with a tightly fastened lid—they may end up living a self-centered, small, and empty life, never experiencing the great joy for which they were destined.

Most people are somewhere in between—neither completely closed nor completely open to love. A spiritual truth is that it takes a lifetime for most people to become totally open to love.

 For **Review**

1. What is the general definition of *morality*?
2. What is the Great Commandment?
3. Why should human beings love others and love themselves?
4. What is the effect on a person of being open to God's love? Closed to God's love?

The Law of Love: The *What* of Christian Morality

Christians believe that the Great Commandment—to love God with our whole being and to love our neighbor as we love ourselves—is the foundation and summary of Christian morality.

Is that it? Is that the end of the the discussion? Imagine someone doing a quick self-check on keeping the Great Commandment of love:

> Well, sure, I really do love God. After all, I go to church on Sundays, and I often ask God for help. As for loving my neighbor as myself, I'm really good to my friends, and lots of people like me because I'm so nice. So I guess I score an A+ on the Great Commandment!

This self-talk illustrates that we can fool ourselves into believing that love is a simple matter. We may believe that if we think we are loving, then we really are. Recall the goats in Jesus' story at the beginning of this chapter. They seemed to think they were very loving, but they missed something important.

The Ten Commandments: Love Spelled Out

How do we know what love really asks of us? The requirements of loving God and neighbor are contained in Scripture and Tradition, coming from a variety of sources. For Jews and Christians, one of the most important sources is the **Ten Commandments**, revealed by God to Moses (recall the story on pages 74–80). The Ten Commandments were what God expected of the Israelites if they were to be

---

Ten Commandments The list of ten norms, or rules of moral behavior, that God gave Moses and that are an important foundation for Christian morality.

faithful to God's covenant with them. These ten norms, or rules of moral behavior, are an important foundation for Christian morality. Jesus' command to love God and neighbor, the Great Commandment, is a summary of the Ten Commandments.

The Ten Commandments

The Ten Commandments are given with somewhat different wording in two places in the Old Testament—Exodus 20:2–17 and Deuteronomy 5:6–21. Here is the wording that has become customary for many Christians:

1. I am the LORD your God: you shall not have strange gods before me.
2. You shall not take the name of the Lord your God in vain.
3. Remember to keep holy the Lord's Day.
4. Honor your father and your mother.
5. You shall not kill.
6. You shall not commit adultery.
7. You shall not steal.
8. You shall not bear false witness against your neighbor.
9. You shall not covet your neighbor's wife.
10. You shall not covet your neighbor's goods.

Reflect on the Ten Commandments. Which ones are the easiest for you to understand? Which ones do you have questions about?

Read "Keeping the Spirit of the Ten Commandments" on pages 321–322. Which of the commandments seems especially hard for teenagers to follow today? What argument would you make for why that commandment is important?

Reflect on the questions in "Keeping the Spirit of the Ten Commandments." What questions would you add to any of the commandments to make them relevant to young people?

You may already have noticed that the first three commandments refer to love of God, and the next seven refer to love of neighbor. All the commandments together spell out the meaning of the Great Commandment.

The Letter and the Spirit of the Law

When Jesus preached that people should follow the commandments, summed up in the Great Commandment, he did not mean that they should follow only the bare minimum of each commandment. He told people that they must go beyond the letter of the law—its literal, obvious meaning—to embrace the spirit of the law—its deeper meaning of love. As an example, consider something Jesus taught in the Sermon on the Mount: "You have heard that it was said to your ancestors, 'You shall not kill; and whoever kills will be liable to judgment.' But I say to you, whoever is angry with his brother will be liable to judgment" (Matthew 5:21–22).

Jesus understood that we can "kill" someone with attitudes and words, not just by literally killing the person. So the fifth commandment, "You shall not kill," is about two things. It is certainly about not taking another's life, but it is also about dispelling hatred and vengeance from our hearts and respecting the dignity of every human being. It does more than forbid us from committing murder. It also calls us to be peacemakers. As Jesus taught, "Love your enemies, and pray for those who persecute you" (Matthew 5:44).

peacemaker

peacemaker *noun* **1**
about peace with the er

Keeping the Spirit of the Ten Commandments

Reflection Questions for Those Trying to Live According to the Commandments

one

I am the Lord your God: you shall not have strange gods before me.

- Do I acknowledge God as the center of my life?
- Do I treat anything or anyone with the honor and reverence that belong only to God? Do I give my whole heart, soul, and mind to other "gods"—like popularity, money, clothes, power, pleasure, good grades, or winning at sports?
- Do I nourish my faith in God by turning to God in prayer?

two

You shall not take the name of the Lord your God in vain.

- Do I have an attitude of reverence to God?
- Do I treat God's name with respect?
- Do I avoid using the name of any holy person or thing casually or offensively?

three

Remember to keep holy the Lord's Day.

- Do I reserve space in my life for rest and relaxation, especially on Sunday (or another day that is sacred in my religion if I am not Christian)?
- Do I worship God with others on that sacred day, participating in the Eucharist on Sunday (or Saturday evening)?

four

Honor your father and your mother.

- Do I show respect to my parents or caregivers?
- Do I try to act with love in my family?
- Do I treat those in positions of authority with respect?
- Do I obey government laws that are in accordance with God's law?

five

You shall not kill.

- Do I treat all human life, my own and others', as a precious gift to be nurtured?
- Do I recognize the dignity and worth of every human being from the moment of conception to their natural death?
- Do I avoid harming others by violent, hateful, or prejudiced words and attitudes, as well as by physical violence?
- Do I foster peace by helping people reconcile differences without violence?

six

You shall not commit adultery.
- Do I treat sexuality, my own and others', with respect and care?
- Do I develop healthy friendships with others, whether of the same or opposite sex?
- Do I refrain from sex outside of marriage?
- Do I keep the desire for sexual enjoyment from ruling my behavior and my relationships?

seven

You shall not steal.
- Do I refrain from taking what does not belong to me?
- Do I refuse to cheat—to try to gain something for myself by manipulation or dishonesty?
- Am I upfront and honest in my dealings with others?
- Do I treat others with justice, allowing them to meet their own material needs and not being selfish with what I have?
- Do I treat the earth as a gift from God for everyone and work to protect it?
- Do I support efforts toward the just distribution of resources and money in society and the whole world?

eight

You shall not bear false witness against your neighbor.
- Do I uphold the truth? Am I honest?
- Do I avoid lying—intentionally telling a falsehood?
- Do I refrain from harming the reputation of others by spreading rumors and gossip about them?
- Do I respect my own and others' privacy by keeping confidential what other people have no right to know?

nine

You shall not covet your neighbor's wife.
- Do I try to see others as precious in God's eyes, not as sexual objects to be used for my entertainment?
- Do I avoid media that exploits people as sexual objects, especially pornography?

ten

You shall not covet your neighbor's goods.
- Do I try to banish greed, envy, and jealousy from my heart?
- Do I try to practice goodwill toward those who have better fortune than I do?
- Do I try to find happiness in things of the spirit, rather than assuming that wealth, material goods, pleasure, and fame will make me happy?

Themes in Catholic Moral Teaching

All Christian churches find the basis for their moral teachings in the Great Commandment, the law of love, which Jesus taught and which sums up the Ten Commandments. The Jewish faith as well sees love of God and love of neighbor as central to morality, and it follows the Ten Commandments. So Christians and Jews have much in common in their teachings about morality. In fact, most of the world's religions hold similar principles about what is right and wrong. For instance, all major religious traditions hold that it is wrong to murder and wrong to steal, although they may define those general principles in varying ways.

The Catholic Church, through its official teaching voice, the Magisterium, has spoken out on issues that especially challenge the society and world of this era. Catholicism is not alone in its teaching on these issues; many of its concerns are shared with other Christians, Jews, members of other religions, and nonbelievers. But in response to these issues, the Catholic voice has been clear and strong.

These issues come under three themes emphasized in Catholic moral teaching in the last few decades:

- protecting the dignity of all human life
- working for social justice
- defending the sacredness of human sexuality

Protecting the Dignity of All Human Life

The Catholic Church has spoken out repeatedly and passionately about the need to protect human life at every stage of existence—from the fetus growing in its mother's womb to the elderly or disabled person being cared for in an extended care facility. Every human being, "from womb to tomb," has dignityand worth because every human is created by God in God's image.

This theme is at the heart of Catholic teaching on issues that involve direct killing: murder, abortion, euthanasia, capital punishment, war. You are likely to study these issues later in a course on morality.

Many other threats to human life exist today besides direct killing, such as racism, discrimination, terrible living conditions, malnutrition and hunger, domestic violence and abuse, reckless driving, alcohol and drug abuse, human trafficking, torture, the military arms trade, and the exploitation of people for economic gain. All these issues are matters of the dignity and worth of human life, and thus they fall within the realm of the fifth commandment, "You shall not kill."

The Catholic Church has consistently called its members to protect human life and human dignity. Through teaching documents, educational programs, and homilies, the Church provides the teaching and motivation to defend human life and

What do you think is the most serious threat to human life in today's world? Explain your answer.

dignity against all attacks. With the help of the Holy Spirit, Catholics then do this important work in their families and communities according to their positions and gifts.

Models of Social Justice

Here are some Catholic individuals and organizations who have modeled Catholic social teaching perhaps better than words ever could:

- **Cesar Chavez.** A cofounder of what became the United Farm Workers union, Chavez was a labor leader and civil rights activist. He organized farmworkers for better pay and working conditions, using direct but nonviolent tactics including pickets and boycotts.

- **Dorothy Day.** As cofounder of the Catholic Worker Movement, Dorothy Day started houses of hospitality for the hungry and homeless, beginning in New York City. She protested war and injustice.

- **Saint Mother Teresa of Kolkata (Calcutta).** Herself a worldwide symbol of charity, Saint Mother Teresa founded the Missionaries of Charity, who minister to poor, sick, and dying people.

- **Catholic Relief Services.** Catholic Relief Services (CRS), governed by the United States Conference of Catholic Bishops, is the largest nongovernmental relief organization in the world. CRS provides immediate help for victims of disasters, and it has hundreds of development projects around the world.

- **Catholic Climate Covenant.** A national organization dedicated to equipping people and institutions to care for creation and care for the poor, Catholic Climate Covenant focuses on battling climate change through education, public witness, and providing resources.

© Sara Fajardo / Catholic Relief Services

The distribution of hygiene kits supplied by Catholic Relief Services to displaced people along the Nile River in South Sudan.

Working for Social Justice

Catholic teaching on social justice builds on the theme of the dignity and worth of every human being. It affirms that everyone's needs in society should be provided for, not just the needs of a few or even of the majority. The goods of the earth are God's gift to all people; it is an injustice when some people and nations have most of the wealth and resources while others have little or none. Immense human misery due to poverty cries out for justice around the world. Following the lead of Jesus Christ, the Church insists that all Christians are called to work for justice so that everyone can share in the goods of the world. The theme of social justice is related to the seventh commandment, "You shall not steal."

Catholic social teaching stresses that we must foster the **common good**—the social conditions that allow for all people to meet their basic needs and find fulfillment in life. Working for the common good has a higher priority than pursuing our own individual good, especially when it is without concern for others.

The Catholic Church has consistently spoken out on behalf of poor and powerless people, through numerous documents by popes and bishops. Here is an inspiring quote on justice from Saint Basil the Great, a bishop born in AD 330:

> When someone steals another's clothes, we call them a thief. Should we not give the same name to one who could clothe the naked and does not? The bread in your cupboard belongs to the hungry; the coat unused in your closet belongs to the one who needs it; the shoes rotting in your closet belong to the one who has no shoes; the money which you hoard up belongs to the poor.

common good The social conditions that allow for all people to meet their basic needs and find fulfillment in life.

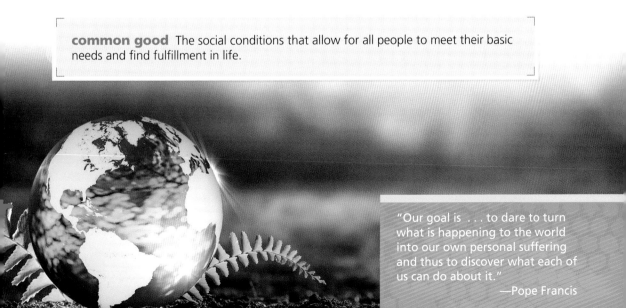

"Our goal is . . . to dare to turn what is happening to the world into our own personal suffering and thus to discover what each of us can do about it."
—Pope Francis

Social Justice in Algebra Class

If action for social justice is central to living a life of love, why should teaching about social justice be limited to theology classes? That's the question students and teachers at Benilde–St. Margaret's Catholic school asked themselves. In response, they created some new courses. One is an Algebra II course that integrates social justice. Instead of tests, the students apply the math they've learned to real-world problems such as housing costs and climate change. The school has also added an English class called "Social Justice and the Written Word." They read works about social justice and write papers on topics such as racism and women's rights. How has or could your school take on the challenge of addressing current social justice topics?

Consider the list of social justice issues mentioned here. What do you think is the most pressing issue in our time? Why?

In recent times, Catholic popes and bishops have addressed issues such as work and employment, poverty and global economics, war and nuclear weapons, national health care, education, racism, the development of the world's poor nations, the problems of farmers and people in rural areas, homelessness, and environmental injustice.

Defending the Sacredness of Human Sexuality

Catholic moral teaching defends the sacredness of **sexuality** in an age when sexuality has been terribly misunderstood and misused. In our society, sex is often used to sell products, to attract attention, to manipulate people, to exert power over another, and for selfish pleasure. Many people regard sexuality as an idol, something to be sought after and almost worshipped, but that does not mean they respect it. Sex is often treated with little respect, as simply a means to a selfish end.

The approach to sexual activity in much of today's media often seems to be, "As long as no one objects, anything goes." Catholicism continues to voice a different message: Human sexuality and its

sexuality The way people experience and express themselves sexually; it involves a person's physical, emotional, and spiritual interactions with other people.

genital expression are sacred; they are one of God's most precious gifts that are to be treated with love and care.

Sexual intercourse is God's way of enabling a man and a woman to express their love for each other and to bring forth the new life of children in a family. That is why intercourse is meant to be part of the permanent commitment of marriage. The Catholic Church asserts that the sacred union of a couple in marriage is meant to be permanent and lifelong. The sixth commandment, "You shall not commit adultery," and the ninth commandment, "You shall not covet your neighbor's wife," are the basis for Catholic teaching on the sacredness of sexuality and its expression in sexual relations.

For this reason, the Catholic Church warns against the dangers of sex outside of marriage. Premarital sex and adultery can have serious physical consequences and wound people's hearts, and they do not satisfy spiritual hungers. The Church also condemns exploitative uses of human sexuality, which have nothing to do with expressing love— rape, sexual harassment, pornography, prostitution, advertising, and the abuse of children and other vulnerable people. In all these teachings runs the theme that as a gift from God, sexual expression is not to be engaged in casually, selfishly, or harmfully.

In what ways do you see human sexuality being misused or treated without the respect owed one of God's most precious gifts?

For Review

1. What do the first three commandments refer to? What do commandments four through ten refer to?
2. List three of the Ten Commandments, and give an example of how to live each of them.
3. What is meant by keeping the spirit of the law, not just the letter of the law?
4. Give brief summaries of the three themes the Catholic Church has emphasized in its moral teaching in recent decades.

Freedom and Grace: The *How* of Christian Morality

We are faced with situations every day in which we need to make choices, many having to do with morality. Think of the possible moral choices high school students have to make:

- whether to join in on gossiping about another person
- whether to copy another student's answers on a test
- whether to have sexual intercourse before marriage
- whether to deceive parents to avoid getting in trouble
- whether to be silent when others are hurting someone in words or actions
- whether to let a friend drive while under the influence of alcohol
- whether to keep buying from a popular company after learning that it treats workers unjustly

© MDV Edwards / Shutterstock.com

Some or all of these issues may seem like common sense to you. "Of course," you may say, "they are all wrong." But another person might not be so sure about the rightness or wrongness of any one of them, claiming, "It all depends." Someone else might think, "Such-and-such action is wrong, but I'm going to do it anyway." Still another person might be tempted to commit an act they know to be wrong, but in the end decide not to do it. In all these cases, Christian morality offers guidelines to help people make wise moral choices.

We Are Responsible

Christian morality does more than offer guidelines for moral choices. It emphasizes the human capabilities that make moral choices possible, and therefore the responsibility for making such choices.

Conscience: Deep in the Human Heart

The Catholic Church teaches that all human beings have a **conscience**, the "inner voice" that helps us recognize the difference between good and evil actions so that we can do good and avoid evil. Thus, Catholics believe they have a responsibility to properly inform their conscience through study and prayer. And they believe they should always follow the judgment of a properly formed conscience. No one should ever be forced to do something that is against the judgment of their conscience.

Free Will: The Ability to Choose Right or Wrong

Furthermore, Catholics believe that God created humans with **free will**, as creatures able to choose freely between moral good and evil, right and wrong. Free will is the basis for Christian morality because having free will means that people are responsible for their actions. However, the freedom of a person's

Think of a time when your ability to freely choose was affected by fear or ignorance. What was the situation, and how did it get resolved?

conscience The "inner voice" that helps us recognize the difference between good and evil actions so that we can do good and avoid evil.

free will The ability to choose freely between right and wrong, which is the basis for moral responsibility.

decisions may be limited by such factors as ignorance, strong emotions like fear, or even psychological problems.

Responsibility: Owning Our Actions

Because we are able to recognize the difference between good and evil (conscience), and we are able to choose between right and wrong (free will), we are responsible for our moral actions, both the good and the bad. We own them. If we perform a deed that is wrong, we cannot simply deny our responsibility, nor can we blame anyone else for our mistakes.

However, our responsibility for an action is lessened if our conscience is incorrectly formed through no fault of our own. For example, a person who steals may have been taught in childhood that stealing is okay, and they carry that attitude with them.

Responsibility is also lessened if our free will is threatened or reduced through no fault of our own. For instance, a terrified person who tells a lie to protect a loved one cannot fully exercise their free will. Fear is making them less free and therefore less responsible. We remain responsible for our actions even if circumstances lessen our level for certain actions.

Mature people are honest people, and honest people take responsibility for their actions. To grow in maturity, we must increasingly take responsibility for what we do. An example that involves a simple mistake, not a moral choice, can illustrate this growth in responsibility:

A one-year-old who spills a cup of milk cannot take responsibility for the spill; an adult will clean up the mess and give the child another drink. A twelve-year-old, however, is mature enough to take responsibility for such an action. They would be expected to clean up the mess and refill the cup.

*I*magine two people facing a similar moral dilemma. One person is fully responsible for their choice, while the other person is much less responsible for their choice. Explain the difference between the two people.

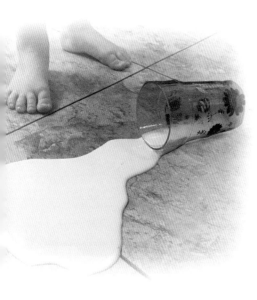

© Taylor E Williams / Shutterstock.com

In the same way, people who are growing in maturity take more and more responsibility for their moral actions. And when they have done something morally wrong, taking responsibility is the first step toward forgiveness.

Forming a Conscience

The Catholic Church teaches that people should always follow their conscience in moral matters, doing what they believe to be right. But people of faith are also responsible for forming their conscience to correctly choose between good and evil. In other words, people must try sincerely to seek out the best knowledge and help they can get to shape their conscience toward God's moral law and not simply toward what they want to think. They cannot just plead ignorance about right and wrong if the ignorance is their own fault.

Catholics believe that deep within the human conscience is a law "written" by God that calls them to love, to do good, and to avoid evil. All people are called to listen for the truth of that law within. Catholics further believe that the best source for forming their conscience is the moral law taught by Jesus Christ, available to them through Scripture and Tradition. Thus, the process of forming one's conscience correctly includes searching out the Church's teachings on moral issues and letting those insights guide one's moral choices.

Parents have the duty and privilege of helping their children form their growing conscience through example, teaching, correction, and the love that is present in their home.

Sin Can Be Overcome by Grace

Sin is the act of knowingly and willingly choosing evil. Evil is the opposite of God, who is the source of all goodness and love. But Catholic teaching emphasizes that sin can be overcome by grace.

What are your thoughts about this question: *What obligation, if any, do teenagers have to help their friends form a correct conscience?*

A Decision of Conscience

Jonas and his friends Lizzie and Marcus were home alone drinking and playing video games when they started talking about a teacher they believed had been treating them unfairly. They decided to play a prank on him. They grabbed a carton of eggs and jumped into Jonas's car. Lizzie had a gut feeling that this wasn't a good idea, but she didn't say anything.

- What might a properly formed conscience be telling these young people? What are some reasons that Lizzie could be ignoring her conscience?

- Jonas's driving was erratic, but they made it to the teacher's house. Lizzie's gut feeling grew stronger, but still she kept quiet. After throwing eggs at the house, they saw lights come on. In their hurry to leave, Jonas hit the teacher's mailbox. After some laughing and high-fives, the car grew silent. Finally, Lizzie said, "That was really dumb."

- How might their consciences hold them responsible for their actions? What could they do to take responsibility and repair the damage?

The Attraction of Sin

To sin is to turn away from God in favor of other things that seem, at the time, more attractive—popularity, thrills, pleasure, safety, convenience, power, money or possessions, a boost to the ego, even the approval of some authority. Not many people sin out of a love for evil itself. Most don't love lying, cheating, or harming life; rather, they are drawn to the benefits of doing evil. Consider these situations, the perceived benefits, and the rationales that might make a person believe the benefits outweigh the harm of the chosen actions:

Situation	Perceived Benefit	Rationale
Lie to your parents about where you are going.	You'll be able to go where you want.	I want to go with my friends, and I'll feel more comfortable if I can just go where they go without my parents making a big deal about it.
Cheat on a test.	You'll get a good grade.	I want to get a good grade, which will pull up my grade point average and help get me into college.
Ignore a popular classmate's cruel social media post about someone.	You'll avoid the ire of the popular students at your school.	I need friends, so I can't risk harming my social life.

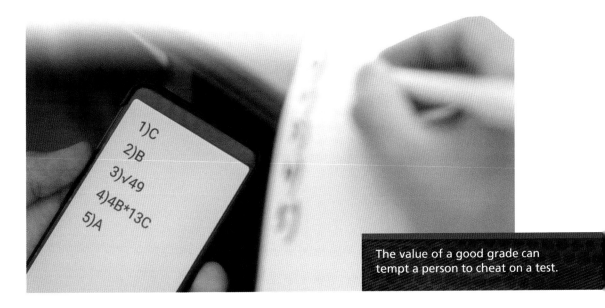

The value of a good grade can tempt a person to cheat on a test.

The apparent benefits of doing evil are really hooks that pull us into committing sin—the temptations of evil. They put a disguise on evil and make it look good so that we deceive ourselves into thinking that doing evil is justified. Unfortunately, many people live in a state of almost constant self-deception, convincing themselves that the wrong they do is really right—according to their needs and wants.

The Degrees of Sin

Catholic moral teaching describes two categories of sin based on how serious the evil is and how much the sin damages the person's relationship with God. **Mortal sin** involves a serious or grave offense, done with full knowledge and freedom, which turns the person completely away from God. **Venial sin** involves a lesser offense that weakens the person's relationship with God but does not turn the person completely away from God.

Imagine that someone you know is being bullied on social media. What are some actions you could take to respond to this wrong?

mortal sin A serious or grave offense, done with full knowledge and freedom, which turns the person completely away from God.

venial sin A lesser offense that weakens the person's relationship with God but does not turn the person completely away from God.

When do you feel like your ability to choose good is weakened or more challenging?

When have you seen a victory, small or great, of goodness overcoming sin in the last few weeks?

Original Sin The belief that every person comes into the world with their ability to choose the good already weakened. All people inherit this spiritual condition because of the sin of the first human beings, Adam and Eve.

Every human being comes into a world where human weakness and sin are already present. Catholics believe that every person comes into the world with their ability to choose the good already weakened. This condition is called Original Sin, and people inherited this spiritual condition because of the sin of the first human beings. **Original Sin** recalls the Genesis story of the first sin by Adam and Eve in the garden. God's grace has the power to overcome even this weakened condition of humanity, saving each person from the tendency to sin.

The Victory of Grace

Sometimes when we look at the world around us, it may seem that evil is winning in the struggle with goodness. Wars go on, violence increases, poverty and injustice abound, human life appears more threatened than ever. You may be wondering where the good news is in all this talk of sin.

Christian faith finds hope in the promise that God's grace is stronger than all the sin in the world. The power of peace, joy, forgiveness, reconciliation, love—God's power—can transform even the worst situations of sin and suffering into new life. This Christian hope is based on the Resurrection of Jesus and the Paschal Mystery. But God needs human beings to cooperate with grace. God never forces people to be good. God invites, and human beings can respond in freedom to God's grace.

Christian faith makes the claim that God's grace will be victorious over all sin, suffering, and death. People of faith believe that even today we can see God's grace triumphing over evil in a world that is burdened with sin and suffering.

1. What does the Catholic Church teach about conscience and responsibility for moral actions?
2. What is sin?
3. How does temptation lure us into committing sin?
4. Define *mortal sin, venial sin,* and *Original Sin.*
5. What do Christians believe about the power of God's grace in the struggle with sin?

Virtue and Character: The *Who* of Christian Morality

This chapter has examined these aspects of Christian morality, which is the law of love:

- the *why* behind the law of love (God loves us first)
- the *what* of the law of love (the Ten Commandments and some themes of Catholic moral teaching)
- the *how* of following the law of love (the dynamics of conscience, free will, responsibility, and sin and grace)

A picture of Christian morality would be incomplete without considering the *who*—the person choosing and doing the moral action.

What Kind of Person?

Perhaps the most important question a person will ever have the chance to answer is the one they are answering every day with their actions:

- What kind of person are you, and what kind of person do you want to become?

This question is not about specific moral issues or decision-making dilemmas. It is about *you*—about what kind of person you are as you consider the issues and decisions you face. The question is about your character.

How would you answer this question: *What kind of person are you, and what kind of person do you want to become?*

character The qualities of a person that are shaped by the good habits and the bad habits they have developed by repetition of good and bad moral actions.

virtue A good moral habit developed by the repetition of good moral actions.

vice A bad moral habit developed by the repetition of bad moral actions.

Character consists of the **virtues**, or good habits, and the **vices**, or bad habits, that a person has developed by repetition of moral acts (each one of us is a mixed bag of virtues and vices). Moral acts, large and small, good and bad, are the stuff of which character is ultimately made. And the moral acts you do tomorrow will be shaped by your character, what you have become as of today. You bring your character to every moral decision and act. In turn, every moral decision and act shapes your character. Here is the way the cycle looks in a simple diagram:

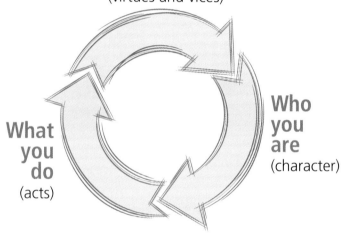

Habits you form
(virtues and vices)

What you do
(acts)

Who you are
(character)

Saint Paul on Virtues and Vices

In several of his letters, Saint Paul lists vices and virtues to instruct Christians on how to live good moral lives. In the Letter to the Colossians, he tells them: "Now you must put them [vices] all away: anger, fury, malice, slander [hurting someone's reputation], and obscene language" (3:8). A few verses later, he encourages Christians to adopt these virtues: "Put on then, as God's chosen ones, holy and beloved, heartfelt compassion, kindness, humility, gentleness, and patience, bearing with one another and forgiving one another" (3:12–13).

Paul concludes with this thought: "And over all these put on love, that is, the bond of perfection" (3:14). The reason for getting rid of vices and developing virtues is simple—to become people of love. People become their best selves, their perfect selves, when their every thought, their every action, is motivated by love. This might seem an impossible goal, but Christians believe that anything is possible with God.

The Character Cycle

Let's say that one day a ninth grader is faced with a choice in school: she can join in on making fun of somebody, she can walk away from the situation, or she can speak up in defense of the person being ridiculed. Suppose she joins in with the others and gets a lot of laughs for her clever, but hurtful, sarcastic comments. The next day, a similar situation comes up. She will probably find it a little easier than the day before to join in on being sarcastic.

If a whole week goes by, and she ridicules somebody every day, she is developing a habit—in this case a vice, not a virtue. She not only pokes fun at others once in a while, but she is also becoming mean. Meanness is starting to be part of her character!

Now every time she is faced with a decision to be hurtful or not, the meanness in her character influences her decision. In fact, she is so used to ridiculing others that it doesn't even feel like she's deciding. It seems to come automatically. Her character is shaping her actions.

The example of this girl illustrates a character cycle in which a vice, meanness, is involved. But we could just as easily (and more happily!) give an example of a virtue, like compassion, being developed, becoming part of a person's character, and shaping the person's later actions. You can probably think of an example yourself.

Once a person has developed a persistent vice that has become part of their character, it is not impossible to change, but it can be difficult. The place to begin changing is in the little actions of everyday life. Becoming aware that one is making choices in doing those actions may be the first challenge. Once aware, a person has a chance to try to make changes.

You told your parents you were going to a friend's house to study for the algebra final, but you actually spent the night playing video games. When you get home, your father asks how the study session went. How would you answer him if you are trying to live a life of virtue? How would you answer him if you are falling into a habit of vice?

Think about the function of a door's hinge. If someone likens a virtue to a hinge, what might that person be trying to communicate about that virtue?

© Artsiom Kuchynski / Shutterstock.com

Christian Virtues: Habits for Living Out the Law of Love

In his life on earth, Jesus showed by his example and by teaching the virtues that enable a person to faithfully keep the law of love. No full and comprehensive list of Christian virtues exists. We could probably come up with dozens of virtues that help people lead a Christian life. But here are some key virtues, which you may consider in depth in a later course on morality:

Theological virtues. The virtues of faith, hope, and love are called theological (from *theos*, meaning "God") because they are given to us by God, who is their source, and are directly concerned with growing our relationship with God and our participation in God's divine life.

Cardinal virtues. Four moral virtues are called cardinal (from a word meaning "hinge") because all other moral virtues hinge, or depend, on them. These are prudence, justice, fortitude, and temperance. Names for these virtues that may sound more familiar to you are wise judgment, justice, courage, and self-control.

Other virtues. Among many possible virtues, honesty, respect for people, compassion, reverence for human life, respect for creation, and peacemaking can be listed.

The virtues and vices we develop through our lifetime will be part of our character. And our character will influence our destiny—what finally becomes of us.

1. What is character? What are virtues and vices?
2. Diagram the character cycle and describe how it works.
3. Name the theological virtues and the cardinal virtues.

Our Final Destiny

What finally becomes of us? How does it all end? What kind of existence or nonexistence are we meant for after we die? These are questions about our final destiny as human beings.

The Christian answer to these questions is this: In the end, people are meant to be united with God in perfect joy and happiness. All those united with God will also be united with one another in a great eternal celebration (the eternal banquet, as it has been called).

Will we *all* end up with God and one another? We do not know. God, who loves us all, would want us all to be united in joy. But human beings, remember, are free. In their lifetime, they can choose to turn away from

God and close themselves off from divine love. Or they can choose to draw closer to God and open up more and more to God's love.

A Christian belief is that at death people will at last have completed the character they have been developing for all the years they have lived. They will be who they are, no more and no less. Their character, with all its virtues and vices, is what they will be able to present to God as the sum of their lives.

The Last Things

Catholic teaching speaks of four "last things": death, judgment, heaven, and hell. Catholic belief is that every human being at death faces God as the person they have finally become.

Mateo's Choice

Mateo's dad left his family when Mateo was only six. Mateo's mom worked as a health care aid and was barely able to pay their bills. It seemed like Mateo and his three sisters were always one step away from being homeless. To make things more complicated, there was a gang operating in their neighborhood, and almost all the boys were pressured to join when they became teens.

Sure enough, when Mateo was fourteen, he found himself cornered one afternoon by several gang members. "Hey, Mateo, it's time to pay your dues," the leader said. "Yeah, join us and keep your family safe," said another. "You don't want your family to get hurt, do you?" They wanted Mateo to break into and rob a neighborhood store after hours. After that, he'd be one of their brothers and they'd keep him and his family safe.

What are your thoughts about the following moral questions related to this scenario?

- Why might Mateo be tempted to accept the gang's offer? What might he gain? What might he lose?

- What moral choices could lead Mateo to a life of virtue? What choices could lead to a life of vice?

- How might the law of love apply in this situation?

Catholics call this facing God after death **particular judgment**. (In this life, a person cannot understand what this facing God will be like.)

If the person has been closed off from God during life and has chosen to turn away from God's love, that person will presumably remain closed off and turned away from God for eternity, losing the perfect happiness for which human beings were created.

The condition is impossible to imagine, calls the experience of the eternal absence of God **hell**. Hell is the state of being separated from God and God's love for eternity—a condition that is a consequence of one's life choices.

If the person chose during life to become open to God's love and has drawn near to God, then at death that person will be united with God and

---

particular judgment The time when individuals face God immediately after death, when they will be either united with God or not for eternity.

hell The state of being separated from God and God's love for eternity.

enjoy perfect happiness eternally. This is **heaven**, and no one can possibly imagine what it will be like. In Saint Paul's words:

> What eye has not seen,
> and ear has not heard,
> and what has not entered
> the human heart,
> what God has prepared
> for those who love him.
>
> (1 Corinthians 2:9)

Catholics believe that God desires all human beings to enter heaven, but that God also respects the choices each person made in their earthly life. People are not "sent" to heaven or hell by God, but they "arrive" in heaven or hell as a consequence of how they lived their lives.

Catholic Tradition holds that some condition of purifying could happen for those who are turned toward God at death but are not yet ready for total union with God because of spiritual obstacles they carry from life. This purification is called purgatory. It is not known how this purifying takes place. In faith, Catholics trust in God's providential care. But Catholic teaching holds that praying for people who have died can help those who at death were not yet ready for union with God.

The Last Judgment

How will the universe end—not just our own individual lives but the life of all creation? What is the final destiny of the whole universe?

The Book of Revelation offers a beautiful, poetic vision of how everything will be transformed when Jesus comes again in glory at the end of time

Reflect on your visions of what happens after death. How do your visions compare with Catholic beliefs about union with or separation from God?

> **heaven** The state of being united with God, enjoying perfect happiness, for eternity.

A mosaic depicting Jesus Christ in glory at the end of time.

for the **last judgment**, the judgment of the whole human race, at the end of time. In this passage, the "new Jerusalem" is an image of the Reign of God, at last come to fulfillment:

> Then I saw a new heaven and a new earth.... I heard a loud voice from the throne saying, "Behold, God's dwelling is with the human race. He will dwell with them and they will be his people and God himself will always be with them [as their God]. He will wipe every tear from their eyes, and there shall be no more death or mourning, wailing or pain, [for] the old order has passed away." (21:1–4)

last judgment
The judgment of the whole human race at the end of time, after which the Kingdom of God will be perfectly established for eternity.

A Parable of Heaven and Hell

A man spoke with the Lord about heaven and hell. "I will show you hell," said the Lord, and they went into a room which had a large pot of stew in the middle. The smell was delicious, but around the pot sat desperate people who were starving. All were holding spoons with very long handles which reached into the pot, but because the handle of the spoon was longer than their arm, it was impossible to get the stew into their mouths. Their suffering was terrible.

"Now I will show you heaven," said the Lord, and they went into another room identical to the first one. There was a similar pot of delicious stew and the people had the same long-handled spoons, but they were well-nourished, talking and happy. At first the man did not understand. "It is simple," said the Lord. "You see, they have learned to feed each other." (In *The Sower's Seeds,* Brian Cavanaugh, TOR)

For Christians, this beautiful passage is a promise that at the end of time all creation will achieve the purpose God intended. Creation—and human life—will have come full circle, from its perfection in the Garden of Eden, when God created Adam and Eve, to the perfection of the New Jerusalem. All creation will live in loving union with its creator.

For Review

1. What are the four last things?
2. Why does someone arrive in heaven or hell after their death?
3. What is purgatory?
4. What is the Catholic belief about what will happen at the end of time?

Learning to Live in Heaven Now

It is not easy to live out Christian morality in today's world, but then it has never been easy. The law of love requires sacrifice. It requires recognizing the dignity of every person, even those who are different from us, who mistreat us, whose values are different from our own.

A modern Catholic Franciscan spiritual writer, Fr. Richard Rohr, describes it well. "*The more we can connect, the more of a saint we are.* The less we can connect, the less transformed we are. If we can't connect with people of other religions, classes, or races, with our "enemies" or with those who are suffering, we're not very converted. Truly transformed individuals . . . see that everything is one" ("Living in Heaven Now," March 12, 2021).

This brings us back to where we started at the beginning of this course. The goal of most religions is to respond to the spiritual hungers of the human heart: the hunger for meaning, the hunger for goodness, the hunger for connectedness. In a nutshell, it is to give and receive love. Father Rohr continues:

> We don't go to heaven; we learn how to live in heaven now. And no one lives in heaven alone. Either we learn how to live in communion with other people and with all that God has created, or, quite simply, we're not ready for heaven. If we want to live an isolated life, trying to prove that we're better than everybody else or believing we're worse than everybody else, we are already in hell. ("Living in Heaven Now," March 12, 2021)

The end goal of Christian morality, really the goal of the whole Christian life, is not about following rules and avoiding punishment. The end goal is to live a life of loving connection, connected with God and one another. By doing this, we make heaven, the Kingdom of God, real in our lives right now.

© Jacob Lund / Shutterstock.com

Glossary

Glossary

Glossary

A

Abba A word meaning "my father," which Jesus sometimes used to address God the Father.

Advent The season in the liturgical year during which Christians prepare for the Christmas season.

Annunciation The angel Gabriel's announcement to Mary that she would be the mother of a son named Jesus.

Anointing of the Sick The sacrament in which a seriously ill, aging, or dying person is anointed by a priest and prayed over by him and others gathered with them. One need not be dying to receive the sacrament.

Ascension The returning to heaven of the Risen Christ forty days after his Resurrection.

Assumption The doctrine that recognizes that the body of Mary, the mother of Jesus, was taken directly to heaven after her life on earth had ended.

B

Babylonian Exile The period in Israelite history during which the Israelites of the ancient kingdom of Judah were held in captivity in Babylon.

Baptism The first of the seven sacraments, by which one becomes a member of the Catholic Church through new life in Jesus Christ.

biblical inspiration The divine assistance guiding the authors of the books of the Bible so the authors could write in human words the truths God wanted to reveal.

biblical interpretation The process and guidelines used to correctly understand the meaning and significance of the Bible.

blasphemy To claim to be divine or to act in a way that is mocking or being irreverent to God.

blessed To receive a favor or gift bestowed by God, bringing happiness.

C

canon The official list of books included in the Bible.

Catholicism The beliefs, rituals, and practices as lived out by those who identify with the Catholic religion.

Catholic social teaching The teachings of the Catholic Church that address social issues and promote justice.

character The qualities of a person that are shaped by the good habits and the bad habits they have developed by repetition of good and bad moral actions.

chief priests Jewish priests of high rank in the Temple, who had administrative authority and presided over important Temple functions.

Chosen People The Jewish people, with whom God chose to have a special bond.

common good The social conditions that allow for all people to meet their basic needs and find fulfillment in life.

Communion of Saints The spiritual union of all those who have been saved by the grace of God, those on earth and those who have died and are with God.

Confirmation The sacrament by which Christians who have been baptized become more fully initiated into the Catholic Church through an outpouring of the Holy Spirit. Confirmation strengthens people to better be like Jesus in the world.

conscience The "inner voice" that helps us recognize the difference between good and evil actions so that we can do good and avoid evil.

contemplation A form of meditation that is so deep that it is purely an experience of being in union with God, without any thoughts or words at all.

covenant In general, a solemn agreement between human beings or between God and human beings in which mutual commitments are promised to each other.

creed A statement that summarizes religious belief.

D

denomination A group of churches or local congregations that are united by a common creed or shared faith under a single governing structure (for example, the Episcopal Church or the Presbyterian Church).

devotion The love and admiration held for a holy person, especially the saints; the prayer to an angel or saint asking for their help.

divine Related to or coming from God.

doctrine An official, authoritative teaching of the Catholic Church based on the Revelation of God.

dogma A doctrine recognized as most central to the life of the Catholic Church; it is defined by the Magisterium and considered definitive and authoritative.

E

Easter Sunday The day on which Christians celebrate Jesus' Resurrection from the dead; considered the most holy of all days and the high point of the Church's liturgical year.

ecumenism The movement to restore unity among all Christians, the unity to which the church is called by the Holy Spirit.

Eucharist The special meal, also called the Mass, in which Jesus nourishes his followers through the consecrated bread and wine that have become his Body and Blood.

Evangelist From a Greek word meaning "messenger of good news," the title given to the authors of the Gospels of Matthew, Mark, Luke, and John.

Exodus The great event in which God led his Chosen People from slavery in Egypt to freedom in the Promised Land.

F

faith The gift of God by which one accepts the invitation to be in relationship with God. It is a matter of both the heart (trusting in God's love) and the head (believing what God has revealed).

free will The ability to choose freely between right and wrong, which is the basis for moral responsibility.

G

Gentile A non-Jewish person.

Gifts of the Holy Spirit The seven gifts received at Baptism and strengthened through Confirmation to help people live as followers of Jesus Christ.

God A name for the supreme being, creator of all that is.

Good Friday The day on which Christians prayerfully remember Jesus' Passion and death on the cross.

Gospels The four books of the New Testament—Matthew, Mark, Luke, and John—which tell about the life, death, and Resurrection of Jesus.

grace The gift of God's unconditional and undeserved love, present in every person's life.

Great Commandment Jesus' summary of the entire moral law as the love of God and the love of neighbor.

H

Hanukkah The Jewish festival remembering the rededication of the Temple after the Jewish victory over Greek occupation.

heaven The state of being united with God, enjoying perfect happiness, for eternity.

Hebrews A tribal people, living in the land of modern-day Israel, who would become the Israelites, and eventually, the Jewish people.

hell The state of being separated from God and God's love for eternity.

hermit A person who seeks to be closer to God by living alone, apart from the world.

high priest One who led the religious services and conducted animal sacrifices at the Temple in Jerusalem. The high priest was appointed by the Jewish king with the approval of the Roman governor.

historical books The section of the Old Testament that tells the story of the Israelites from the time they enter the Promised Land until the time of the Maccabean revolt. The accounts combine historical information with religious interpretation.

Holy Orders The sacrament by which baptized men are ordained as bishops, priests, or deacons for permanent ministry as leaders in the Catholic Church.

Holy Spirit One of the three persons of the Holy Trinity, along with the Father and the Son. Also called the Spirit of God and the Spirit of Jesus.

Holy Thursday The Thursday before Easter, on which Christians prayerfully celebrate Jesus' Last Supper.

Holy Week Beginning on Palm Sunday, the weeklong remembrance of the final days of Jesus' earthly life.

I

Immaculate Conception The Catholic teaching that the Blessed Virgin Mary was free from sin from the first moment of her conception.

Incarnation The mystery of Jesus being both God and human. It literally means "in flesh." The term refers to the belief that God took on flesh in Jesus in order to become united with people.

Israelites The descendants of Abraham and his son Isaac, who become God's Chosen People.

J

Jerusalem The city that King David established as the capital of the united kingdom of Israel.

Jewish Diaspora The settling of Jews outside the Promised Land, usually during times of war and foreign invasions.

judges The eleven men and one woman who served the Israelites as tribal leaders, military commanders, arbiters of disputes, and inspirations of faith.

K

Kingdom of God A realm Jesus proclaimed, characterized by love, in which God's will for all creation is brought about and justice reigns.

L

Lamb of God A title for Jesus Christ recalling the Passover lamb, whose death brought about freedom and salvation for the Jewish people. The title highlights the Christian belief that Jesus' death brought salvation for all people.

last judgment The judgment of the whole human race at the end of time, after which the Kingdom of God will be perfectly established for eternity.

Last Supper Jesus' final meal with his disciples before his death, in which he instituted the Eucharist.

Lent The forty-day period in the liturgical year that is preparation for Easter, recalling the forty days that Jesus spent in the desert in preparation for his mission.

liturgical year The annual cycle of holy days and seasons that celebrates the events and mysteries of Jesus' birth, life, death, Resurrection, and Ascension.

liturgy The Catholic Church's official, public, communal prayer. The most important liturgy is the Eucharist, or the Mass.

Lord's Prayer Another name for the Our Father, the prayer Jesus taught his disciples.

M

Magisterium The Catholic Church's official teaching voice, which consists of all bishops in communion with the pope. The Magisterium interprets and preserves the truths revealed in Scripture and Tradition.

martyr Someone who dies with courage for their religious faith.

matriarch The mother of a tribe, clan, or tradition. Sarah, Rebekah, Rachel, and Leah were the primary matriarchs of the Israelite people.

Matrimony The sacrament by which a baptized man and a baptized woman establish a lifelong partnership and commit to faithfully loving each other for life.

meditation A form of prayer that focuses a person's attention on God and the mysteries of God with their thoughts, feelings, and imagination.

Messiah Title based on a Hebrew word meaning "anointed one" given to the saving leader hoped for by the Jews. The equivalent Greek term is *christos*. Christians apply the title Christ to Jesus.

metaphor A word or phrase for one thing that is used to refer to another thing to show or describe some trait or characteristic of the second thing.

monasticism A way of life in which people seek holiness by living apart from the normal society, either living alone or in community.

monotheism The belief that there is only one God.

morality A system of principles guiding how we live our lives. Christian morality helps define what is right and wrong with the goal of motivating people to choose what is right.

mortal sin A serious or grave offense, done with full knowledge and freedom, which turns the person completely away from God.

Mosaic Law (or Law of Moses) The laws given to the Israelites by God as part of the Sinai Covenant. It describes the Israelites' responsibilities in keeping the sacred covenant.

N

New Testament The name for the second main section of the Bible, which contains the books whose central themes are the life, teachings, Passion, death, Resurrection, and Ascension of Jesus Christ and the beginnings of the church.

O

Old Testament The Christian name for the first main section of the Bible, which contains the writings that record God's Revelation to the Chosen People.

Ordinary Time The period in the liturgical year during which Christians reflect on the things Jesus taught and lived so that they might make their values and attitudes more like his.

Original Sin The belief that every person comes into the world with their ability to choose the good already weakened. All people inherit this spiritual condition because of the sin of the first human beings, Adam and Eve.

P

Palm (Passion) Sunday The Sunday on which Christians remember Jesus' triumphal entrance into Jerusalem and his Passion and death.

parable A short story used to communicate religious messages, based on everyday events and often with surprising endings. Jesus used parables frequently to teach about the Kingdom of God.

particular judgment The time when individuals face God immediately after death, when they will be either united with God or not for eternity.

Paschal Mystery The reality that Jesus has gone through death to new life and that those who are united with him will experience the same.

Passion The suffering of Jesus during the final days of his life: his agony in the garden at Gethsemane, his trial, and his Crucifixion.

Passover The feast that celebrates the deliverance of the Chosen People from bondage in Egypt.

patriarch The father or leader of a tribe, clan, or tradition. Abraham, Isaac, and Jacob were the primary patriarchs of the Israelite people.

penance Asking for and receiving forgiveness for sin, with the intention to not repeat the sin.

Penance and Reconciliation The sacrament that celebrates God's forgiveness of sin, through which the sinner is reconciled with both God and the Catholic Church.

Pentateuch A Greek word meaning "five books," referring to the first five books of the Old Testament.

Pentecost The descent of the Holy Spirit upon the Apostles, Mary, and the disciples gathered with them, empowering them to continue Jesus' mission.

petition A form of prayer asking God for help for oneself or others.

pilgrim A person who travels to a sacred place for a religious purpose.

polytheism The belief that there are many gods.

pope The name for the leader of the Catholic Church. He is the successor of Saint Peter, the person Christ appointed to lead the Apostles.

prayer Lifting up of one's mind and heart to God and communicating with God in a relationship of love.

Promised Land The land God promised to his Chosen People, which has been known in different times as Canaan, Judea, and Israel.

prophet A person God chooses to speak his message. In the Bible, primarily a person who called the Chosen People to change their lives, not necessarily a person who predicted the future.

prophetic books The section of the Old Testament that contains the words of many, but not all, of Israel's prophets.

Protestant Reformation The movement that began in the early sixteenth century and sought changes to the Catholic Church. It eventually led to the formation of separate Protestant denominations.

R

reason The power of the human mind to think, analyze, and form logical judgments.

reconciliation The process of restoring broken relationships with God, the faith community, and those hurt by one's sin.

religion An organized system of beliefs, rituals, and ways of living that gives expression to a particular people's faith in a god or gods.

Resurrection The passage of Jesus from death to life on the third day after his death on the cross; the basis of our hope in the resurrection of the dead.

Revelation The communication from God through which human beings come to know who God is.

ritual Words and actions that have symbolic meaning for a group or community.

Rosary A devotional prayer that honors the Virgin Mary and helps people meditate on Christ's life and mission.

S

Sabbath A sacred day of rest and worship, kept by Jews from Friday evening to Saturday evening, and by most Christians on Sunday.

sacrament A visible sign of God's saving love, instituted by Christ, by which spiritual gifts are given.

sacramental The sense that God and the sacred are encountered in the ordinary things and events of everyday life.

saint A person trying to live the Gospel of Jesus Christ, especially those who have died and who live in full union with God.

salvation history The pattern of events in human history in which God's presence and saving actions are revealed.

scribes People who were able to read and write in the Hebrew language. They were teachers of the Jewish Law and Scripture.

Seder The Jewish ceremonial meal, celebrated at home during Passover, in commemoration of the Exodus of the Chosen People from Egypt.

sexuality The way people experience and express themselves sexually; it involves a person's physical, emotional, and spiritual interactions with other people.

sin A deliberate thought, word, or action that ignores God's will or turns a person away from God.

Sinai Covenant The covenant God made with the Israelites through Moses at Mount Sinai.

spiritual Relating to the nonphysical, or nonmaterial, aspects of human life and experience.

spirituality Ways of tending to the part of the self that is not physical. It is expressed through actions, beliefs, values, and attitudes that characterize a person's life.

symbol A tangible, physical reality that represents an invisible reality.

synagogue A Jewish center for worship and community life.

T

Temple The building complex in Jerusalem where the Israelites' religious sacrifices and worship were performed.

Ten Commandments The list of ten norms, or rules of moral behavior, that God gave Moses and that are an important foundation for Christian morality.

tradition A religious practice, often rooted in a specific culture, that can change or even disappear over time.

Tradition The process by which the Catholic Church reflects on, deepens its understanding of, cherishes, and hands on to every generation the teachings and practices that are essential to the faith, as interpreted by the Magisterium under the guidance of the Holy Spirit.

Triduum The last three days of Holy Week, from the evening of Holy Thursday to the evening of Easter Sunday. This period is the high point of the liturgical year.

Trinity The central Christian mystery and dogma that there is one God in three divine persons: Father, Son, and Holy Spirit.

U

unconditional Having no conditions or limits placed on it.

V

venial sin A lesser offense that weakens the person's relationship with God but does not turn the person completely away from God.

vice A bad moral habit developed by the repetition of immoral actions.

virtue A good moral habit developed by the repetition of moral actions.

W

wisdom and poetry books The section of the Old Testament that contains collections of wise advice and prayers.

worldview How a person sees and understands the world. A person's wordview is influenced by their experiences and beliefs.

Index

A

Abba, 47, 116
Abraham, 65, 70, 72, 73, 194
absolution, 264
Acts of the Apostles
  Apostles' mission in, 158
  Ascension accounts, 158
  content descriptions, 158, 201
  early Christian communities, 161, 163
  Easter liturgical readings from, 278
  Holy Spirit appearance in, 159–161
Acutis, Carlo, 180, 181–182
Adam and Eve, 194, 334
adolescence, 17–19
adultery, 322, 327
Advent, 274–275
Advocate, 157
afterlife, 60, 184, 340–341
Alexander the Great, 91
Allah, 38, 46
Amos, 85, 197, 198
Analects, 191
Andrew, 114–115
Annunciation, 107–109
anointing
  in sacramental rituals, 257, 258, 266,
    269
  symbolism of, 247, 257, 258
  traditions of, 258
Anointing of the Sick, 250, 264–267
Antioch, 163
Apocalypse of Peter, 209
Apocrypha, 204
Apostles. *See also* Paul; Peter
  discipleship of, 114–115
  Gentile conversions, 163
  Jesus' resurrected appearances to, 143
  mission of, 60, 158
  teachings of, 43
  Tradition origins, 222–223

Apostles' Creed, 45, 229–231, 301
apostolic exhortations, 225, 226
Aquinas, Thomas, 31, 239
artistic prayers, 305
Ascension, 158–159, 278
Ash Wednesday, 276
Assumption, 167, 227
Assyrians, 86
Augustine of Hippo, 234, 239

B

Babylonian Exile, 86–89
Badano, Chiara, 180–181, 182
Bahá'í faith, 29, 38, 315
Baptism
  of adults, 254
  of babies, 253
  definition, 252
  in early Christian church, 253, 257
  of Jesus, 111–112
  meaning of, 252–253
  oil used for, 258
  ritual descriptions, 253–254, 277
  sacrament type, 250
  through Trinity, 234
  water symbolism, 254
Baptism of the Lord, 275
Baruch, 197
Basil the Great, 325
beatification, 176
Beatitudes, 61, 121, 200
belief, 54, 59–60
Benedict, 174
Benedictines, 174
Bhagavad Gita, 191
Bhagavati, 38

Bible (Scriptures). *See also* Gospels; New Testament; Old Testament
  authors of, 189–190, 193, 209–210, 211–212
  canonical status, 204, 209
  Catholic *vs.* Protestant, 204
  cultural context of, 146, 187
  descriptions, 193
  development of, 206–209
  God's Revelation through, 43, 222–223
  historical time line of, 71
  idolatry themes, 203
  impact of, 193
  importance of, 214
  interpretation of, 205–206, 210–211, 238
  literary genres in, 69, 193
  in liturgical readings, 260, 278
  messages of, 212–213
  salvation history in, 68
  as Word of God, 188–190
biblical inspiration, 211–212
biblical interpretation, 205–206, 210–211
bishops, 257, 268–269
blasphemy, 130, 135
blessed, 31
Body and Blood of Christ, 129, 132, 139, 151–152, 259, 260
Body of Christ, 169
Brahman, 38, 46, 65
brain remodeling, 17–18
bread
  sacramental rituals with, 129, 132, 139, 259, 260
  symbolism of, 247, 259
Buddhism, 28, 33, 65, 315
butterflies, 184

C
calendar, 61, 273–278
Canaan, 70, 75–76, 80–81, 91, 195
canon, 204
canonization of saints, 176
cardinal virtues, 338
Catechism of the Catholic Church, 225

catechumens, 254
cathedrals, 170
Catherine of Siena, 176–177
Catholic Church
  buildings of, 170
  butterfly parables describing, 184
  calendar of, 61, 273–278
  descriptions, 165–166
  gifts of, 235–240
  images of, 168–170
  leaders of, 171, 268–269
  levels of, 167
  moral teachings of, 323–327
  Mother of the, 167
  origins of, 161–165
  purpose, 166–167
  as sacrament, 249–250
  splits in, 171
  teachings of, 43, 221–228, 238, 241–242, 323–327
  traditions of, 220–221
  unity and diversity of, 218–220
  worship practices of, 260, 273, 303
Catholic Climate Covenant, 324
Catholicism
  beliefs of, 29, 45–46, 59–60
  definition, 6
  divine creator of, 46
  gifts of, 235–240
  practices of, 61
  worldview of, 58–59
  worldwide statistics, 165
  young Catholic statistics, 60
Catholic Relief Services (CRS), 324
Catholic social teaching, 238, 323–327
Catholic Worker Movement, 324
chapels, 170
character, 335–338, 339
Chavez, Cesar, 324
chief priests, 93, 130
Chosen People, 66. *See also* Israelites
chrism (sacred oil), 247, 257, 258, 266
Christ, 258
Christian Initiation Sacraments, 249, 251–260

Christianity
  affiliation statistics, 33, 165
  beliefs of, 29, 142, 229–231
  denominations of, 171
  divine creator of, 38
  early Christian communities, 161–165, 166, 253
  Golden Rule of, 315
  non-Christian religion relations, 65, 67, 172
  rituals of, 129
  roots of, 65–67
"Christ Is Alive" (Pope Francis), 226
Christmas, 275
church buildings, 170
circumcision, 71, 111, 163
Clare, 175–176
Clarke, Maura, 139
climate change, 324
Colossians, 336
common good, 325
communal sense, 235, 237–238
Communion, Holy, 277
Communion of the Saints, 182–183, 239
community prayers, 306–309
confession, 263–264
Confirmation, 250, 255–258, 277
Confucianism, 28, 33, 191, 315
connectedness, 12–13, 30–32, 343–344
conscience, 329, 330, 331
contemplation, 301
conversation prayers, 294–296
Corinthians, 147, 169, 281, 341
councils, 106, 163, 225
courage, 257, 338
covenants
  with Abraham, 70–72
  with David, 83
  definition, 66
  during Exile, 88
  with Moses, 76–77, 81
  sacraments as, 271

Creation
  biblical stories on, 194, 209, 210
  as Catholic belief, 59
  divine, 29, 38, 45–46
  goodness of, 190
creators, divine, 29, 38, 45–46. *See also* God
creeds, 45, 106, 229–231, 301
crosses and crucifixes, 277
CRS (Catholic Relief Services), 324
Crucifixion, 60, 136–139, 149–152, 277
Crusades, 67, 175

D

Daniel, 197
David, 82–83, 195
Day, Dorothy, 324
deacons, 253–254, 268–269
death
  and afterlife, 60, 340–341
  of Jesus, 60, 136–139, 149–152, 277
  as last thing, 339
  sacraments for, 266–267
death penalty, 227–228
denominations, 171
depression, 11, 12
devotion, 239
Diego, Juan, 240
disciples, 114–115, 142–143, 146, 154
diversity, 216–220
divine, defined, 29
doctrines and dogmas, 226–228
Donovan, Jean, 139

E

early Christians, 161–165, 166, 253
earth, 46
Easter Season, 278
Easter Sunday, 142
Easter Vigil, 255, 257, 277
ecumenical councils, 106, 163, 225
ecumenism, 171
Elijah, 85, 197

Elisha, 197
Emmaus, road to, 142, 154–155
emotional development, 18–19
end of time, 312
enemy love, 119, 198, 320
Ephesians, 169, 309
Epiphany, 275
eternal banquet, 339
Eucharist
    for dying people, 267
    meaning of, 259
    origins, 129, 132
    ritual descriptions, 259–260
    sacrament type, 250
    significance of, 133, 151–152, 155, 273
    word meaning, 132
Evangelists, 198
evil, 10–11, 212, 331–334. *See also* sin
Exodus, 76–78, 129, 194–195
Ezekiel, 85, 197

F

faith
    commitment to, 236, 238–239
    definition, 9, 52
    Jesus' presence as, 153
    life's meaning leading to, 9
    as response to God, 50–57
    Resurrection beliefs as, 147–148
    sin overcome with, 334
    testimonies of, 62–63
    as theological virtue, 338
Father, 47, 48, 59, 116, 231–234
fear, 284–285
Felicity, 173
Festival of Lights, 91
figurative stories, 69
fire, 244, 246
Floyd, George, 123
Focolare movement, 181
foot-washing rituals, 132, 277
Ford, Ita, 139
forgiveness, 31, 49–50, 200, 213, 263–264
fortitude (courage), 257, 338

Francis, Pope
    Eucharist meaning, 133
    foot-washing rituals, 132
    Holy Spirit as comforter, 162
    modern Samaritans, 123
    prayers for peace, 309
    unity, 218
    young people advice, 226
Franciscans, 175
Francis of Assisi, 175, 176, 307
Frank, Anne, 62–63
free will, 33, 51, 54, 212, 329–330
friendship, 270, 291–293

G

Gandhi, Mahatma, 104
Gautama, Siddhartha, 65
Genesis
    Abraham's call, 71, 194
    Creation, 190
    Jacob wrestling angels, 72
    Original Sin, 334
    stories of, 194
    word meaning, 194
Gentiles, 163, 201, 210–211, 253
gestural prayers, 305
Gifts of the Holy Spirit, 256–257
God. *See also* God's love; God's presence; God's relationship
    belief statistics, 60
    biblical authorship, 209–210, 211–212
    covenants with, 66, 70–72, 76–77, 81, 83
    definition, 29
    disbelief in, 57, 60
    the Father, 47, 48, 59, 116, 231–234
    Incarnation, 100, 102, 103, 104, 244
    judgment of, 37, 312–313, 340–343
    justice expectations, 198
    names and titles of, 75, 321
    natures of, 44–50
    scientific proof of, 30
    as Trinity, 231–234
    trust in, 52–53, 285–289
    Word of, 188–190

godparents, 253
God's love
  afterlife, 340–341
  commandments on, 318–320
  creation as, 29
  effects of, 306, 316–317
  human connection as, 29–34, 55, 306
  Jesus' teachings on, 117–118
  as unconditional, 281–285
God's presence
  in everyday experiences, 40, 248, 281
  as grace, 102, 244–245
  as sacramental sense, 235, 236
  in sacraments, 279
  symbolism of, 245–248
  wonder and awe of, 257
God's relationship. *See also* God's love
  as biblical message, 212
  as Catholic worldview, 59
  commitment to, 292–293
  descriptions, 232–233
  faith as response to, 52–57
  grace as gift of, 102
  with Israelites, 66, 72, 77
  prayers for, 31, 293
  Revelation and knowing, 38–43, 244
  sin affecting, 102
Golden Rule, The, 315
Good Friday, 139, 277
goodness, 10–12, 190, 212, 331
Gospel of Peter, 209
Gospel of Thomas, 209
Gospels. *See also* John's Gospel; Luke's
  Gospel; Mark's Gospel; Matthew's
  Gospel
  content descriptions, 68, 198–199
  definition, 98
  religious traditions in, 98
  synoptic, 199, 207–208
  writing of, 144–145, 198–199,
    207–211

grace, 102, 244–245, 331, 334
gratitude, 297–299
Great Commandment, 126, 213,
  314–322, 323
Great Spirit, 38
greed, 322
Greeks, 91

H
habits, 336–338
Hail Mary, 240, 302–303
Hanukkah, 91
Healing Sacraments, 250, 261–267
health, 12
heaven, 46, 158–159, 339, 342,
  343–344
Hebrews
  biblical books as letters to, 202, 240
  definition, 70, 72
  lifestyle descriptions, 95
  members of, 70, 72
  religion of, 95
  sacred writings of, 68, 89, 165, 192,
    194
Hebrew Scriptures, 68, 89, 165, 192,
  194. *See also* Old Testament
hell, 339, 340, 342
hermits, 174
high priests, 135
Hinduism
  affiliations statistics, 33
  beliefs of, 29, 142
  divine creators of, 38
  Golden Rule of, 315
  origins, 65
  sacred writings of, 191
  as worldwide religion, 28
historical books, 195
Holocaust, 62–63, 67, 96
Holy Orders, 250, 267–269
Holy Saturday, 277

Holy Spirit (Spirit of God, Spirit of Jesus)
 Baptism and action of, 254
 as Catholic belief, 59, 60
 Church as Temple of, 169–170
 definition, 158
 descriptions of, 160
 disciples and appearance of, 159–161
 in early Christian communities, 161
 fruits of, 310
 Gifts of, 256–257
 guidance of, 157–158, 173, 213,
  241–242, 249
 as person of Trinity, 231–234
Holy Thursday, 129, 277
Holy Week, 276–277
hope, 11–12, 281, 289, 334, 338
Hosea, 85
house churches, 170
humans
 connectedness of, 12–13, 30–32,
  343–344
 dignity of all, 323–327
 God's relationship with, 29–34, 55,
  102, 212, 232–233, 306
 life's meaning and purpose, 7–9, 32–34
 love and, 30–31
humiliation, 136
hypocrisy, 120

I

idolatry, 80, 84, 203
Ignatius of Loyola, 177–178, 290
Immaculate Conception, 109, 227
Incarnation, 100, 102, 103, 104, 244
Indigenous religions, 33, 38, 128, 172,
315
infallibility, 227–228
Isaac, 72, 73
Isaiah, 48, 49, 84, 197, 198
Ishmael, 72
Islam
 affiliation statistics, 33
 beliefs of, 29, 72, 142
 Christianity connections with, 65,
  72, 109
 divine creator of, 38, 46
 Golden Rule of, 315
 sacred writings of, 31, 191

Israelites
 Babylonian Exile, 86–89
 covenants and laws, 76–79
 definition, 72
 Exodus, 74–76
 God's relationship with, 66, 72, 77
 kingdoms of, 82–84
 post-exile freedom of, 90
 Promised Land of, 70, 75–76, 80–81,
  91, 195
 tribes of, 81
 wilderness wandering, 80
Israel (Jacob), 72, 73
Israel (kingdom), 82–83, 195

J

Jacob (Israel), 72, 73
Jainism, 315
James, 114, 202
jealousy, 322
Jeremiah, 85, 197
Jerusalem
 as capital city, 83, 84, 91
 destruction of, 87
 early Christian communities in, 161
 rebuilding of, 90
 Temple in, 83, 87, 90, 91, 93, 165
Jesuits, 177–178
Jesus. *See also* Resurrection
 arrest of, 135
 Ascension, 158–159, 278
 baptism of, 111–112
 betrayal of, 134
 birth of, 109–110, 210–211
 burial of, 139
 conception of, 107–109
 Crucifixion and death, 60, 136–139,
  149–152, 277
 early years, 111
 ethnicity, 65, 66–67
 fear and, 286
 Gandhi on, 104
 for genuine spirituality, 290–291
 at Gethsemane, 134–135
 Gospel portraits of, 199, 200, 201
 Incarnation, 100, 102, 103, 104, 244
 justice expectations, 198

Last Supper, 129–132
love commandments of, 126, 213,
    314–322, 323
as Messiah, 92, 94–95, 98–99,
    105–106
natures of, 100, 104–106
oil symbolism, 258
origins of, 107
prayers of, 116, 200, 301
presence of, 153, 159, 166
public response to, 124–125, 130, 186
religion of, 65, 66–67, 98
second coming, 166
teachings of, 114–123, 186–188, 198
temptation of, 112–113
titles of, 59, 100, 108, 151–152, 201,
    231–234, 258, 313
Tradition revealed through, 222–223
unity prayers of, 171
Jewish Diaspora, 86
Jews. *See also* Israelites; Judaism
beliefs of, 29
Christian relations with, 67
culture of ancient, 146, 187
early Christian communities of,
    161–166
God's name, 75
God's relationship with, 66
groups among, 93
Messiah prophecies, 92
oppressors of, 91–92
sacred writings of, 68, 89, 165,
    192, 194
statistics, 33
survival of, 96
wartime destruction of, 62–63, 67, 96
word origins, 90
John, 114, 198, 201, 202, 203. *See also*
John's Gospel
John's Gospel
Christian unity, 171
content descriptions, 201
Crucifixion, 138
disciples, 114
genuine spirituality, 290
God's love, 117

Holy Spirit guidance, 157
Jesus' portrait in, 201
Last Supper, 132
love commandments, 126, 316
Resurrection, 142, 144–146
writing of, 198–199, 201, 203
John the Baptist, 111–112
Joseph (Jesus' foster father), 110, 111
Joseph of Arimathea, 139
Joseph (patriarch), 73
Joshua, 81, 195
Judah, 84, 86, 90, 195
Judaism
affiliation statistics, 33
beliefs of, 29, 142
Christianity connections to, 63, 65, 72
development of, 90–91, 95–96
divine creator of, 38
feasts of, 76, 91
gifts of, 95–96
Golden Rule of, 315
in Gospels, 98
origins of, 72–73
rituals of, 76, 128, 129
sacred writings of, 192, 194
word origins, 90
as worldwide religion, 28
worship places, 93–94
Judas Iscariot, 114, 134, 135
Jude, 202
judges, 81
Judges, Book of, 81, 82, 195
judgment, 37, 312–313, 340–343
Julian of Norwich, 48
justice, 61, 198, 324–326, 338

K

Kazel, Dorothy, 139
Keller, Helen, 7
killing, 320, 321, 323
Kingdom of God, 115, 117–122
kneeling, 304
knowledge, 257
Kolbe, Maximilian, 139
Koran (Qur'an), 31, 191

L

Lamb of God, 151–152
Lamentations, 87, 197
last judgment, 341–343
Last Supper, 129–132, 277
last things, 339
laws
  commandments, 61, 78–79, 314–323,
    325, 327
  hypocrisy confrontations, 120
  as literary genre, 69
  of Moses, 78–79
laying on of hands, 266, 269
Leah, 73
Lent, 276
letters, 69, 201–202, 225
life
  after death, 60, 184, 340–341
  meaning of, 7–9
  protection of human, 323–324
  purpose of, 32–34
literary genres, 69, 193
liturgical year, 61, 273–278
liturgy, 260, 273, 303
Liturgy of the Eucharist, 260
Liturgy of the Word, 260
Lord, 75
Lord's Prayer, 116, 200, 302
Love. *See also* God's love
  as biblical message, 213
  commandments of, 126, 213, 314–322,
    323
  connection and, 12
  enemy, 119, 198, 320
  humans and, 30–31
  for knowing God, 39–40
  laws as expression of, 79
  as theological virtue, 338
Luke, 201. *See also* Luke's Gospel
Luke's Gospel
  Annunciation, 107–109
  audience for, 201
  content descriptions, 201
  Crucifixion account, 138
  disciples, 114
  Jesus' conception, 107
  Jesus' early years, 111
  Jesus' portrait in, 201
  Jesus' synagogue readings, 99
  Jesus' temptation, 113
  justice, 198
  lost son parables, 186–188
  love commandments, 119
  Nativity narratives, 109–110, 210–211
  prayers, 302–305
  Resurrection, 144–146, 155
  trust in God, 286
  writing of, 198–199, 200, 207–208
Lwanga, Charles, 179–180
lying, 322

M

Maccabean revolt, 195
Magisterium, 224–227, 323
major prophets, 197
Mark's Gospel
  audience for, 200
  Crucifixion, 137–138
  disciples, 114–115
  Gethsemane, 135
  historical context and themes, 200
  Jesus' portrait in, 200, 201
  Jewish authorities, 130
  Resurrection, 144–146
  writing of, 198–199, 200, 207–208
martyrs, 139, 146, 164, 173–174
Mary Magdalene, 141, 142
Mary (Mother of God)
  Annunciation, 107–109
  appearances of, 240
  Assumption, 167, 227
  at Crucifixion, 138
  doctrines on, 227
  as Immaculate Conception, 109, 227
  Jesus' early years, 111
  nativity narratives, 110
  Pentecost, 159
  prayers to, 240, 302–303
  as role model, 167
  titles of, 106, 109, 167
  veneration of, 240

Mass
  as Catholic practice, 61
  on Pentecost, 162
  prayers at, 302–303, 308
  ritual descriptions, 132, 260, 303
  sacraments during, 260, 272
  significance of, 273
  symbolism of, 259–260
  yearly cycle of, 273
matriarchs, 73
Matrimony, 250, 270–272
Matthew's Gospel
  audience, 199
  content descriptions, 199
  disciples, 114
  Jesus' baptism, 112
  Jesus' conception, 107
  Jesus' portrait in, 199, 201
  Last Supper accounts, 131
  love commandments, 314, 316
  Messiah, 99
  nativity narratives, 109, 110, 210, 211
  religious legalism, 120
  Resurrection, 141, 144–146
  Sermon on the Mount, 121
  writing of, 198, 199, 200, 207–208
maturity, 330–331
meditation, 31, 299–301, 304–305
Merton, Thomas, 284
Messiah, 92, 94–95, 98–99, 105–106
metaphor, 45
Micah, 85, 203
Miller, James, 139
minor prophets, 197
miracles, 118
monarch butterflies, 184
monasticism, 174
monotheism, 29, 72
morality
  as Catholic practice, 61
  Catholic teaching themes in, 323–327
  character development for, 335–338
  choices and responsibility, 328–331
  commandments as, 314–316, 318–322, 343–344

  definition and description, 313–314
  religions and, 315
  sin *vs.,* 331–334
mortal sin, 333
Mosaic Law, 78–79
Moses, 74–81, 195
Mount Sinai, 76–77
Muhammad, 191
Mukasa, Joseph, 179–180
musical prayers, 304
Mutesa, King, 179–180

N

Native Americans
  beliefs, 38
  Golden Rule of, 315
  miraculous appearances to, 240
  religious affiliation statistics, 33
  rituals of, 128
  as saints, 178–179
nativity, 109–110, 210–211
neighbor love, 79, 318, 319, 320, 323
New Testament. *See also* Acts of the
  Apostles; Gospels; Paul
  canon of, 204
  Church's images, 169–170
  Communion of Saints, 240
  content descriptions, 58, 193
  definition, 68
  forgiveness themes in, 200
  last judgment, 341–343
  letters of, 164, 202, 209
  perception of, 192
  prayer, 306, 309, 310
  sections of, 198–204
  Trinity, 232
  virtues and vices, 336
Nicene Creed, 231
Noah, 194
non-Christian religions. *See also*
  Hinduism; Islam
  Christian connections, 65, 72
  Christian relations with, 128, 172
  creation beliefs of, 46
  divine creators of, 29, 38, 46

Golden Rule, 315
intermarriages, 272
largest, 28
salvation of, 172
worldwide affiliation statistics, 33

O

oil, 247, 257, 258, 266
Old Testament (Hebrew Scriptures). *See also* Genesis
Babylonian Exile, 86–89
canon variations of, 204
content descriptions, 68, 193
covenants in, 70–72, 76–79, 83
definition, 68
early Christian communities readings of, 165
Exodus, 74–76
forgiveness, 200
judges of, 81
meditation, 300
Messiah prophecies, 92
modern perception of, 192
patriarchs and matriarchs of, 72–73
prophets of, 84–85
sections of, 194–197
sin, 102
wilderness wandering, 80
writing of, 89
Ordinary Time, 275, 278
ordination, 269
Original Sin, 59, 109, 226, 227, 334
Our Father (Lord's Prayer), 116, 200, 302
outsider inclusion, 118, 123, 186

P

Palestine, 91
Palm Sunday, 130, 276
papal encyclicals, 225
parables, 69, 121–123, 184, 186–188, 342
parents, 47–48, 321
parish churches, 170
particular judgment, 340
Paschal Mystery, 149–152
Passion, 134–139, 277

Passion Sunday, 130
Passover, 76, 129, 130–131, 149
pastoral letters, 225
patriarchs, 73
Paul (Saul)
biography, 163
Church images, 169–170
community prayers, 309
conversion of, 164
early Christianity development, 161, 164
fruits of Holy Spirit, 310
God's love, 341
Jesus' humanity, 104
journeys of, 201
letters of, 164, 202, 209
martyrdom of, 164
Paschal Mystery, 149
Resurrection, 146–147
unity in diversity, 218
virtues and vices, 336
Word of God, 190
peace, 320
Penance and Reconciliation, 250, 263–264, 302
Pentateuch, 194–195
Pentecost, 159–161, 162, 278
People of God, 169
Perpetua, 173–174
Persian Empire, 90
Peter
biblical books featuring, 201
discipleship, 114–115
early Christian communities, 161
as first pope, 171
Holy Spirit appearance to, 160
Jesus' appearances to, 143
Jesus as Messiah, 99, 105–106
Jesus' relationship with, 106
letters of, 202
martyrdom of, 164
People of God, 169
petitions, 296–297
Pharisees, 93, 120, 130, 142, 186
Pilate, Pontius, 135
pilgrims, 218–219, 240

poetry books, 196–197
polytheism, 29, 72
Poor Clares, 175–176
popes, 171, 225, 226, 227–228.
  See also Francis, Pope
praise, 297–299
prayer groups, 309
prayers
  as biblical literary genre, 69
  body postures for, 303–304
  for Christian unity, 171
  community, 306–309
  of conversation, 294–296
  of dedication, 290
  definition, 281
  formal, 301–303
  forms of, 293–294
  Jesus, 300
  Jesus' teachings on, 116
  to Mary, 240
  of meditation, 299–301, 304–305
  for peace, 309
  of petition, 296–297
  physical movement for, 304–305
  private, 306
  purpose of, 31, 293
  of sorrow, 302
  of thanks and praise, 297–299
  walking, 304
  written, 305
priests, 253–254, 263–264, 266,
  268–269
prodigal son parables, 186–188
Promised Land, 70, 75–76, 80–81,
  91, 195
prophetic books, 197
prophets, 84–86, 197
Protestant Reformation, 177
Protestants, 204
protests, 123
Proverbs, 69, 196
prudence (right judgment), 257, 338
Psalms, 197, 303
purgatory, 341

Q
Qur'an, 31, 191

R
Rachel, 73
RCIA (Rite of Christian Initiation of
  Adults), 254–255
reason, 40–42, 235, 236, 238–239
Rebekah, 72, 73
reconciliation, 263, 264
redemption, 151
religion. *See also specific religions*
  affiliation statistics, 6, 33
  conflicts between, 28
  conversations on, 27
  core beliefs of, 29
  definition, 6, 26
  development of, 28
  Golden Rule, 315
  life's purpose, 32–34
  questions about, 21, 28
  quick judgments on, 37
  for spiritual guidance, 35
  spirituality vs., 15, 25–27
religious history, 69
Remnant, 90
responsibility, 328–331
Resurrection
  belief in, 60, 147–148
  biblical accounts of, 140–142,
    144–145, 213
  evidence for, 145–147
  Jesus' appearances after, 142–143, 153,
    154–155, 157
  liturgical celebrations on, 277, 278
  significance of, 149–153, 213
resurrection of dead, 142
Revelation, Book of, 203–204, 341–342
Revelation of God, 38–43, 244
reverence, 257
ridicule, 136
right judgment, 257, 338

Rite of Christian Initiation of Adults
 (RCIA), 254–255
rituals
 purpose of, 31
 Sabbath, 88–89
 of sacraments, 253–254, 257,
  259–260, 277
 as symbolic actions, 246–248
 symbolism of, 248
Rohr, Richard, 343–344
Romans, 91–92, 125, 136, 164,
 173–174, 253
Romero, Oscar, 139
Rosary, 240, 303

S

Sabbath, 88–89
sacramental sense, 235, 236, 239, 244
sacraments
 categories of, 250–251
 as Catholic practice, 61
 as Catholic Tradition gift, 236–237
 of Christian Initiation, 249, 251–260
 Church as, 249–250
 of Healing, 250, 261–267
 Jesus as original, 249
 as liturgy, 273
 living, 279
 purpose of, 61, 251
 of Service, 249–250, 267–272
Sadducees, 93, 120
saints
 Communion of the, 182–183, 239
 definition, 182
 female, 173–174, 175–177
 Franciscan, 175
 indigenous, 178–179
 Jesuit, 177–178
 martyrdom of, 164, 173–174
 monastic, 174
 official declarations of, 176
 teenage, 180–182
 Ugandan, 179–180
 veneration of, 61, 239–240

salvation, 151, 172, 213, 233
salvation history, 42–43, 68
Samaritans, 123
Samson, 81
Samuel, 82
Sarah, 70, 72, 73
Saul. *See* Paul
Scholastica, 174
science, 30, 59
scourging, 136
scribes, 89
scriptures, 191, 222. *See also* Bible
second coming, 166
Seder, 76, 128, 129, 149
self-control, 338
Sermon on the Mount, 121, 198, 200,
 320
service, 31, 61, 249–250, 267–272
sexuality, 271, 326–327
Sikhism, 315
Simon of Cyrene, 137
sin
 attraction of, 332–333
 confession of, 263
 consequences of, 212, 264
 definition, 103, 331
 degrees of, 333–334
 Original, 109, 226, 227, 334
 overcoming, 331–332
 reconciliation for, 263
Sinai Covenant, 77–79, 195
sitting, 304
social justice, 324–326
Society of Jesus, 177–178
Solomon, 83–84
"Song of Miriam", 207, 208
Son of God, 59, 100, 108, 201, 231–234
Son of Man, 312–313
Spirit of God. *See* Holy Spirit
Spirit of Jesus. *See* Holy Spirit
Spiritual Exercises (Ignatius of Loyola),
 178, 290
spiritual hungers, 7–15, 22–27,
 343–344

spirituality
  benefits of, 14–15, 310
  conversations on, 27
  definition, 14
  genuine, 290–291
  during good times, 289–290
  growth of, 20–27
  religion as guidance for, 35
  trust in God, 285–289
  of young Catholics, statistics, 60
standing, 304
stealing, 322
Stein, Edith, 139
Sunday, 142, 321
symbols and symbolic actions
  of Baptism, 254
  crosses and crucifixes, 277
  definition and descriptions, 245–246
  as God's presence, 236, 244
  literary genres featuring, 69
  rituals as, 246–248
synagogues, 93–94
synoptic Gospels, 199, 207–208

T
Tanakh, 192
Taoism, 28, 29, 33, 315
Tekakwitha, Kateri, 178–179
temperance, 338
Temple, 83, 87, 90, 91, 93, 165
Temple of the Holy Spirit, 169–170
temptation, 113, 332–333
Ten Commandments, 61, 78–79,
  218–323, 325, 327
Teresa of Ávila, 39–40, 239
Teresa of Kolkata (Calcutta), 245, 324
Tertullian, 233–234
thanksgiving prayers, 297–299
theological virtues, 338
Thérèse of Lisieux, 293
Timothy, 149, 190

Torah, 194
Tradition, 43, 221–228, 241–242, 341
traditions, 220–221
Triduum, 277
Trinity, 69, 158, 231–234
trust in God, 52–53, 285–289
Twelve Tribes of Israel, 81

U
Uganda, 179–180
unconditional, defined, 281
understanding, 257
Unitarianism, 315
unity, 171, 216–220, 273, 301, 306–309

V
Vatican Council II, 225
venial sin, 333
vices, 336–338
Virgin of Guadalupe, 240
virtues, 336–338
vocations, 268–269

W
walking prayers, 304
water, 247, 253, 254
weddings, 272
White Fathers, 179–180
wine, 129, 132, 139, 259, 260
wisdom, 256
wisdom books, 196–197
women, 146
wonder and awe, 257
Word of God, 188–190, 192
worldview, 58–59
written prayers, 305

Y
Yahweh, 38, 75

Zealots, 93
Zoroastrianism, 315

Acknowledgments

Scripture texts used in this work are taken from the *New American Bible, Revised Edition* © 2010, 1991, 1986, 1970 Confraternity of Christian Doctrine, Inc., Washington, DC. All Rights Reserved. No part of this work may be reproduced or transmitted in any form or by any means, electronic or mechanical, including photocopying, recording, or by any information storage and retrieval system, without permission in writing from the copyright owner.

All formal prayers contained herein have been verified against authoritative sources.

The sociological data on page 6 and the quotation by a young adult on page 21 are from the research presented in *The State of Religion & Young People 2020: Relational Authority* (Bloomington, MN: Springtide Research Institute ®, 2020), pages 38 and 60. Copyright © Springtide Research Institute.

The quotation on page 12 is from "The Health Benefits of Hope," by Ander Bonior, in *Psychology Today,* March 30, 2021, at www.psychologytoday.com/us/blog/friendship-20/202103/the-health-benefits-hope.

The social isolation study referred to on page 13 is from Kassandra Alcaraz et al., "Social Isolation and Mortality in US Black and White Men and Women," in *American Journal of Epidemiology,* volume 188, issue 1, January 2019, at https://academic.oup.com/aje/article/188/1/102/5133254?login=true.

The quotation on page 29 is from *Angelus* (Saint Peter's Square, August 18, 2013), at www.vatican.va/content/francesco/en/angelus/2013/documents/papa-francesco_angelus_20130818.html. Copyright © LEV.

Saint Thomas Aquinas's five proofs for God on page 31 are paraphrased from his *Summa Theologica.*

The data about world religions in the pie chart on page 33 is from Pew Research Center's 2015 study "The Future of World Religions: Population Growth Projections, 2010-2050," at www.pewforum.org/2015/04/02/religious-projections-2010–2050.

The prayers by Alaine Gherardi on page 40, by Michael Elmer Bulleri (adapted) on page 248, by Megan O'Malley on page 285, by Kaitlyn Pratt on pages 289–290, by anonymous students on pages 297 and 298 are from *More Dreams Alive: Prayers by Teenagers,* edited by Carl Koch (Winona, MN: Saint Mary's Press, 1995), pages 80, 86, 75, 59, 30, and 89, respectively. Copyright © 1995 by Saint Mary's Press. All rights reserved.

The excerpt on page 45, the excerpt and quotation on page 152, and the text in the chart on page 230 are from the English translation of *The Roman Missal* © 2010, International Commission on English in the Liturgy Corporation (ICEL) (Washington, DC: United States Conference of Catholic Bishops, 2011), pages 528, 667 and 669, and 528, respectively. Copyright © 2011, USCCB, Washington, DC.

All rights reserved. Used with permission of the ICEL. Texts contained in this work derived whole or in part from liturgical texts copyrighted by the International Commission on English in the Liturgy (ICEL) have been published here with the confirmation of the Committee on Divine Worship, United States Conference of Catholic Bishops. No other texts in this work have been formally reviewed or approved by the United States Conference of Catholic Bishops.

The quotation by Julian of Norwich on page 48 is from "Julian of Norwich: Revelations of Divine Love," in *The Culturium* (blog), October 28, 2016, at www.theculturium.com/julian-of-norwich-revelations-of-divine-love.

The excerpt by Dag Hammarskjöld on page 56 is from *Markings,* translated by Leif Sjöberg and W. H. Auden (New York: Alfred A. Knopf, 1976), page 205. Translation copyright © 1976 by Alfred A. Knopf and Faber and Faber.

The sociological data and the quotation by a young adult on page 60 are from *The State of Religion and Young People 2021: Navigating Uncertainty* (Farmington, MN: Springtide Research Institute®, 2021), pages 21, 48, and 57. Copyright © Springtide Institute.

The quotation by Anne Frank on pages 62–63 is from *The Diary of a Young Girl: The Definitive Edition,* edited by Otto H. Frank and Mirjam Pressler, translated by Susan Massotty (New York: Doubleday, 1995), pages 261–262. Translation copyright © 1995 by Doubleday, a division of Bantam Doubleday Dell Publishing Group.

The quotations by Mahatma Gandhi on page 104 are from "My Life Is a Message," at www.mkgandhi.org/whatjesusmeanstome/05jesus.htm and at www.mkgandhi.org/mynonviolence/chap114.htm.

The quotation by Pope Francis on page 123 is from "In conference address, Pope Francis praises George Floyd protesters as 'collective Samaritans,'" by Nate Tanner-Williams, in *Black Catholic Messenger,* October 17, 2021.

The excerpt on page 133 is from "Homily of His Holiness Pope Francis" (Saint Peter's Basilica, June 6, 2021), at www.vatican.va/content/francesco/en/homilies/2021/documents/papa-francesco_20210606_omelia-corpusdomini.pdf. Copyright © LEV.

The excerpt on page 150 by a student from La Salle High School, Pasadena, California, is adapted from *I Know Things Now: Stories by Teenagers 1,* edited by Carl Koch (Winona, MN: Saint Mary's Press, 1996), pages 94–95. Copyright © 1996 by Saint Mary's Press. All rights reserved.

The excerpt on page 162 is from "Homily of His Holiness Pope Francis" (Saint Peter's Basilica, May 23, 2021), at www.vatican.va/content/francesco/en/homilies/2021/documents/papa-francesco_20210523_omelia-pentecoste.html. Copyright © LEV.

The excerpt on page 179 is from *Saint of the Day: Lives, Lessons and Feasts,* edited by Leonard Foley and Pat McCloskey (Cincinnati: St. Anthony Messenger Press, 2001), page 154. Copyright © 2001 by St. Anthony Messenger Press.

The information on Chiara Badano and the brief quotations from her on page 181 are from the Chiara Luce Badano website, at www.chiarabadano .org/?lang=en.

The information on Carlo Acutis and the brief quotations from him on pages 181–182, are from Catholic News Agency, at www.catholicnewsagency .com/news/46048/who-was-carlo-acutis-a-cna -explainer.

The excerpt on page 218 is from "Homily of His Holiness, Pope Francis" (Saint Peter's Square, June 9, 2019), at www.vatican.va/content/francesco /en/homilies/2019/documents/papa-francesco _20190609_omelia-pentecoste.html. Copyright © LEV.

The excerpts on page 226 and on the back cover are from "Christ Is Alive" ("Christus Vivit"), by Pope Francis, numbers 143 and 197, at www .vatican.va/content/francesco/en/apost_exhortations /documents/papa-francesco_esortazione-ap _20190325_christus-vivit.html. Copyright © LEV.

The sidebar on page 237 is loosely based on the article "Holy Family Students serve the homeless," at www.hfchs.org/hfchs-service-simpson-house. The student quoted is from Holy Family Catholic High School, Victoria, MN.

The excerpt on page 254 is from the English translation of *The Order of Baptism of Children* © 2017, International Commission on English in the Liturgy Corporation (ICEL), number 23. All rights reserved. Used with permission of the ICEL. Texts contained in this work derived whole or in part from liturgical texts copyrighted by the ICEL have been published here with the confirmation of the Committee on Divine Worship, United States Conference of Catholic Bishops. No other texts in this work have been formally reviewed or approved by the United States Conference of Catholic Bishops.

The excerpt on page 257 is from the English translation of *The Order of Confirmation* © 2013, International Commission on English in the Liturgy Corporation (ICEL), number 9. All rights reserved. Used with permission of the ICEL. Texts contained in this work derived whole or in part from liturgical texts copyrighted by ICEL have been published here with the confirmation of the Committee on Divine Worship, United States Conference of Catholic Bishops. No other texts in this work have been formally reviewed or approved by the United States Conference of Catholic Bishops.

The letters to God by Alinda and "Anonymous" on pages 283–284 and 288 are used with permission of Michael Dowd, who does youth retreat ministry, 34 Winsor Way, Weston, MA 02493.

The quotation by Thomas Merton on page 284 is from *Thoughts in Solitude* (New York: Farrar, Straus and Cudahy, 1958), page 83. Copyright © 1956, 1958 by the Abbey of Our Lady of Gethsemani.

The prayer by Ignatius of Loyola on page 290 is from *The Spiritual Exercises of Saint Ignatius Loyola,* translated by Elisabeth Meier Tetlow (Lanham, MD: University Press of America, 1987), page 79. Copyright © 1987 by the College Theology Society, University Press of America.

The excerpt by Thérèse of Lisieux on page 293 is from the *Autobiography of St. Thérèse of Lisieux,* translated by Ronald Knox (New York: P. J. Kenedy and Sons, 1958), page 289. Copyright © 1958 by P. J. Kenedy and Sons; copyright renewed.

The excerpt on page 302 is from the English translation of *The Order of Penance* © 2023, International Commission on English in the Liturgy Corporation (ICEL), number 45. All rights reserved. Used with permission. Texts contained in this work derived whole or in part from liturgical texts copyrighted by ICEL have been published here with the confirmation of the Committee on Divine Worship, United States Conference of Catholic Bishops. No other texts in this work have been formally reviewed or approved by the United States Conference of Catholic Bishops.

The Prayer of Saint Francis on page 307 is quoted from *The Fire of Peace: A Prayer Book,* compiled and edited by Mary Lou Kownacki, OSB (Erie, PA: Pax Christi USA, 1992), page 8. Copyright © 1992 by Pax Christi USA.

The excerpt by Pope Francis on page 309 is from "Invocation for Peace," (June 8, 2014), at www .vatican.va/content/francesco/en/prayers/documents /papa-francesco_preghiere_20140608_invocazione -pace.html. Copyright © LEV.

The Pope Francis quotation in the photo caption on page 325 is from "On Care for Our Common Home" ("Laudato Sí"), number 19, at www.vatican .va/content/francesco/en/encyclicals/documents /papa-francesco_20150524_enciclica-laudato-si .html. Copyright © LEV.

The parable on page 342 is quoted from *The Sower's Seeds: One Hundred Inspiring Stories for Preaching, Teaching, and Public Speaking,* by Brian Cavanaugh, TOR (Mahwah, NJ: Paulist Press, 1990), pages 33–34. Copyright © 1990 by Brian Cavanaugh.

The excerpts by Fr. Richard Rohr on pages 343 and 344 are from "Living in Heaven Now," Center for Action & Contemplation, March 12, 2021, at https://cac.org/living-in-heaven-now-2021-03-12/.

To view copyright terms and conditions for internet materials cited here, log on to the home pages for the referenced websites.

During this book's preparation, all citations, facts, figures, names, addresses, telephone numbers, internet URLs, and other pieces of information cited within were verified for accuracy. The authors and Saint Mary's Press staff have made every attempt to reference current and valid sources, but we cannot guarantee the content of any source, and we are not responsible for any changes that may have occurred since our verification. If you find an error in, or have a question or concern about, any of the information or sources listed within, please contact Saint Mary's Press.

Chapter Opener Image Credits:
Chapter 1: © Helena Lopes / Unsplash.com,
Chapter 2: © Creative Travel Projects / Shutterstock.com
Chapter 3: © Poleznova / Shutterstock.com
Chapter 4: © NPL - DeA Picture Library / Bridgeman Images
Chapter 5: © Laura James. All Rights Reserved 2022/ Bridgeman Images
Chapter 6: © ASDF_MEDIA / Shutterstock.com
Chapter 7: © Anastasiia Stiahailo / iStockphoto.com
Chapter 8: © cge2010 / Shutterstock.com
Chapter 9: © Bernardo Ramonfaur / Shutterstock.com
Chapter 10: © Zac Durant / Unsplash.com
Chapter 11: © Arthur Poulin / Unsplash.com